WHY EVER
I WANT TO WRITE

Paul K. Lyons spent many years as a Euro-journalist, writing about energy, environmental and transport policies. His business publications were among the first to focus exclusively on these issues from an EU perspective. His experiences in Brussels led him to write and publish *Kip Fenn – Reflections* (re-published in paperback as the *Not a Brave New World* trilogy). This is the bold fictional biography of a high-level UN official who lives throughout the 21st century working to improve international cooperation and reduce the rich-poor divide. Lyons was an early enthusiast for psychogeography, with his online book, *London Cross*, describing a 30 mile straight line walk across Greater London. The History Press published his two local history books: *Brighton in Diaries* and *Brighton & Hove Then & Now*. Most recently, his passion for diaries has led him to create three diary websites, all freely available and non-commercial: *The Diary Junction* (a database of 500 diarists), *And So Made Significant . . .* (possibly the world's greatest diary anthology), and *The Diary Review* with over a thousand news-type articles on diaries and diarists. His own colourful diaries, spanning more than half a century, can also be found online. In late 2018, Wiley-Blackwell published his comprehensive essay on diaries in *A Companion to Literary Biography*. He has one adult son, and now lives in Brighton with his wife, Hattie, and their two young sons.

WHY EVER DID
I WANT TO WRITE

PATCHWORK OF A WRITING LIFE

Paul K. Lyons

PIKLE
PUBLISHING

Published by Pikle Publishing 2019

ISBN 978-0954827045

Copyright © Paul K. Lyons 2019

* * *

Pikle Publishing
44 Shaftesbury Road, Brighton BN1 4NF, UK

www.pikle.co.uk

Beneath the hot incurious sun,
Past stronger beasts and fairer
He picks his way, a living gun,
With gun and lens and bible,
A militant enquirer,
The friend, the rash, the enemy,
The essayist, the able,
Able at times to cry.

W. H. Auden *As He Is*

For Adam, JG and Albert

WITH MANY THANKS TO HATTIE, ADAM AND MARY

CONTENTS

WHY EVER DID I WANT TO WRITE?

Why am I writing this autobiography of sorts, this collection of stories about myself, this patchwork of a life? I'm no celebrity, and I've done nothing of importance in or with my life (other than bring up three amazing boys), nothing that would warrant public attention, promotion or explanation. But I am a writer, and writing has been such a consistent thread running through my life and how I've lived it that I feel this gives me purpose in putting together a collection of autobiographical swatches, to show this interweaving of living and writing.

Much of my writing has been so-called 'life writing', for I've kept a lively diary from the age of 11, but much has been other forms of writing, journalism in particular. I've also written novels, plays, short stories, poems, local history, psychogeography, and children's fiction. I am not society's idea of a 'writer', a published author with a portfolio of commercial or literary books behind me. No, I am my own idea of what a writer is: someone who enjoys the process of writing, the translating of thoughts and ideas into communicable language; someone for whom writing infuses their daily life; and someone whose mind and soul is affected – infected even – by how and what they write, and by the need to use words to explain, to expose, to imagine, and to play.

So, why ever did I want to write? Where did this want come from? I don't think it was anything to do with my background. My father, Fred, who I hardly knew and certainly didn't admire, did write two crime novels in the 1950s, but he never published again. My step-grandmother, Vera Caspary, was a famous American writer (*Laura* being her most celebrated book and film), but I didn't even meet her until writing was already a part of how I defined myself, or at least how I hoped to define myself. And there's no point in looking to my schooling for any inspiration since I failed English at O-level, and my teachers didn't even think it was worth me going on to university (where, in fact, I studied maths and physics, two subjects which needed zero writing ability). Nor is it worth glancing at my friends, since I don't recall knowing anyone who wrote, at least not before I was in my mid-20s.

However, I can in retrospect see how, at three different stages in my young life, this passion for writing unfolded and emerged. Chance, I believe, played its part early on; this was followed by a kind of inner impetus to express myself more; and, thirdly, there was conscious decision and wilful effort.

Firstly, as to chance, aged 11, I was given a five-year diary. This consisted of 366 pages, one for every date in the calendar, and five lined sections on each page for different years. I wrote regularly in bouts, but then skipped months and years. The book is quite full, but the entries come from a dozen different years, right up until 1974, when I was in my early 20s, which is when I started travelling and writing a diary more consistently.

Secondly, as to the inner stimulus, while travelling in New Zealand I found myself writing poems into my diary, and while in South America I began composing, also for the diary, very short fictional stories, often inspired by characters and events around me. It was as though I wanted or needed to record a deeper, richer set of thoughts and responses to my daily experiences, and the wider range of thoughts, ideas, imaginations that came with them.

And, thirdly, sometime in the late 1970s I made an intellectual decision: of all the art forms (and I was trying a few), I decided, writing was the most interesting, useful and challenging. And I didn't want to set myself any minor challenge. In June 1978, came a eureka moment: I was so inspired by seeing Ballet Rambert perform *Cruel Garden* that I wrote a first lengthy short story with the same title. During the following months two further pieces followed – all three were vaguely autobiographical and written in a stream-of-consciousness style. At the time, I had a professional job (and potential career) but daily life in an office was not matching whatever expectations I had of myself, and so I resigned – with the conscious ambition to become a 'writer'.

My first sustained piece of fictional writing was a stage play about Aleister Crowley, dubbed the most evil man in Britain between the wars. I had access to the Yorke Collection which held many of Crowley's occult writings; and I also managed to interview Gerald Yorke, by then he was old but he had been one of Crowley's close friends. I sent the manuscript off to the very few theatres which put on new plays, and heard nothing, of course. Nevertheless, I can see now that it was no minor achievement to have had the discipline and the craft to complete a full length stage play, even if it would do nothing more than gather dust throughout my life.

Soon after comes a crucial period in my writing life, my life – Corsica! I was living at the time – 1979 – in a lovely garden flat in north London, along with Harold, a magical character from South Africa, and Roser, a delightful Catalan girl. They were exciting times, full of people, rich in experiences. Years later, in fact, Roser told me that on reading

Justine, the first book in *The Alexandria Quartet* by Lawrence Durrell (my literary hero at the time), she had suddenly understood how Harold and I had been affected, infected even, by Durrell's fictional society. I was certainly aspiring to his literary achievements, and to the richness of his characters' lives.

Unexpectedly, we had to move out of the garden flat thanks to an unscrupulous developer. We ended up far away, on an outer rim of London. I hated it. And I hated the cold which was fast encroaching with winter. I devised a plan to escape from both while at the same time furthering my plans to be a writer. I'd go to the Mediterranean (Durrell's literary habitat) for a few months, find somewhere special (and cheap) to live, and do nothing but write, write, write. The future was in my hands, and this is what I had to do. I packed up my Remington typewriter (portable but still 5kg), clothes, books, a few silk scarfs which I'd collected from jumble sales, and headed off for Corsica.

Why Corsica? I think I decided on France because I thought I might try to learn French (having absorbed none of the language from school lessons) in my spare time, and on Corsica itself because it was an island, a defined geographic area, one I knew nothing about. I arrived towards the end of November 1979, full of hope. I spent a week searching for a clean, comfortable, self-contained studio, costing no more than 300 francs a month – and failed.

> 15 November 1979
> Bastia. I am wrecked, physically crippled by a week of sleepless nights. The spots begin to crawl across my face, the hairs on my chest and under my armpits fall out, rotted by fermented sweat. Fingernails feel as though there's a war between them and the cuticles. I dare not take my shoes off. At least my neck remains clean constantly chaffed by a scarf, like the innards of a bicycle wheel and a rolling leather loop. The scalp itches. My legs are heavy plumb lines after one night of walking non-stop to keep off the sea-cold air. My eyes shitter and shutter and my head can only manipulate the simplest of thoughts. Wrecked.

I gave up, and took the ferry back to Marseilles. I was very depressed, as though it was my writing future that had also failed. On the ferry, which sailed through the night, I met two Dutch girls. They told me they had been living in a well-equipped, modern studio flat, not far from Ajaccio, costing exactly 300 francs a month; and it had a view of the sea. I wrote about this meeting in my diary as if it had been a dream, and continued on to Aix-en-Provence where, after a day or two, I found the resolve to return to Ajaccio.

> 23 November 1979
> The Mediterranean. I am on the boat back to Corsica. I am headed for Terra-Bella. Wait without hope for hope would be hope for the wrong thing, Eliot

says. But, I say, he should tell us how to wait without hope. And, any way, it would make more sense if he were to say: wait without hope for hope would be hope for the right thing. But imagine how endlessly right things could go.

28 November 1979
Porticcio. My new home: Studio 110, Terra-Bella, Porticcio 20166, Corse, France. Where to begin? Everything went right. There really were apartments for Fr300 a month, they really were furnished with brooms, knives, pillows, tin-openers. The view from my window is across the gulf to Ajaccio. Aeroplanes come and go, but they can be fun to watch. It is a 20 minute walk to the main road and to the beach, and then a half hour hitch into town. The walls are of rough concrete and painted white; the beds are bright orange; the drawers don't open properly; and now there are decorative scarfs everywhere – covering the cushions and the fuse box, long ones dangling, square ones half-mooning from the ceiling, and an arabesque shade for where my head is at night. Ties and hats and a dressing gown also adorn the walls. One blanket carpets the cold tile floor, the other is on my bed, as is my poncho. There is a cooker/fridge sink unit in one corner; a door leads to a shower/washroom/toilet. I am determined to live without cigarettes or coffee. I shall run a little along the beach each day, and walk lots.

I settled down quickly to various routines, eating, sleeping, reading, walking – and writing. I'd already decided to try my hand at a radio play thinking I could trust the BBC to give it a fair reading. My walks often took me to the beach, where I'd do my best thinking. Out of nowhere, a title came to me, all complete and finished – *The Brittle Rhapsody of Silence on a Winter Beach*. I took five days to write a first draft. It was about – guess what? – a man who had come to Corsica to be a writer.

7 December 1979
I went to the beach, but the sky never got blue, the sea never twinkled, so I came back to the clickety clack, and finished off the play – just like that. I think it has an interesting plot, although it's a bit too poetical at times. It took five days to write. Not bad. Amazing what you can do when you get down to it. Then I went to the tower on the beach for sunset. The middle level has a dome roof and it echoes beautifully. I recited *Prufrock* there; and then, on the roof, I went through *Little Gidding*. Felt good.

8 December 1979
I read the play over. It's pretty crummy.

Some months later, I did send the play to the BBC. It was read, and returned. At the time I thought it was a damning rejection, but years later – when I'd accumulated more experience of rejections – I realised that the letter had actually given ideas on how to revise the script, implying that, if I did so, it might be worth resubmitting. Just now, I've dug the densely typed tatty papers out of a box, and reviewed the play. It IS pretty crummy.

After completing the play, I reverted to writing short stories. Many of these were inspired by a glorious book about Corsica, *The Granite Isle*, by Dorothy Carrington, otherwise known as Frederica, otherwise known as Lady Rose at La Cave bar, downtown Ajaccio. Oh, she was glorious too, with luscious hair full of curls, natural or unnatural I never knew, a picture, lips always over-painted with bright red lipstick which would keep drawing one's gaze away from the faded blue eyes. We chatted sometimes, and when we did I was carried away by her intensity, whether talking of minor plans for the weekend, or the reasons for her love of Corsica. She introduced me to the Mazzeri, or dream-hunters, who secretly hunt at night, kill an animal, and then, from the face of the animal, recognise someone from the village who will die soon. And her writings introduced me to the island's colourful history, the ancient and beautiful statue-menhirs at Filitosa, the age-old traditions of Corsican vendettas, and Miguel Manara, the original Don Juan. Other regular drinkers at La Cave I described in my diary as a 'pacing owl', a 'munching hippopotamus', a 'black sparrow', and a 'singing zebra'.

In mid-December, I suddenly realised the strangest thing. There I was in Corsica trying to do two things: to write and to learn French. Yet these were the very two subjects I had found so difficult and distressing during my school years.

Christmas came and went. I spent Christmas Day itself eating and drinking with a generous couple, English Monica and Corsican Ange, and their young children. This only served to remind me how lonely I was, and so my thoughts were already imagining how endlessly right everything would be when my friends – Harold and Roser – showed up. I had been expecting them by boat on 30 or 31 December. When they didn't arrive on any of the scheduled sailings (for each one of which I was at the harbour side), I found myself again with Monica and Ange on New Year's Eve. Declining an offer to stay over, Ange lent me his car so I could return to my studio. Arriving back, I turned on the light – Harold and Roser jumped out from hiding places with a joyous bundle of laughs and smiles. They had come by plane and a hired car (given the poor state of our finances, I'd never even considered these possibilities). Right away – at 3am – we went to the beach, and to the old tower to drink champagne that Harold had brought, to toast the full moon, to dance, and to celebrate the new year and our friendship.

In the morning, the three of us set off on a mad dash around the island. Southward, to an ancient penitentiary with vast kilns and cellars, to Filitosa where the olive trees seemed as old as the menhirs, and to Sartene, with its narrow alleys roofed by arches, in time for tea. At Bonifacio we bargained for a room, and disturbed everyone in the hotel with our screams and laughter. Onwards we went to mountains where we encountered snow and pine forests and lakes. At Zonza we found a bust of some general with his nose broken off, and met Isabel who invited us to dinner; over Col de Bavella we went, where it seemed no man had been before; and then slowly down to the clementine fields, to dawdle along the coast.

And before I knew it, my friends were gone. I'd focused myself so determinedly, for a winter of hibernation, for a winter of clickety clack, and there I was only half way through and my resolution was in tatters. Not only had I discovered I was wasting my time trying to write, but I was also feeling very alone, and more lonely than I could have imagined. I lasted less than four more weeks.

So my stay on Corsica came to an end. It was the start of a process that would lead me to a mental breakdown of sorts over the next six months. I was a very lost individual. Yet I believed then, and I believe now, that some breakdowns serve a useful purpose. I was broken for a reason. I'd been living in a world of false and unrealistic expectations of and for myself. It was only by falling down, that I could start the process of picking myself up again. I could have done so in any number of ways, but I chose to try and become a journalist, conscious that I needed to learn, by experience and more experience, the craft of writing.

* * *

The swatches in this patchwork take a roughly chronological line, starting, more or less, with my own birth and finishing in the mid-1980s when I am 34, just before the birth of my first son (but with occasional forays into more recent times). Together, I believe, they sketch a picture of myself moving inexorably towards, first, wanting to write, and then hoping to be a 'writer'. In consequence of this development, I would say, I eventually became competent and versatile enough to write all kinds of material – business books, novels, fiction for children, short story collections, local history, psychogeography, literary/historic diary anthologies – all of which will provide structure and substance for a second autobiographical volume, a second patchwork.

Writing infuses this volume, though, mostly simply because many of the chapters are underpinned by entries from my diaries – not great writing, but characteristic of me all the same. Unlike those who burn/shred their childhood diaries for containing embarrassing detail or youthful journals for being impoverished in a literary sense, I'm a fan of my own diaries from every stage of my life. Generally, I consider them a reliable witness, for I have mostly tried hard to be straightforward and honest with myself – what would have been the point in leaving behind unreliable accounts of who or what I was? Obviously and self-evidently I have often – chronically, indeed – argued the case for myself when it comes to friction, disputes, arguments with the world around me. We all engage in this kind of self-justification, and without it most of us would be utterly lost psychologically. I have always claimed to myself, and occasionally to others, that the act of writing down the internal dialogues about external difficulties has helped keep me balanced. After all, I need to make what I write down in black and white sound sensible, I need my self-justifications to work in written language. It's when they don't work very well, and I find myself writing long convoluted explanations, that I sense myself out of sync, and, if not lying to myself, then twisting evidence.

My early diaries are desperately bare of the kind of detail that would interest me today, but nevertheless they are an invaluable source of information – through their content and the manner of the writing – as to who I was.

Which brings me to the topic of memory. For most people, their memories serve as the primary source of information about their past. Not so for me. I remember almost nothing about my pre-teenage years, and very little about my teenage years. The memories I do have are fixed stories about (or pictures of) myself: when brought to mind I cannot root around for further detail. Therefore, as I've long told myself and friends, my diary is my memory. A good example of this is the journal I kept for three years while travelling round the world: almost all of what I think I know about myself during that time can, in fact, be found in the journal. Over the years, I've had occasion to re-read it several times – typing it onto the computer, editing it for a printed copy, editing it for uploading to my website and so on. This means that if any of the travelling stories in my memory get altered (exaggerated), re-reading the diary serves to reset them.

However, I believe that those memories I do have and can write about are important for having survived, as it were, though I judge it necessary to put them in context (not dissimilar to facts in a news article) by qualifying them with phrases like 'my impoverished memory' or 'I have no memory of. . .'. For example, I have no recollection of any journey at all away from my home in Hampstead until I was 11 – not a single holiday, or day trip, or visit, not one. But I can't say: 'As a child I was deprived of holidays and outings' because I don't know that. Instead, I have to record that 'I have no memory of ever going away from home, even on a day trip.'

Writing permeates through the chapters in other ways. Having divorced Dolly, my grandfather, Igee, married Vera Caspary, and she wrote an autobiography which is a key source of information I have about Igee for chapter one. I also have Igee's eloquent, heartfelt but suicidal letters. Vera was an inspiring character who I only met in her old age; I write about her more in a later chapter (twelve) on the Goldsmith identity alongside my cake-making grandmother, and her journalist son, my uncle who was imprisoned and tortured in the Central African Republic.

Chapter two is reserved for my 'flip-flap' father, desperately trying to be a novelist (and being helped by his step-mother, Vera) in the same period as becoming a father. His letters to my pregnant mother are full of fun and word play, and reveal a dislike for one particular possible name for his new son – Paul! He left me, my mother and England while I was still a toddler, and never came back, so our relationship, or lack of, existed sketchily, pathetically, in occasional letters. Much later on, as an adult, I did meet him, only for us to fall out irreconcilably (chapter twelve). Oddly, there is more of him in this patchwork than there is about my mother. In fact, I even have more to say about my stepfather, Sasha, than about my mother. As an adult, I gave Sasha filial, uncomplicated respect, largely because I was grateful that he'd brought me up, more or less, on a par with his own children, and because our upbringing had been materially comfortable and without want. But, throughout my childhood, I believe he unconsciously repressed much of what might have been creative, or imaginative, or different from him. He certainly did little to grow me into a confident human being. I don't have much written evidence for this, apart from a few diary entries and a revealing letter from him which is the centrepiece of chapter five.

Chapter three focuses on Hampstead where I spent the first half of my childhood, but where I returned time and time again in my 20s drawn by the charms of Hampstead Heath. My very first diary entries from the age of 10 (about comics, board games, football, TV) contrast strongly with those from my mid-20s by when a literary pretension had infiltrated my diary writing ('I, in my handsome trance, climbing walls and tramping whimsical pathways'). And chapter four focuses on the Hertfordshire commuter towns of Hoddesdon and Broxbourne where I spent my secondary school years, and where I believe I was effectively bonsaied by teachers, parents and religion. Only on escaping to university (chapter six) did I start to flourish, allowing friends with richer backgrounds and interests to influence me, mostly in positive ways. Suddenly, I was becoming keen on the theatre, photography, magazine production; and towards the end of three years studying I discarded – in a kind of anti-conversion – any belief in religion, freeing me even further to do whatever I wanted.

But I didn't know what I wanted or wanted to do, had no idea. Instead, with what must have been an astounding degree of naivety as to the potential risks, I set off to travel the world (chapter seven). Keeping a diary – recording the myriad experiences of every day – was, for the first time, an absolutely essential part of this new life. The diary became the most valuable possession in my backpack along with my passport and money, and the most protected, and remains to this day a treasured possession, providing a far fuller account of where I went and what I did than I can possibly remember. It charts a myriad of adventures, from hitchhiking across the Saudi Arabian desert to chanting with Tibetan monks in the Himalayas, from swimming in a crocodile infested Malayan river to bathing in the hot springs of a Sumatran volcano, and from seeing Nureyev perform in Swan Lake to being nearly wiped out by Cyclone Tracy in Darwin.

Six months of hard travelling across Asia was followed by a year of living in the South Island of New Zealand (chapter eight), far, far away from everyone and everything I'd ever known previously; and I loved it. I blossomed. Life was magic. And this shows clearly in my diary, where news of my Kiwi travels and bustling social life compete with poetry for space. And then off again, across the ocean to spend a year travelling in South America. But now I found myself engaging more confidently, more intimately with other travellers, which made for a very different travelling experience. My diary reflects this too, as it becomes more taken up with emotions, and self-questioning about those emotions. Also, mini-stories begin to appear in the pages, each one an imagined scenario based on something observed. It's as though I wanted, through my writing, to bring more depth to how I was experiencing people and places. I have an acutely impoverished record of my first three months in South America because the diary for those months was stolen. The loss made me deeply depressed (still does). I remained in the same ugly town for days trying to recover it (even by advertising on the local radio), without success.

The return to London was far from easy. I tried to fit into my old shoes, and it didn't work. I may no longer have been travelling topographically, but I still wanted movement, exploration, excitement. The world of performance seemed full of bright lights, so I gravitated there (chapter ten); and, no longer afraid of intimacy, I sought out intoxicating love affairs (chapter nine). Drama and passion both fuelled my writing, in different ways, the former inspiring me to write plays, and the latter (by dint of uncritical encouragement from lovers and the emotions sparked) towards exploratory forms of writing, both in my diary and in short stories. I took up photography too, no longer worried (as I had been when I set out on my travels) about a conflict/tension between writing what I saw/experienced and photographing it. Instead, photography brought a new dimension to my creative self (chapter thirteen).

Before long, as I've outlined above, I found myself on Corsica believing I could be a 'writer'. Then came what I called an existential crisis, and the subsequent drive to find a proper job, that led me to journalism (chapter eleven). My first post as a journalist proved a trial of my ability and my personality to begin with, but, in time, led to me being better able to craft words (which did help my other writing), and to another colourful venture – two years as a freelance journalist in Brazil (chapter fourteen).

The final chapter (fifteen) traces – mostly through diary extracts – the first ten years of my relationship with Bel, and how we came slowly to the idea of wanting to have a child, but without any intention of marrying or even living together. Becoming a father would prove to be the most wonderful of adventures, and this new stage in my life would have a profound impact on my writing – both in the diary and in other writing – all of which I must leave for a second patchwork.

Chapter one

IGEE
THE STARS LOOK DOWN

Where do I come from? What's in my blood or, less metaphorically, what's in my genes? Much of me – both looks and character – seems to come from my father, Fred. Beyond him, I only know a little about my grandparents. I knew my grandmother Dolly well, but I never knew my grandfather, Isidor Goldsmith, Igee (or I. G.) as he was called later in life. However, he was such a vivid man, and lived such a kaleidoscopic life, with many ups and downs, that I feel it's only right to begin my own story with his. And if anyone in my known genetic history could be even slightly considered a 'star' then it's Igee, and I am not going to miss out on writing about any stars in my firmament.

Isidor Goldschmid (anglicised to Goldsmith) was born in Vienna in 1893. His parents – Josias and Laia (Laura) – came, probably, from Lviv (now in Ukraine, but in different times part of Poland but also Austria-Hungary) which had a large Jewish population. Aged only 17, he was posted to Smyrna, then part of the Austro-Hungarian empire, as a consular aide involved with the issuing of passports. According to Fred, Igee had suggested that he'd been given these duties because he was a Jew, and because no one else wanted to bother with the new-fangled camera technology. He remained with the consular service through the First World War, serving in various Middle East countries. Many years later, on seeing the film *Lawrence of Arabia*, he remarked to his second wife, Vera Caspary: 'If the Royal and Imperial Court had given me as much gold to bribe the Arabs as England gave Lawrence, I'd have been Goldschmid of Arabia.' According to Vera, he was a natural raconteur, my grandfather, and told many tales of his early days, especially in Smyrna.

After the war and the downfall of the Hapsburg Empire, Igee worked as an assistant and then a managing director for Apollo Film Company of Central Europe. In 1920, he married Dolly Schoham. Their two sons, Gustav (later Michael or Mike) and Fred were born in Vienna. From there the family moved to Berlin where Igee became general manager for a company called Sued Film, the German subsidiary of British International Pictures Ltd, which not only made films but owned cinemas. In the early 1930s, he was responsible for showing Walt Disney films; but, he also screened the strongly socialist movie, *All Quiet on the Western Front*. The Nazis were not yet in power but the Brown Shirts began picketing theatres showing the film, and Igee himself was high up on Hitler's list of undesirables. With mounting troubles, both political and financial, plus a wife and two young sons, he decided in 1931 to decamp to London. Dolly, however, returned to Berlin to organise the secret removal of their possessions. The following comes from a letter written by Dolly to a friend several years later.

> I went back to Berlin alone to arrange the secret removal of our furniture, promising with a pounding heart an inquiring income-tax man that my husband would be back soon, trembling all the time that he may look into the adjoining room, where everything had been already packed. He did not look, but that night I lay awake all alone in our house, listening to the Nazis shooting in the next house – arresting people in the middle of the night, hunting for them with guns and big dogs – knowing that my husband too was on the black list.

In London, Igee formed Grafton Films Ltd, and tried his hand at producing. He was responsible for one of the great pre-war British movies – *The Stars Look Down*. Based on a novel by A. J. Cronin, a Scottish doctor and novelist, it is certainly considered one of the finest film portrayals of working class life at the time. Cronin is best remembered for creating Dr Finlay, the title character in a long-running TV series; and for his book *The Citadel*, also made into a film, which is said to have contributed to the establishment of the National Health Service in Great Britain by exposing the injustice and incompetence of medical practice at the time. *The Stars Look Down* is set in a fictional town in the northeast of England, and weaves a story around a coal mine called Neptune and three men: a miner's son who is studying to become a doctor; a miner who becomes a businessman; and the son of the mine owner. Apart from being thoughtful and telling a great story, the film has thrilling scenes in which shaft constructions give way and the mine floods, trapping a group of miners deep below the surface. There is a clear socialist message, in the book and the film, suggesting that such accidents were inevitable so long as the coal industry was run by a large number of small owners rather than operated by the government within a nationalised industry. Carol Reed, who went on to make *The Third Man* which is considered the greatest British movie, directed the film version; and the cast included several young actors who would go on to become famous: Michael Redgrave, Margaret Lockwood and Emlyn Williams.

To jump forward briefly in my own life, the first time I remember being conscious of Igee in anything but a cursory way is when in

1981 Fred took me to the Museum of Modern Art (MOMA) in New York. Unbeknownst to me, he'd hired the small cinema for a showing of a copy of *The Stars Look Down* that Igee had donated many years earlier. MOMA's film department had a sheet of notes about the film, written by the famous American film critic Pauline Kael, who says: '[*The Stars Look Down*] has an understanding, an achieved beauty, that Carol Reed was never again able to sustain.'

At this point in his life, Igee would not have minded much about the stars looking down on him in an uncaring universe. He was on top of the world. The success of *The Stars Look Down* in the UK led him to the United States, where he was fêted, and offered work by Metro-Goldwyn-Mayer and Columbia (although, as it happens, he never actually finished a movie production for either of them). And new love came his way too. While attending a party at the house of Dr Cronin, who had moved to the US in the 1930s, Igee met a writer called Lillie Messinger. Dolly, his wife, found out, and the marriage, such as it was, collapsed. The same year (1942), it seems, Igee fell in love with another, but far more successful, writer – Vera Caspary, author of *Laura* (which was made into a film by Otto Preminger starring Gene Tierney).

Dolly of course was devastated. It had not been an easy life with Igee, but now he was deserting her. She wrote to a confidante.

> I have been happily married, except the last two years, for 22 years to a man which I love with all my heart – a man who always had ups and downs in his life, a man – I am sorry to state, who is absolutely unreliable and changeable in his character, who dismisses his best friends the moment he has no use for them anymore, but – I am sure – deep in his heart, devoted to me and our two magnificent boys, aged 20 and 17. It is not the first time that his financial state is in a mess and I am left behind alone, to face his creditors. Matter of fact, it is the 4th time in our married life, but I will not say it is his fault, I just state the fact he always tried very hard to make a success of his life and helped by his tremendous ambition, enthusiasm and overwhelming power of persuasion, he has been always successful till his financial position, based on borrowed money, collapsed once more and he had to look out for a new start somewhere else.

Soon after, though, Igee was called back to the UK. If he hadn't heeded the summons, he might have lost his British citizenship, and without it he would have reverted to his original Austrian nationality. However, against all the odds, and the difficulties of crossing the Atlantic, Vera managed to travel to England to be with her new lover. And, thereafter, they were rarely separated again. Poor Dolly.

After the war and back in the US, Igee tried and tried again to develop film projects. One of them was sparked by Fred (this was a little before I was born). Vera had been involved in writing a screenplay for a popular movie entitled *A Letter to Three Wives*, and Fred suggested a sort of sequel with the title *Letter to Three Husbands*. Igee set to work, and soon had the capital, a contract for release by United Artists and studio space at Motion Picture Centre. Vera too became heavily involved in the project, not least through providing finance out of the funds made from her own career. The film was shot and produced, Vera says in her autobiography *The Secrets of Grown-Ups* (McGraw-Hill, 1979), previews were shown, distribution dates set, and, 'once again, Mr and Mrs Goldsmith gave in to addiction; a pair of optimists indulged in happiness'.

But all was not well in Hollywood, and a fierce power battle was raging within United Artists. According to Vera, this led to serious delays in the release of *Three Husbands*, and only one tenth of the promised promotion budget being spent. Consequently, the film and Igee's company sank into serious financial difficulties. Other companies similarly affected went bankrupt. By doing so, they could be free of their contracts with United Artists, and sign with healthier distributors. Igee, though, could not take this route out of financial trouble because, according to California community property law, a wife was responsible for her husband's debts: all of Vera's future royalties on past writing and all reprint payments would be sucked in to pay them. In the end, Vera says, the mortgages Igee had raised to keep the company afloat were foreclosed, and he lost all his film rights – including that for *Three Husbands* – to his creditors.

Vera's autobiography again: 'The sorriest effect was Igee's remorse. He had wanted so much to take care of me, to free me for work I enjoyed. So painful the wound, so deep the scars that I had constantly to console him for losing my money.'

The stars were still looking down, unflinchingly, but this time on a desperate Igee. He'd lived a boom and bust life with his first wife, and now it was the same with Vera, only the ups and downs were still more dramatic. On 2 May 1952 (just four weeks now before I was born), Igee wrote a letter to Vera. I have a copy. It starts as follows.

> My Darling Vera, this last thing which I am doing in my life is meaner than anything I have ever done or sinned before. But I can't go on any longer and have no courage to face the consequences of my mistakes. Let me tell you first that I have done nothing dishonest except killing myself and leaving you in the end without money and without a loving devoted husband. This is the only crime I have committed in my life with you. This crime is of such magnitude that still – while writing this here – I don't know if I shall have the guts to do it. Once more now in these last days or perhaps minutes of my life I swear to you that had I known at the beginning of my work as independent producer that my signature would involve you I'd never have started at all. When I realised that my signature involves you . . . it was too late to withdraw and from that moment I piled mistake on mistake, sin on sin, until disaster has become una-

voidable. Everything that I did, right or wrong, was aimed to get out of my responsibilities and to save you disappointment. I only succeeded to delay it for a time but ultimately I failed. Why do I run away like this? Because I can't face you any more and can't look you in the eyes. I am afraid of you not because you'd be mad or scream or even cry. I am afraid because no greater injustice could ever be done to a woman like you than what results from my business transactions. I have been unfair to you . . . I should have known better before I dragged you into this. I feel guilty towards you to an extent where that feeling of guilt becomes unbearable.

He didn't kill himself, but trouble followed trouble. With financial difficulties dogging Igee and Vera, the early 1950s also brought the worst excesses of the McCarthy period. Vera was asked to write a letter disclaiming any sympathy for communism but refused, and, in consequence, was greylisted by the film industry. Greylisting was a more subtle means of ostracising artists than blacklisting, but, nevertheless, Vera (and Igee) were forced abroad, to Europe, for a few years. Vera was able to sell scripts back to the American studios, but often under an assumed name. Igee pursued more projects, none of them successful. 'Plans, hopes, disappointments and rejection formed the pattern of his life. The mysterious element, the magic that creates success, had departed,' Vera says.

One project, in particular, led Igee into spirals of despair. The film *Wunderkind* had been a great success in Germany, and Igee had high hopes for the US market. He invested Vera's money and took out loans to fund promotion and marketing, yet across the Atlantic the film was a huge flop. Its failure and the ensuing debts led Igee to write at least two more letters to Vera expressing suicidal sorrows. This is from 1960: 'This *Wunderkind* loss . . . this dreadful disappointment is the reason for my depression during this last year. I shall never get over it.'

One of Igee's failed projects in Europe is worth mentioning if only because he might have been responsible for the career launch of a movie icon. This is how Vera tells the story.

A young American friend told us he was soon to be married and hoped we could come to the wedding. "Here? How exciting. A wedding in Paris." Igee's big fist smote the frail cocktail table. "What a title." Wedding, Paris – box-office words. All we needed was a story. I doubt we had a glimmer of plot when Igee told the title to Robert Clark of Associated British Pictures. Mr Clark was looking for a light comedy for a talented young girl under contract to the studio. If I could give them a good idea I could write the screenplay and Igee produce a picture for Audrey Hepburn.

Wedding in Paris never made it to the screen but, instead, was turned into a hit musical comedy for London's West End with music by Hans May (who had written the score for *The Stars Look Down*).

My grandfather Igee suffered several heart attacks in 1964, the first after a strenuous day's walking and an argument with his old German friend Fritz Lang. Another came from over-excitement on listening to the Clay-Liston boxing bout. Despite these setbacks, and his poor health, he wanted to travel again to Europe. Vera diverted him, first to Las Vegas, and then to Vermont, New England, to stay at a house in a maple grove. Here are Vera's words again.

> For our pleasure the trees put on an early show. From glossy green they changed to crimson, gold, copper, orange and flame against backgrounds of dark pine and the yellow leaves and white trunks of the birches, all under a sky of polished blue. Igee had never seen its like, nor the white serene villages of New England. Just before dusk on 7 October, he asked me to stand under a flaming maple. It was for the last film in his camera. The light of the setting sun filtered through the maples dyed the white houses and our faces were as pink as June roses. We were saddened that day by the news that a friend had died in Hollywood, yet we could not restrain our joy in the beauty of the living world. The next morning he died. . . How can a man stride through a room, decide to sit in the sun and half an hour later not be there any longer?

Although I never knew him, Igee lives on in my history, in my story. And I am somewhat comforted – not saddened – to know that just as the stars looked down dispassionately on the characters in his film, and on his life, so those same stars (with him among them now) look down on me.

Chapter two

Fred
Flip-flap fatherhood

I have a dilemma in starting out on this chapter, the first of two which feature my father (Fred, Frederic, Freddy, Freddie), which is to understand why I have so much more to say about him than I have about my mother, Barbara (née Todd).

Fred left my mother and the UK when I was four, to live in the United States. He never came back, at least not for 20 years, and when he did I was on the other side of the world. I did meet him during two trips to New York in the early 1980s, but during the second visit he turned against me, for no apparent reason (which I will come to in chapter twelve), and that turned out to be an absolute end to our relationship. Since I have no memories of him from my childhood, the only ones I do have are from the few days spent together in New York. By contrast, I lived with my mother full-time for 18 years, and, thereafter, when I wasn't travelling, I would see her often, and speak to her regularly (at least once a fortnight, probably). I've struggled with how this can be, how I can have so much more to say about my almost non-existent flip-flap father and my homely ever-present ordinary mother. I use the word 'ordinary' guardedly, but need to insist it be taken without any negative connotation. I mean ordinary in the sense of being opposite to extraordinary. It was an ordinary day at work, no emergencies; John's a fairly ordinary guy, but his wife Jill is excruciatingly dull; etc.

A doctor writing up notes about his patients will have nothing to say about the healthy ones, but might have lots to say about those with unusual symptoms. A scientist might learn nothing from experiments or investigations that yield nothing strange, but write scores of academic papers about unusual or unique results. And, similarly, writers are inevitably drawn more to flip-flapness than ordinariness.

Born on 2 February 1925 in Vienna, Fred, along with his older brother, Mike, moved to London from Berlin in 1934 with his father Igee and mother Dolly. He went to University College School until 1941, spent a year at Willesden Technical College studying mechanical engineering, and was even apprenticed to the aircraft manufacturer, De Havilland, for a short while thereafter. He undertook military service with the Home

Guard in Hampstead and as a driver for the Army's Royal Engineers between 1943 and 1945. He then decamped to Los Angeles to study English literature and other subjects at University of Southern California. Back in London he found odd jobs in and around the film industry, in which his father, Igee, was working. Fred's positions, as recorded on his CVs of the time, before and after his studies in Los Angeles, included 'staff screenwriter' at Elstree Studios and 'camera assistant'.

In 1951, Fred met my mother Barbara. It may well have been at the Cosmo cafe, Finchley Road, near Swiss Cottage, where many Jewish émigrés, artists, poets and writers, often congregated. Barbara was still married to her first husband, Frederick Abel, not a love match for my mother, but a ticket out of and away from working class Stockton-on-Tees. They had moved to Manchester, but my mother left him there, seeking even brighter lights in London.

As far as I know – this is a story my mother did not tell me until I was in my 30s – she and Fred met in the middle of one week, and journeyed to Brighton the following weekend. Amazingly, I have a photograph of Fred and Barbara then on the Palace Pier, happily lounging in deckchairs – amazing because I must have been conceived within hours of that photograph being taken. According to Barbara, as a result of the pregnancy, Fred agreed to get married because it would be 'a new experience', something he hadn't done before. But his letters from that time show he was also in love with my mother. Here are three of them.

> May 29th (Baby's first day)
> Darling Barbi, This is just a little note to tell you I love you very much and miss you (and baby). There's a lot of things to think of at the moment, especially what to bring you (Quackum Ducks – Sleeping pill? – paper – pen – book – fruit – flower) in about two hours/and to shave and other unpleasant things, oh yes, and to go and have tea with mother. But I love you and want to say so . . . Before going on to tell my adventures. . .
> Barbi-Darling, I loves ye. The flap, the great big first-father-flap has subsided a little, just a little. I wants my family home, I does. Yesterday (kiss darling) I went to meet Tommy (who sends you his congrats) Morrison, but he didn't turn up as per telephone conversation (Quack-Quaack) which I expected because the telephone had said that Mr Tommy might or might not be detained with other first-flap-fathers or film-flap-floogers at the Old Horses Club where screenwriters go. Instead at the 'C' or 'K' – osmo (dive-bomber kids) I saw Pat and Henry who send you their love. (As they didn't incidentally, offer to lend me money, I was disdainful and never mentioned the subject.) . . . and me on to Leicester Square at the all night post-office. I've wrat the letter to OILSHELL, but would rather gather exotic shells on some pacific beach, musing in the sand, while Barbi and Baby look for diamonds in nearby rocks. One day we must do this in Brighton. Flip-flap has done a lot really, but not yet made a start on Arthur Dent work, naughty be'nt it? Flip Flap anti-aircraft duck thinks it waste to devote to Arthur Dent good writing paper to Arthur Dent flip-flap assignment. I loves ye and the baby . . .

I loves yer now just as mooch as I did when I started wratting this letter and before, I expect however soon for you to say ye loves the baby, and, as an afterthought, ye loves me too. Has it gone meow again? Very important this, to be noted down against future psychopathic inquisitions from neurotic psychoanalyists. I discover writing you the exquisite peace of no flip flap about spelling and such other terriblenesses of civilisation. I loves ye with an XXXXXX and etc. (This etc. is an very important one, and shows how extreme weight can be attached to such a little.) Yours Freddy

Tuesday
Darling Barbi, I've just got twenty minutes before I take Mrs Dixon a-driving. Past the ciggie shop to get my Barbi some sweeties and only incidentally perhaps a few cigarettes for Flip-Flap. The drive yesterday was lovely and I really enjoyed myself. I gave a lift to a dangerous looking tramp, all the way to Brighton, where there was a furious wind . . .

Flip flap loves darling and misses family. I shall sees yer later this afternoon, and wonder if up-and-abouting again suits you. How is Baby Goldsmith? Can he say AGGAGA ix AGAG ix ix yet? Or does he still go meow?

Everybody has been offering to feed me. I could accept fifteen meals a day, and still have other offers to refuse. I think of these offers rather ironically at this moment for I am ravenously hungry, and eating bread and margarine. Tonight Joan Abse will feed me, and Danny and I'll play a game of chess, and then flip flap must flip flapping back to flap flip work – must be finished in week or thereabouts; for that is what flip flap letter says to Arthur Dent.

Sunday 1pm
Darling Barbi and Baby, You looked so beautiful yesterday when I flip-flapped quacking into the ward. But I was a bit depressed by the world, and couldn't see further than my own glasses which no Barbi had cleaned for me lately in the piccies. When I got home I howled for about three minutes, and then got down to Dent work, writing wise-cracks; no longer working for the twenty odd pounds, ten of which am spent already, but thinking that with a good bit of work done, Flip-Flap could say to Dent, now give regular work to Goldsmith family . . .

I think darling, that when you come out of the hospital, we will have ahead a few rough weeks, a month or two even, during which time it may be necessary to rely on mother and friends. But I know that we three being together forged together now with a strong hand, we, and especially you, will pass through the difficult time, if it comes so, with strength and good heart. Honestly, I feel very optimistic. I will find something, tomorrow or the next day, and soon settle down, that we may live as well as we can. If flip-flap finds square peg in round hole work, then Barbi will help him cut off the corners. . .

I should get back to the wise-quacks, but I love Barbi and want to carry on writing, while an egg fries in the pan for a flip-flap lunch. I want to think more names

Lee Goldsmith, Leon Steven Goldsmith, Sam Goldsmith, Maxwell Goldsmith, Larry Goldsmith, Paul Goldsmith (awful sound), Felix Goldsmith, William Felix Goldsmith, Charles Goldsmith, Henry Goldsmith, etc

Oh darling, you think of some. It's most cross-making when names whirl around in the mind, and the intellect makes lightening attempts to disassociate them from their false associations. I think we should consider the matter perhaps along the following lines: In view of heredity and environment (that's us) what sort of boy might it become, and ergo what sort of name would then

suit it. For instance TITO GOLDSMITH would be a good name for a trapeze artist, but would hardly suit an ear, nose and throat specialist who would better
be named HENRY. Enough. It is better for baby to have no name for a few
days, than for Daddy to go mad.

. . . My life is altogether confused without Barbi – one big flip-flap from
morning to night. So I still love, love you very much my darling, and I hope it
will not be long before I can bring you good news that I have work. And the
baby will be sun-tanned on the Heath, and we'll take it rowing in Regent's
Park, and in a few months I will teach it to drive the Dixon's car; for it will certainly be no worse on the road than other drivers. Around the time you had
the baby, about 3pm on Derby Day, I slowed down for some pedestrians to
cross, and a posh car driven by a swanky man passed me, the swanky man
yelling at me to wake up. As loud as I could I shouted 'SHUT UP YOU OLD
CLOT' and since he was aged about thirty he was obviously upset about the
OLD, and threatened with a motion to stop his car and dispute the matter further. But Flip-flap not wishing to do battle, quickly took a side turning.

How odd, I think some 65 years later, that my father should
pick out just one name for comment ('Paul Goldsmith – awful sound')
and that I should have been given that very name. I have no information as to why my mother or father or both chose that one. It has
served me reasonably well, I should say, except that when I took on my
stepfather's surname, Lyons, the sound of the two names conjoined
was ugly – it being linguistically awkward to provide a gap between the
last 'l' of Paul and the first 'l' of Lyons. But, at least, I wasn't branded a
Tito, and forced into clownhood.

Not long ago, when I got married in fact, I discovered that on
being born I had first been listed in the birth index as Paul Kenneth
Abel. This must have been because my mother's divorce papers had not
yet come through and/or she had not yet married Goldsmith. My
parents must have wed a few weeks after I was born; and only then
was my birth certificate – with the name Goldsmith – issued.

Back to my father, my flip-flap father. He hung around for three
or four years. He and my mother moved into a garden flat at 21 Fitzjohn's Avenue, and he took one of the small bedrooms for a study,
determined to become a writer. He never had any money, and one of
the few things my mother told me as an adult about him was that he
was good at conjuring up flashy gifts, like smoked salmon, but often
could not afford basic food supplies.

Nevertheless, this period of Fred's life turned out to be the most
productive, at least in terms of his ambition to be a writer. In 1954, W. H.
Allen published his novel *Murder in Mayfair*, a thriller. I first read it in the
British Library, but I've since acquired a couple of copies, one from a
jumble sale, and one from my mother's bookshelves. This latter copy has
a dust jacket, showing a young woman wrapped in a huge fur coat,

standing outside a club called Camellia. Apart from the title and Fred's name, the front cover also notes that the novel is 'Based on a short story by Vera Caspary'. Vera, of whom I will have more to say later, was already successful by this time, and Fred benefited doubly from his father's second marriage. Not only did Vera gift him the story, but her name and connections certainly helped the book get published. Inside, there's an inscription – although I'm not sure who to. It says: 'Sept 54, With my very best wishes, Freddy'. A year later, while I was still in toddlerhood and no doubt doting on my parents, W. H. Allen published Fred's second (and last) book – *The Smugglers*. This is an adventure story, and is dedicated to 'I.G.' According to Fred's own CVs, both books were 'excellently reviewed nationally in England and Canada'.

I had never known anything about *The Smugglers* but then, out of the blue in 2016, I received an email. It began: 'I am Anna, daughter of Tiya and Jack Kendall.' I had never heard of her or them. She had found my contact details online, she said, and went on to explain that her parents had been friends with my father long ago. 'According to papers found in my mother's archives, my father had made an arrangement to have his smuggling times story written down by writer Frederic Goldsmith.' We exchanged a couple of emails, and I put her in touch with Peter the Girl and Tony, elderly friends of mine who had once been friends with my father, and who, I later found out, had also been involved in the smuggling. Anna's last email to me contained a few extra details: 'The war had broken [my parents'] lives. When it ended Tiya was a painter and textile designer and Jack was a poker player and a tool factory worker. I believe his smuggling story ended in 1953 or 1954 when they left London for Paris, after his "partner" got caught with all the money and stuff...'

In the second half of 1956, Fred left me, my mother and the UK to follow Igee, his father, to the US. Having flip-flapped to New York, his first letter to my mother promised everything, as usual:

> 'My sights are set very high. It is important for me for the time being to go all out to make the maximum amount of money possible because I desire very much to pay everything off in London, to send you money, and to go ahead with the analysis which, like everything else here, is ten times as costly as in London.'

The reference to analysis is a surprise, since I never heard my mother mention this. The letter also gives good descriptions of the boat journey (including how 'the boat finally gave in and produced for me the inevitable girl friend') and of his new digs in New York. He calls me 'Pauli' in this and other letters, and signs himself 'Freddie'.

Three months later, he writes to my mother that he hopes to start regular payments for me soon, though they might be a bit 'erratic' for a while. And here also is Fred's view as to why the marriage broke down. It's worth quoting the whole paragraph.

> I am relaxing somewhat with the postcards to Paul because I feel that the impact of my going away must have settled itself by now, and I hope the postcards helped bridge the gap. It was the best I could do, and I will continue with them, but not so frequently. For one thing, I don't want him to get bored with hearing from me. Mother [Dolly] suggested I was easing my conscience in this way. My conscience, and I wish you would tell her this, is quite clear. I think we were unfortunate, we hurried into marriage and tried to love each other, but it just did not happen that way. If Mother were to say that I sent the postcards because of a sense of loss, that would be quite true. Big love to the little man.

Big love to the little man! Postcards! I don't know anything about his big love or postcards. If any question marks hang over my life, then, this is it: did the loss of my father at the tender age of four affect me a little, a lot, not at all? As an adult, I questioned my mother about this several times but she always claimed the answer was 'not at all'. I have no memories of him from my early life, none. And it's certainly true as far as I know that I've never possessed any conscious traces of him within me, whether physical or emotional. But what about deep in my psyche? I have wondered at times if a deep sense of insecurity I felt through the first half of my life came from having had a father who flip-flapped out of my world so early. So flippantly.

As I say, I don't know anything about postcards either, but I do have a sequence of letters written by Fred and sent to me directly while I was still living at home (1961-1969). Mostly they are dated May (my birthday) or December (Christmas) and sometimes mention a present (small amounts of money, or coins, or stamps – I still have a set of Kennedy half dollars and a collection of Hungarian stamps). At the beginning of this period he'd just married a dancer called Judy, and was still trying to be a writer. By the end of the period he was working mostly as a tour guide. In the first letter, dated May 1961, he suggests he might come to England next year. In 1962, he again says he might be coming to England soon. He also writes this: 'We don't know each other very well, but that means that some time in the future we have a marvellous experience before us – to get to know each other again.'

It would be nearly 20 years before I met Fred, and a marvellous experience it was, briefly, before he threw me out his house, saying he never wanted to see me again (the explanation for this, though, fits better in chapter twelve).

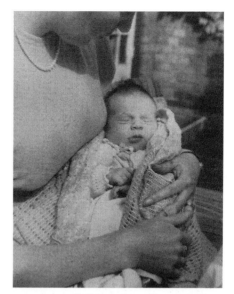

Top left: Fred and Barbara on
Palace Pier, Brighton;
Top right: Barbara and baby me;
Middle left: toddler me; Middle right:
Barbara, Dolly (my grandmother) and
me; Bottom left: Igee Goldsmith

Chapter three

HAMPSTEAD
SECRET GARDENS

Secrets can be dark and forbidding or magical and full of promise. Much of my childhood is a secret garden, now so overgrown that I visit it rarely and know little about it. I was born in Hampstead, and lived there until I was 11, when, in the summer of 1964, my parents moved to Hoddesdon in Hertfordshire. If, in this chapter, I were to include every single memory-story I know about myself from those first 11 years, they would barely fill two pages. But then there's Hampstead to consider too, an area of London that for a long time felt more like home than any other part of the world, and a place I never tire of revisiting – not the narrow streets, nor cutesy shops, nor atmospheric cafes, particularly, but the Heath, magnificent Hampstead Heath. Much as I love the Heath, its ponds and paths, its wildnesses and tamenesses, its gardens and its hills, there is one part I love more than any other. I call it my secret garden, but it's full of light and magic not darkness and shame.

I was born right in the middle of Hampstead, at New End Hospital, on 28 May 1952, the same day the Aga Khan's horse *Tulyar* won the Derby, and a race pundit wag said 'What did I tulyar!' Originally founded in 1800, part workhouse, part casual ward and part infirmary, the institution was rebuilt in 1845 and until the First World War served the unemployed, the destitute, unmarried mothers and their children, and psychiatric patients. During the war, it was used for soldiers who were wounded or shell-shocked. After the war, it was modernised and renamed New End Hospital serving acutely sick patients. Because of the pioneering work of Jack Piercy, Surgeon Superintendent for over 30 years, it became well known as a centre for endocrinology. It remained in use as a hospital until 1986, when the building was sold, and the profits funded redevelopment of Queen Mary's Maternity Home, also in Hampstead. Across the road, the hospital's mortuary, dating from 1890 where Karl Marx was once laid out before being buried in Highgate Cemetery, was converted to a theatre in the 1970s.

I know that when I was born we lived in my grandmother Dolly's house at 13 Bracknell Gardens, and that for a few months we also stayed in a flat in Platts Lane, but from the age of about one until I was 11, I lived at Flat 1, 21 Fitzjohn's Avenue. This is the long road that runs uphill from Swiss Cottage to Heath Street in Hampstead. It was built in the late 1870s with large houses set well back from the road, and plantings of alternate red and white chestnuts. In 1883, *Harper's Magazine* called it 'one of the noblest streets in the world'. There were steps down to our front door from the drive in front, and steps down from the garden to French doors at the back of the flat. An alley ran round the side of the house (and our flat) from back to front. Apart from the French windows, I recall nothing at all about the inside.

The earliest memory I have . . . I can't honestly call it a memory, it's the earliest story I know about myself. I was four or five and had been playing in the garden when I wanted to come inside. The French doors were closed, and I was knocking on them for someone to let me in. No one did, so my knocking got louder, until I broke the glass.

Most of the garden was laid to lawn with flower beds all around. In one of the back corners was a tree which had two different kinds of leaves growing from its branches. It was possible to walk along the wall at the back past several other gardens. I must have played in that garden a thousand times, often with my neighbours and friends – Nicky and Sherry. I have a tiny photo of them standing on the grass. We had pets, cats and dogs, throughout my childhood, so they must have made good use of the garden. And, oh yes, I had a tortoise, or more than one, since I seem to remember them not coming back after a winter of supposed hibernation. My stepfather, Sasha, once laid out a rope on the lawn, and demanded that I be able to cycle along it before he allowed me out on the road. There's another vague story-memory about Sasha and a bicycle, a few years later. I must have left it in the street one day, and it got stolen. Sasha made me go along the street knocking on everyone's front door to ask them if they'd seen it. The story always surfaces with feelings of acute shame and embarrassment.

I know a few, very few, details about my early life. After Fred, my father, left for the USA my mother took in lodgers; and she also worked as a typist near Belsize Village. Before long, though, she met and married Sasha Lyons.

I was still called Paul Goldsmith when I went to Holy Trinity, a Church of England school on Trinity Walk, a steep pedestrian alley which runs up from Finchley Road (opposite where John Barnes Department Store used to be, and where Waitrose is today) to Maresfield Gardens. I have no memories of, or stories about, this school at all – no teachers, no pupils, no classes, nothing. But, because I've walked up or down Trinity Walk many times in my life since then, I have an image of a school dominated by an impressively tall stretch of wire fencing between the playground and the steep alley, presumably to keep balls in rather than uninvited guests out. Apparently, the school was founded in 1873 to educate the children of the men building the Metropolitan Railway at Finchley Road.

I do have one report sheet from Holy Trinity. It's dated July 1958. There were 40 pupils in the class, but I was absent during tests and so wasn't given a 'position in class'. According to this report my 'reading' and 'memory words' were 'good', and I was 'very good' at 'missing words'. I was also 'good' at art, writing, handwork, and 'very good' at arithmetic and PE. Miss or Mrs Hatton, the class mistress, wrote: 'Paul has done an excellent year's work. He is bright and helpful in class and behaves fairly well.'

I was taken out of Holy Trinity and sent to Lyndhurst House Preparatory School when I was about seven, because I couldn't read very well. Interestingly, but not surprisingly, there was a marked difference in standards between the state and private schools. My first Lyndhurst report (I was being called Paul Lyons by this time) has these comments about my ability: 'English – Very weak at present'; 'Reading – Weak. When he tries he can do better. He needs constant hard practice.'; 'Mathematics – He is slow and lacks perseverance, but has made some progress. Knowledge of tables weak.'

I have a couple of story-memories connected with Lyndhurst House. There was a time when I was listening to a cricket Test Match secretly in class, thanks to a little transistor radio with an earphone. But I gave myself away when I involuntarily let out a cry of pleasure at something that had happened in the match, and my radio was confiscated. Another time, the whole class was lined up in the corridor outside the deputy headmaster's study. We were all queuing to be caned by Mr Wilcox (on the hand, I think) for some joint sin we must have committed. I have an imprinted impression that Mr Wilcox caned us often.

The neat handwritten Lyndhurst School reports I've managed to keep for over 50 years do give me a little extra, if rather dull, information about the form or shape of my academic abilities at the time. I am bottom of the class when I first arrive, but slowly climb the form rankings to fourth (out of about 20). Then, apparently at the same time as we get a new form teacher, I slip back to a position somewhere in the middle of the class. At the end of 1962, when I'm 10, for one report only, I am ranked as top of the class. Even so, my form master, Mr Gilbert, feels it necessary to draw attention to my 'quick and violent temper'. His comments in previous years were almost always negative or begrudging, 'must work harder', 'can do better', 'badly behaved', 'too talkative' and 'inattentive'. One teacher complained of me being 'over-cheerful', which is nice. My favourite comment, though, is probably this one about history: 'Having squandered most of the term in total indolence, he has recently started to do some work. If he allows this trend to become a habit, he is in danger of rising rapidly.' Thank you, Mr Dunlop, thank you, I'm sure your comments spurred me on.

What else about school? Very little. I learned to play chess at Lyndhurst House. And, once, I went to a large house in Swiss Cottage, to a party being given by the diplomat father of a friend.

Here is the last of these story-memories from the secret garden of my Hampstead childhood. Right opposite 21 Fitzjohn's Avenue, there was a pedestrian crossing – perhaps it's still there. I used to walk home from Lyndhurst School on my own, but I wasn't allowed to cross Fitzjohn's Avenue alone. So I would arrive on the side of the road opposite to our flat and wait for my mother, or shout to her. One day, I was desperate for the toilet, and despite shouting and shouting my mother did not appear. Eventually, I just peed there, standing by the side of the road, the warm liquid dribbling down my shorts and leg. When my mother was still alive, I asked her whether she recalled anything about this, but she didn't. The story I've always had in my head – and it's quite a sure one – is that I could easily have crossed the road on my own but that I deliberately wet myself out of revenge, in order to get back at my parents for insisting on such a stupid rule. But now, as I am writing down this story for the very first time, I'm wondering whether, at that age (was it 8 or 10? I've no idea), I would have been prepared to put up with the shame of wetting myself to make such a point. Perhaps. Or perhaps, I just didn't dare break the rule.

What else about my childhood in Hampstead? Peter the Girl, a contemporary of my parents but also a friend of mine in later life, said she gave me a key to her flat in case I needed a refuge – the implication being that I wasn't always happy at home. Incidentally, I never knew exactly why she was called Peter the Girl, but even in old age there was something of a tomboy about her.

One summer I went on holiday to Alderney with a friend who lived in the same block of flats as Dolly. I seem to recall the Isle of Raz, with its tide-dependant causeway, and rusty World War II armaments, and swatting flies in the kitchen of wherever I was staying. I'm sure I must have been on other holidays, but any trace of them has gone. I know I used to go to Cubs in a hall by what is now the Everyman Cinema, and sail a model yacht on Whitestone Pond. I went regularly to the Saturday Morning Pictures at the Swiss Cottage Odeon; and on Saturdays and Sundays there was an outdoor art market along Heath Street, and donkey rides near the pond.

For the last few months of my childhood life in Hampstead, I have a more reliable – yet rather paltry – source of information. For Christmas, in 1962, I was given a five-year diary. There are very short entries for most days in January, February and March 1963, and a few from July. Here's a brief selection.

1 January 1963
Went to see *The Magnificent Seven* . . . Had swimming lesson and learnt to do back stroke.

8 January 1963
Washed windows and cleaned brass, got 2/6 for doing it.

9 January 1963
Nicky and Sherry came to tea and as usual we were interrupted to have tea in the middle of *The Terrible Ten*.

10 January 1963
Went to Grandma's and played Scrabble, poker, gin and roulette.

14 January 1963
Had two fillings and found out that drilling is horrible.

23 January 1963
Played Sir in chess. He won. We did not get English prep.

1 February 1963
Went to see *Oliver* with Caroline. It was a lovely play but it did not have [my schoolmate] Martin Stephens as Oliver Twist.

10 February 1963
Did homework in afternoon and evening – watched *XL5* and *Candid Camera*. . . Went to Sunday School, and answered a lot of questions.

16 February 1963
Got my *Valiant and Knockout* there was a 2d bar of toffee as a free gift. Went to the pictures and saw *The Life of Tommy Steele*. Found my penknife which I lost the other day.

17 February 1963
Sorting out my Hungarian stamps.

23 February 1963
Went to the pictures. The big film was *Ma and Pa Kettle at Home*. Went to the football match – Arsenal v Spurs. Spurs won 3-2. It was a very exciting game. Daddy taught me how to play Steve Canyon.

26 February 1963
Half term. Sherry came to my house for lunch and we played Steve Canyon and Scrabble, neither of which we finished. We played Monopoly – it was a lovely game and I won. I then went to Sherry's house for tea and did a jigsaw puzzle and watched television. Had pancakes for lunch and tea.

24 April 1963
In morning watched Princess Alexandra get married to Angus Earl of Ogilvy. The programme lasted about three hours.

25 July 1963
Had a bleeding nose early in the morning and prize giving in the afternoon. Mummy came and after prize giving went to see some of the work I did during the term. Watched *Criss Cross Quiz*, *Space Patrol* and *The Alfred Hitchcock Hour*. Had my last Lyndhurst House school lunch. It was horrible. Had big tea – 11 pieces of bread, two cakes and strawberries.

That summer, July 1963, we moved out of London, to Hoddesdon in Hertfordshire, and it would be some years – after school, university and travelling – before I found myself living in the area again. In December 1977, the friend I've already mentioned, Peter the Girl, and her husband Tony decided to move to Germany (where Peter originally came from). In doing so, they let me take over their garden flat in Kilburn, in Fordwych Road, a stone's throw from West Hampstead, and two stones' throws from Hampstead. By then, the so-called village of Hampstead really was long past its Bohemian heyday, and had become an expensive suburb, a commercial hub with designer clothes shops, and pretentious cafes. There wasn't much there to attract me, except, of course, Hampstead Heath.

Once upon a time – it must have been 1978 – I was re-exploring, re-discovering the Heath a little north of Whitestone Pond when I came upon a hole in a fence. I was 26 at the time, the same age at which my parents had become parents with me, yet there I was still in my childhood, climbing trees and crawling through holes in fences. Inside, I found brambles, and an iron circular staircase that led me up and onto a long raised walkway with a pergola covered in mature and characterful climbers, their thick stems curled and twisted round the pergola's posts and rafters, the leafy stems hanging down, rich in buds and flowers, mostly old roses, but clematises too, honeysuckles . . . To one side of the walkway was the imposing Inverforth House, once Lord Leverhulme's residence, with its formal gardens, lawns and ponds, all slightly lower than the walkway. To the other, much lower down, were the wild, wooded, dark parts of the open heath. I assumed I was trespassing, but as there was no one about, I strolled along the walkway, walking on air almost through the picturesque landscape, until I reached a cute bridge, over a path below, and passed through an elaborate gateway to an even more impressive walkway possessed, it seemed, by a most beautiful and ancient wisteria. At the other end, I could see a summerhouse of sorts, and expected I'd soon have to turn back or find another hole in the wall to return to the public parts of the heath. As the walkway neared the summerhouse, a wall on the right gave way and suddenly there was a view, looking down onto another beautiful garden, this one dominated by wide beds of mature shrubs, wonderfully shaped and coloured, a gently rolling lawn, and a fish pond. It was heavenly. I thought I was still trespassing but, as there were no other people, I walked down the stairs and wandered around the new garden, in wonder. For a moment, I lay down on the grass, and found the slope was just perfect for the child in me to tuck his arms in tight by his side, and roll, roll, roll.

On the far side of this secret garden, I eventually discovered a gate, and a notice informing me that it was called The Hill, and that for set hours every day it was open to the public! No matter. It was still my secret garden and my favourite place in all of London, and has remained so for more than 30 years. Until the hole was repaired and the walkways modernised, whenever I took friends, especially girlfriends, to see the garden, I always took them through the hole in the wall, and I usually persuaded them to roll on the lawn too. Mostly though I went there alone, to think, to read, to watch, to play, to dream.

> 2 Jan 1979
> Yet another magical afternoon in the secret garden. The sky incandescently blue, the sun incandescently yellow . . . I, in my handsome trance, climbing walls and tramping whimsical pathways through corridors and time tunnels briared by the dying thorns of ramblers and crawlers. And alone in the garden, dancing in the snow. The very first time, I have seen it so, covered in snow. Almost undisturbed – sleeping snow – magic – colours shining through the multi-greens, outlined by brilliant white – shapes sharpened and more roundly framed by the glistening powder. Like feathers the snow lies on the grass, tempting one to fall into a floating dream on its surface. But I am surprised, because no people come or go – the snow and I, and my ecstasy of life. I read out loud from Eliot's *Burnt Norton* and *East Coker* for an audience of deaf snowflakes. How alive, how vibrant, dancing and reciting, uncaring of interruptions, and yet there are none. Garlic and sapphire in the mud – the children laughing in the bushes – and the stillness shall be the dancing – splendid, splendid, splendid. The park keeper finally throws me out: he explains the garden has remained closed because there are no staff to clear the paths. He tells me to leave the way I came in – very friendly he is. Splendid.

Here is another diary entry from a decade later.

> 13 Oct 1989
> She talks completely without inhibitions, and asks me direct whether or not I have lusted for her, and tells me she has liked me since we first rolled down a hill together at the secret garden.

Hampstead is not only Hampstead Heath for me, but it is mostly; and Hampstead Heath is not only the Secret Garden for me, but it is mostly. Yet I do have other experiences of the Heath – tramping from one end to the other, in rain, sun, wind and snow, and not always knowing exactly where I am; the magnolia tree in Kenwood garden, picnics, and open air concerts; watching my son Adam fly his kite from Parliament Hill, and sail his model boat in one of the nearby ponds; all the fun of the Easter fairs, sometimes by the Vale of Health, sometimes in South Hampstead; Golders Hill Park with its aviary and bands playing in the summer; and swimming in the mixed pond. How I loved to cycle over to South Hampstead from Kilburn, of a spring or summer evening, to swim in the bathing pond – didn't matter to me if it was wet or sunny, except that when it was a warm sunny evening there'd be others at the pond too, and when it wasn't, I'd be alone, wonderfully alone. I have always loved to swim in fresh or sea water – it seems to make me feel more alive than almost any other activity. And to be able to do this in the middle of London, to wash off the urban heat, dirt and tribulations, meant these swims were even more intensely pleasurable.

I did, though, have concerns about the water because it always looked so murky. I knew the ponds were fed by running water, from the underground river, and that it smelled good and sweet. In July 1989, one of my testicles nearly doubled in size. Various doctors thought it was only an infection, but because they could not rule out cancer, I was admitted very quickly to the Royal Marsden Hospital for a testicular biopsy. It was a horrible experience – so much waiting, so much anxiety, and lots of pain/discomfort – from beginning to end. Worst of all, though, was meeting a man in the next bed, so fit, so strong, so young, who had been diagnosed with testicular cancer a year earlier. He had had the testicle removed, had had loads of chemotherapy, but the cancer was still inside him and he was back in the ward. A surgeon, and half a dozen other doctors in tow, arrived at his bedside, closed the curtains, but I could hear them talking about an ensuing operation in which more of the young man's organs – such as a kidney – might need to be removed, depending on just how far the cancer had spread. It sounded like his luck had run out in his mid-20s; I was in my mid-30s, and my luck was definitely in – the biopsy proved there was no cancer. Antibiotics soon removed the infectious swelling. I remain convinced to this day that the infection was most likely caused by something in the pond water, though no doctor I talked to would give this idea any credence. Consequently, though, I never swam in the Heath ponds again.

Also in Hampstead, a couple of years earlier, Adam was born, in August 1987, at the Royal Free Hospital, which coincidentally is the hospital closest to where I was born. Not everything in the ward went as well as it should have done, though, so my memories of that time are a little tainted. The Royal Free Hospital is also where my mother died in January 2007.

But to close this chapter I wish to return to more pleasure-full memories of Hampstead, and thus to my secret garden. A few years ago, when I was living in Surrey, I signed up as a volunteer photographer, one of hundreds, for English Heritage which was running a huge project to photograph all the listed buildings in the country, and to put one picture of every building on the internet – *Images of England*. I took a lot of photographs in Surrey villages, but when I'd completed the task, I asked English Heritage if there were any targets in northwest London still waiting to be photographed – at the time, I was spending a lot of time in Willesden. When I got my first batch of target buildings, I was astonished and thrilled to find I'd been allocated the listed buildings and structures in and around The Hill, and that the archive of England's listed buildings would include MY photographs of MY secret garden.

Chapter four

HODDESDON AND BROXBOURNE
BEING BONSAIED

In 1963, my parents moved to Hoddesdon, Hertfordshire, a commuter town with an efficient train service from its neighbour Broxbourne into London's Liverpool Street station. I have no recollection of the change or move. While my stepfather went to work every day from Broxbourne Station, I went to study at Broxbourne Grammar School. Reflecting back on these years with few real memories, a few diary entries, and a sprinkling of facts, I suspect I was bonsaied. I know there is no verb to bonsai, so I've had to stretch the English language in conjugating it, with a past form and past participle (bonsaied), an 'ing' form (bonsaiing), and an associated noun (bonsaier).

I think, one way or another, I was fed too little, my roots were clipped regularly, my twigs and branches were pruned, and restraints were wrapped around my trunk to bend it into shape. I am not blaming the places, Hoddesdon and Broxbourne themselves, even though once away from them, my roots and branches found more fertile ground and healthier air, and my trunk grew round its restraints. But where else should I look – my parents, my school, my friends, my teenage self? Perhaps a psychologist should write this chapter.

For this period of my life, I have a variety of information sources. The least useful, probably, is the five-year diary, into which I began writing short entries even before the move. There are entries in the diary from every year from 1963 to 1968, but the total adds up to only around 15,000 words, and the vast majority of them are a catalogue of what I did in school lessons, what I ate, and what I watched on television. A fairly detailed Broxbourne School report book provides third party evidence about my academic ability and my behaviour in class. There is my family, of course, but my parents are dead, my brother and sister were ten and eight years younger than me respectively, and I had too little contact with other relations for them to know much about my life. There is Colin, though, the only school friend with whom I'm still in touch. He has a phenomenal memory of those times, and certainly remembers far more about our school life than I do.

We moved from our basement flat on a busy London road to a three-storey, four-bedroom detached house with a large garden on a (very rutted) private road. Behind, there was an orchard (at least until a housing estate was built); 100 yards up the road was a copse, where once I found wild strawberries; and a five minute walk would bring me to fields, where once I lost our dog. The house – at 23 West Hill Road – had a white-painted pebble dash front, a large lounge with French windows, and a huge attic with secret tunnels. I was given the room at the top of the house, next to the attic, with a dormer window, and a large cupboard, useful for games, storage boxes and hiding in.

My head is buried in my hands as I try to find memories connected with that room. There are only three. Seven years of my life lived in that room, and all I have are three very foggy recollections or evocations of myself. Astonishing.

One evocation is of having to listen to my transistor under the bedclothes for fear of being caught by my parents. I was keen on a group called Dave Clark Five, and was determined to listen out for plays of their latest record. I didn't like the Beatles, because everyone else did. Sandy Shaw was another favourite – it's just a coincidence that she didn't wear shoes, and, once I'd escaped to university, nor did I. Rigid early bedtimes were imposed on me through most of my early teenage years – for what purpose?

The second is of sitting at the desk under the window, pen in hand, exercise book in front of me, and crying over having to write an essay. I found it so very difficult. The third is difficult to confess, but in so doing I ask for forgiveness. For a short while, I had a girlfriend called Ann King. She was very pretty, and her father had a very old car, an A10 I think it was, with running boards, and doors that opened the wrong way. I drove the big heavy thing once or twice. I have other memories connected with Ann, but this one sees her in my room. She was very fond of a Rolf Harris hit at the time – *Two Little Boys* – which I hated. In order to bring her round to my way of thinking, I recorded the song onto a loop of tape, and when she was in my room I let it play again and again and again and again . . .

All of which is to skip too far forward, too quickly. As it happens, about a year after moving to Hoddesdon fate decided to have a go at bonsaiing me, in a truly physical sense. I was already small for my age (12) at the time, but three months of daily antibiotic injections into my bum served to bring further growth to a near standstill for several years – my nickname Titch was very apt. My mother always maintained that a few years later I was given a growth hormone, but I have always been convinced, in my own mind, that I'd never wanted this. I've checked my medical records, which do in fact go back to childhood, and there's no evidence to support my mother's belief. At 5ft 8, I reached a reasonable height, though significantly smaller than my father, and about the same height as my mother.

The problem started with a pain in my groin. I reported it to my parents, and in time a doctor was consulted. My memory, my story is that no one believed how much it hurt. The doctor passed it off as a sprain, and my parents trusted him rather than my expressions of agony. Eventually, though, it became so unbearable that the adults around me could no longer ignore it, and I was rushed off to hospital in an ambulance. I may have first gone to Hertford, but I ended up in Bishop's Stortford Hospital, and stayed there for the best part of three months (including Christmas 1964) on my back with the leg in a traction. I had a rare infection called septic arthritis which was so advanced (or so the story in my head goes) that I was within a day or two of losing the whole leg. Afterwards I was on crutches for a month or so. I don't recall being in hospital, or anyone coming to visit me, or being ill. I just know it happened. I also have a singular collection of letters. My English teacher at the time, a Mrs Cregan (wife of the playwright David Cregan), obliged all my classmates to spend one lesson writing to me. The letters are mostly formal, lacking any real warmth, but the occasional spark of humour and hints of fondness come through. Here are a few extracts, starting with a line I have never forgotten.

> The class is very quiet without you and I hope it stays that way a lot longer! – Catherine Connell

> Take your time in hospital. None of us mind you staying in hospital. We have been twanging catapults all over the class. If you were here you would be one of the favourite targets. – Phillip Burrell

> We have been told to write these letters in our English lesson, and so I don't know what to say. Don't believe I want to write this flipping letter. I don't, I was forced into it. – Anne Mather

> The last few days at school have been awful, what with the end of term, marks coming in, tests and other disgusting things. – Fiona Bartlett

> Susan is missing hitting you, although she doesn't admit it. – Janet Ball

> Susan Gregory said she would come and see you to give you a kiss (I think she was joking). – Catherine Mogg

> We are all missing you, especially your 'darling' Susan Gregory. – John Vyse

> I hope you are getting better and will soon be coming back home, and that you will be back to school (cough)... Best wishes (cough). – Susan Gregory

I hope you are being taken care of by those gorgeous nurses. You lucky devil. – Graham Phillips

If you're in the Herts and Essex General Hospital, and a Mr Kraaij works on that ward I've a shock in store for you – that's the mental ward. – Glynis Kraaij

Here is the most interesting of the letters.

Dear Paul . . . I couldn't think of anything else to write, so I'm going to write a compo called: Lions. Paul woke in the middle of the night. Outside, in darkest Africa, it was pitch black, and the crickets were fidgeting. Paul had only just arrived in Africa and so was not used to the noises. At 14 years, he was QUITE small for his age, at only 4ft 10in.

Suddenly, he heard a crackle, and then a muffled roar. He jumped out of bed, that was in the visitors' room of the missionary hut, and looked out of the window. Outside was a MONSTROUS lion, over 6ft tall at the shoulders. Following it was a troop of lions, over 60 so calculated Paul. There was something unusual about this lion, it was PURE WHITE!!!!!

Now Paul had never seen lions before, so it did not strike him as unusual. Paul called Bwana-Bongee, his native servant, and told him about the procession. When Paul looked out of the window, the lions had their forefeet on one another's 'near-quarters' and were proceeding round in a circle around the white lion. 'That', said Bwana-Bongee, 'is the dance of the lions. It only happens when the moon is high and sends the moon spirit which is the white lion!'

NB: That is only Bwana-Bongee's story. [Coloured pictured]
Yours sincerely, M. S. Wallis

And here is the friendliest, the kindest.

Dear Paul, I sincerely hope that the fault in your leg will be quickly located. For the history lesson (much to the approval of most of the boys) Mrs Dodderidge asked the boys to make models of siege weapons used in the middle ages. The next lesson when Mrs Dodderidge entered the classroom humps of chalk were flying left right and centre. After Burrell had constructed one, the following lesson, almost every boy in the class had one, and the battle raged fiercely. [. . .]

Perhaps this will cheer you. When we received that private work on Brazil back (today Wednesday), I got 8/20 and Mr Edwards positively exploded at me and the whole classroom shook (exaggeration).

I hope you have enjoyed reading my letter, and also that you will enjoy reading the remainder of the class's letters.

Your affectionate friend, Colin (Harper)

Much as I would like to believe otherwise, I feel sure – from this distance in time – that school did effectively bonsai me (along with many others, which is not to say that some lucky pupils didn't flourish well). Of me, in my first school report from Broxbourne School (February 1964), the form mistress, C. Boyd, says: 'Paul shows great enthusiasm and interest in his work; but he must also take more thought and care over it. He is far too often misbehaving. Far more self discipline is required.'

And nothing much changed over the next seven years, such comments were ever present in the twice yearly reports, if not in the form master's summary then among the individual teacher comments somewhere. Occasionally, teachers reported on my 'ability' or my 'liveliness' or my 'enthusiasm' or my 'quickness', but too often, it seems, these good qualities were marred by erratic work, poor concentration and childish behaviour. Were these my fault? Could I have acted differently? Could I have been different?

School life was full of boring lessons, boring tests, boring homework. My diary provides evidence that we had a surprising amount of homework – evenings and weekends usually revolved around it. There were punishments galore, lines, detentions and report cards. Being 'on report' meant I had to carry around a card from lesson to lesson and get each teacher to comment on my behaviour in class and sign it. Not only was this embarrassing, but I couldn't ever race away, to the lunch table or tuck shop or to play football. Once, our whole class was put on report, which was extremely tedious for the other teachers, but a laugh for us, especially as we turned it into a competition to see who could get the most colours on the report card. It was just a matter of thrusting a pink or purple or turquoise pencil into Sir's or Miss's hand at the right moment.

My academic record never sparkled. I was usually graded 2B or 3B for most subjects, although there's an occasional 2A or 1B. Once or twice I came first or second in an exam (there were 60 or 70 exams in the seven year period) for maths or chemistry. There were usually about 30 in the class, and 17th or 22nd was a normal position for me.

Here's a couple of typical examples from my diary.

7 February 1966
In biology we talked about digestion and did a lot of experiments. In maths we did more parabolas and in history we drew a map of India and for hwk we had to write about Plassey. In French started new chapter – *La Pauvre Felicite*. Went running round junior course and did it in 15 minutes with Harper. Watched *The Rat Catchers* and did geog and bilge hwk.'

23 November 1966
Had another quarrel with Mum, father joined in. Again got to school late. In English we did the press, got questions on it for hwk. In Latin wrote down nouns, third declension. Was forgiven by Susan. Ah! In chemistry went over atomic weights etc. Had three fourth year girls on my lunch table and we had kidney plus apricot tart. In PE had possession rugby, terrible. In maths did horrible sums which were set the day before. Drew map of South Africa. Mark came over, did maths and terrible English.

And here is the school's very last report on me, dated June 1970, by my form teacher L. E. Anderson:

> Most disappointing in the light of the promise he showed at the commencement of his Sixth Form career and represents an opportunity thrown away. Unless the results he is likely to gain in these examinations are a severe jolt to him and make him realise what committed study involves he will be extremely ill-advised to take a full time course of higher education.

Thanks Broxbourne School for all those years of behavioural clipping and pruning. By your very own words, it didn't work. What would work later – at least in an academic sense – was escape from the bonsai factory.

I'm sure school wasn't all bad. I know it wasn't. There were, after all, games and sport. I hated rugby, because it was way too physical for titchy me. When possible, I and other inadequate youths chose to go cross-country running instead. I think I liked time in the gym best, and was reasonable at basketball despite the handicap of my size. I liked cricket, and played for a school team. I've no idea how often I played, although I seem to believe I was the weakest of the 11. All I recall is this one story – presumably because of the scar of embarrassment it left behind. I was due to play in a match, and I couldn't find any white shirts. They hadn't been washed. So my mother – bless her – rather than give me an unwashed shirt insisted I take a pink one – at least it was clean. Was I not aware of the laughter my kit would generate, the fool it would turn me into?

Swimming was no fun at Broxbourne School. From around May, we used to be taken once a week to the unheated open air pool in Hoddesdon.

> 4 May 1964
> Went swimming for the first time this season with the school – it was freezing. I got a headache and was shivering all through next lessons.

But, interestingly, I have an identifiable psychological scar which relates back to my experience in that pool. At least once a year there was a swimming gala, and the stands around the pool were full of parents, teachers and other pupils. I had been entered into a race, whether press-ganged or voluntarily I don't know. But, in the event, I could not complete the two or four lengths, and gave up half way. To this day, every time I'm doing lengths in a swimming pool, I have to deal with unbidden thoughts that I'm being watched.

I never felt there was anything geekish about me as a teenager, but perhaps there was, for I had some talent at chess – is it a geekish game? I'd learned to play at Lyndhurst Preparatory School, and was a keen member of the chess club at Broxbourne School. We had a team and played in a league, and used to travel to other schools, many of them private, like Haberdashers, for big matches. Andrew Cooper and David Storey used to play on boards one and two, Daniels, Cutts-Watson and I used to vie for boards three, four and five. I also belonged to the Hoddesdon Chess Club. One year, I won not only the club's handicap competition (which took account of my age), but also its main competition as well. I brought home two large silver cups, and my parents wanted to show them off in the lounge. But there was no way I would let them do this for they had very pointedly, and meanly to my mind, refused to pay my club subscription fees (believing it should come out of my pocket money).

And then there was football, the beautiful game that brings so many people together, at so many different levels. The grammar school did not lower itself to teaching or organising football games in the 1960s, but nevertheless we played most days, most break times, in the school playgrounds. We would form teams in a moment, and kicked a ball about, ever passionate, ever determined to score and win, whether the game was lasting five minutes or an hour. Every game was my chance to shine, to win, to be as tall as everyone else.

As tall as Langley, for example, who may have been a bit of a bully. I remember – but I may be completely wrong in this – that he used to punch me in the ear just for fun. In the sixth form, I developed a strategy to deal with him, which worked in the sense that it narked him: during free times I'd make a point of walking out of any room that he entered. Not as tall as Hutchings, who lived near me, and had a table-tennis table set up in his conservatory. I must have played him hundreds of times, and never once did I win a game. I was certainly not as tall as Dick Davies, who went on to set up his own portable DJ service called The Undertakers, using an ex-hearse to transport his equipment around. I was nearer in height to some of the girls, Susan Gregory, for example, with whom I must have anti-flirted a lot, in a childish schoolboy kind of way, and Christine Speller who once turned me down when I invited her to dance at a school gig with another line that has stuck in my memory: 'You can't dance, you can't sing, you can't even whistle.'

Happier school-related memories are those with Colin. One set of recollections, in particular, relate to our history teacher Bill Wyman (and a couple of other teachers also). They provide the only example, I can summon up, of Broxbourne school actually encouraging an activity, an interest that was useful and rewarding later in my life. But, I believe, this was down to Mr Wyman et al, rather than the school, for they took it on themselves to organise and lead summer holiday expeditions to the Lake District or the Yorkshire Moors, always staying in Youth Hostels. How old were we, Colin and I, when we first joined Wyman on these hiking trips? 14 maybe. There were several over the years. I have a couple of small b&w photographs, and a log book of youth hostel stamps.

On leaving Broxbourne School, in the summer of 1970, Colin and I organised our own ambitious hiking trip along what is surely the premier walking trail in the UK – The Pennine Way. The *Pennine Way Companion* hand written and drawn by the great Alfred Wainright was our guide. Colin insists I stole our copy from a public library; in any case I do still have it. We started in the north, at Kirk Yetholm in Scotland, and finished, after three weeks, at Edale in the Peak District. At times, it was a strain on our friendship, and at other times a strain on our calves, but what an achievement for our young, and newly independent selves. Here is part of an email from Colin reflecting back on the trip.

> We hadn't wanted to carry the 35 lbs plus pack necessary to do the PW properly and had tried to do it on the cheap. Plastic bags instead of proper sleeping bags, a flimsy tent with NO sewn-in groundsheet and no way to heat/prepare food – the idea being to just eat out of tins when obliged to camp out between hostels. Once at Once Brewed we had to sleep rough, Once again, in the field opposite the Youth Hostel and for Once my sage counsel prevailed. It was decided to go from hostel to hostel, using each hostel as a starting point to walk along the Way; then hitch back to base at the end of the day. In this way, we did the greater part of Way, just leaving out some flat isolated sections but doing ALL the peaks with the exception of Black Hill.

It was to be a decade or more before I returned to the joys of hiking in Britain, along its coasts, up and down its modest mountains, and through its moors and national parks, but walking, often alone, has since remained a regular and necessary way of refreshing my spirit.

It must have been in our sixth form years that Colin and I, along with our friends Chris West and Rob Cutts-Watson, created rival teams: Colin and I formed the Samantha Consortium, while Rob and Chris were the CW Consortium. The moniker Samantha came from the name Colin and I had given a car – a grey Standard 10 – we'd bought for £30. We shared ownership, each of us taking possession for a few days at a time, until, that is, one of us had an accident, not far from the school gates no less. Of course we had no funds to repair the dysfunctional doors on the crash side, so we replaced them with a sheet of plastic – unthinkable in today's safety conscious culture. The two consortiums were friendly rivals in two-a-side football, of course, tennis, cards, and any other sports or games we happened to be playing. Friday night was reserved for pub crawls, we'd tour a series of pubs drinking at least a pint of bitter in each one.

Away from school, I was involved in a more caring, more comforting social world. It came with a price, and the price was being exposed to another bonsaier – god! Within weeks of arriving in Hoddesdon, the local vicar from St Paul's had called at our house, and I was thenceforth dispatched to Sunday School. On Easter Mondays, the group used to go on a mass pilgrimage to St Albans Cathedral. I have a sense that these days were good fun. In autumn 1967, I attended weekly confirmation classes, which led to my being confirmed on 22 February 1968. By then, though, the Sunday School had evolved into St Paul's Youth Fellowship, or SPYF as we called it, partly thanks to the curate, Geoffrey. As we grew older, our unofficial but very regular meeting place was a pub called The Sun, where we'd congregate sometimes in the evenings, but definitely after church on Sundays. SPYF certainly became far more social than religious, and the easy companionship between boys and girls attracted several of my school friends to join. Once I'd left home for university in Cardiff, it was these friendships that had me hitching back home through the night every few weekends rather than hang around with fellow undergraduates. Having largely escaped the constraints of home and school, though, I found myself turning more and more seriously to god – as though I wanted or needed someone to keep clipping my roots and branches.

And, finally, a last word about feeding, or lack of, since a sustained lack of nutrients can also lead to bonsaidom. It seems, in my impoverished memory, I was starved of culture as a teenager. I watched a lot of television, according to my diary, occasionally went tenpin bowling, but had no exposure at all to the theatre, music other than pop, literature (other than books studied at school which, by definition, meant they were dull), or art as in painting, photography, sculpture. In fact, as a teenager, I don't even recall going to the cinema, except once, when I was taken – against my will, because this was an outing for my younger brother and sister – to see *Chitty Chitty Bang Bang*!

Chapter five

SASHA
IF YOU HAD ANY BRAINS YOU'D BE A HALF-WIT

When I started thinking about Alexander (Sasha) Lyons, my stepfather, and collecting information about him for this section, from diaries and letters and from my memory, I found myself trying to weigh him up, the good, the bad, the ugly . . . the kind. In fact I was trying to assess his life as it impacted on me, trying to criticise him, trying to judge him as a father. But then I asked myself why? Why was I doing this, mentally composing material about him, rather than me? It seemed all wrong. I shouldn't be judging him, I should be judging myself. This book is about me, not about him. Except – I went on to argue with myself – I've spent most of my adult life judging myself, believing that where difficulties arise around me, especially in relationships, they are my fault, or if not necessarily my fault then I should be able to do something about them.

As an adult, I've also been too ready to critique, able to see positives, yes, though always counter-balanced by a prevailing cynicism if not pessimism. But it is the negatives I see more often, I'm quick to see the glass half empty rather than half full. I've always justified this hyper-rational side of me as stemming from a strong dislike of hypocrisy, and a vivid belief in truth and truthfulness. But I understand now, with perspective, that human kind cannot bear very much reality (Eliot again), and it should never have been incumbent on me to be loaded down with reality all the time.

I do not think I was like this as a child or teenager – judging and critical. It's possible I have a genetic predetermination towards this way of being since, I've no doubt, there are swathes of a person's character set down by genes. If so, I don't believe it's the whole story, and I suspect Sasha played his part. He was fond of telling me, for example, that if I had any brains I'd be a half-wit. I think he stopped the day I told him I'd been awarded a First Class Honours degree, but, by then, if he'd had a role to play in the forming of my character, he'd performed it. This is all by way of explaining why I decided, after some thought, not to struggle too hard in this section against criticising him, judging him.

Considering his position in my life I know very little about Sasha's background. His mother, Valla (or Mutti as I knew her) married Litzinsky, a Russian who, after the revolution, had emigrated to Berlin.

He may already have been married, and had children. Valla was young, 20 or so, and possibly pregnant when she met him. A year or so after Sasha was born, they separated, and Sasha was given to the care of Valla's mother, who I knew as Mummi. It was Mummi and her husband, Uncle Fietje, who brought Sasha up. They came to England as Jewish refugees and were interned on the Isle of Wight for a short time. Valla remarried a man called Ernest Poncelet and went to live in the Congo. My mother says she once asked Uncle Fietje about Litzinsky, and he observed that one should not talk ill of the dead but that there was nothing good to say about him.

My mother Barbara met Sasha, who had anglicised his surname to Lyons by then, at The Freemasons Arms in South Hampstead in the late 1950s. Before long he had moved into her flat at 21 Fitzjohn's Avenue, and my half-brother Julian was on his way. Friends tell me that Sasha was very much in love with my mother (he must have been, I suppose, to be willing to take me on as well) and that they were happy together. I've already mentioned, in the Hampstead section, a couple of vague negative memories about my new step-father from this time. But in trying to be as fair as I can, I must stress two things: he paid for me to go to a private school, something my mother alone would never have been able to afford; and, according to my mother, he played with me a lot in those early years, thus I might well have benefitted from more paternal playfulness than either of his own children. It is certainly true that once we moved out of London his work (marketing and promotions) and the commuting occupied him more and more, and his home life less and less.

By the time we had relocated to Hoddesdon, Sasha had fathered two of his own children, Julian and Melanie, so we were a family of five – except that Julian was packed off to boarding school when still quite young. Melanie went later. According to Sasha's own words (in a letter to me and I've no reason to disbelieve him), he gave me the chance to go to boarding school too. This would have been when we first moved to Hoddesdon, when I was 11. He says I, myself, chose to go to a local grammar school instead. I wonder. I wonder if I could really have made such a choice on my own; or indeed whether my parents would have put such responsibility in my own hands. Is it possible he wanted to pack me off, away and out of sight of his new cosy suburban life; but perhaps my mother said no, because of me, and/or for me, and/or through me.

I have little information about my relationship with Sasha during our Hoddesdon years – from 1963 to 1970. My diaries reveal some of the routine of our life. I used to cycle to school or take a bus, but since the station was near the school, Sasha used to give me a lift sometimes. There's no indication in the diaries of any warmth or kindness from him, nor do I remember any in this period. They do, though, reveal some undercurrents. In 1965, I started calling him 'Father' instead of 'Dad'. In November 1966, I wrote this: 'Had another quarrel with Mum, father joined in.' In September 1967, there's this: 'Father very unfatherly.' In February 1968, this: 'I have just lost my respect for my mother and stepfather.' Normal teenage stuff perhaps. But there's other information in my hazy memory.

It's possible I was a bit clumsy as a teenager (as many teenagers are) but when I broke something or caused a difficulty, according to Sasha, it was always because of my stupidity. Here's an example I do remember. He bought me a large spool tape recorder for my birthday once. It was bigger and grander than I'd hoped for. I even remember the brand, Roebuck – one I'd never heard of at the time. Unfortunately, it broke down very soon. I was fearful to tell him, but did so eventually. He blamed me of course, but, nevertheless, went to the trouble of seeking a replacement. This one also broke down in exactly the same way. I was too frightened to tell Sasha so I took the machine to pieces myself and uncovered, what I considered to be, a design fault. Armed with proof that I wasn't stupid, I endeavoured to explain this all to Sasha. He wasn't interested.

A small man, slightly overweight, he always dressed well, in good quality shirts and suits. One year, my diaries reveal, I went to great lengths to find him hand-stitched silk handkerchiefs for his birthday. His face was always clean shaven and there was usually a whiff of expensive after-shave about him. He liked his food, so much so that some of the fiercest arguments that raged around me in Hoddesdon were sparked at meal times – he hated plates that hadn't been warmed, or a roast that had been cooked too long. My mother was a marvellous cook, but even she couldn't get everything right all the time.

Fond of sport, he held two season tickets to Arsenal football club, and would drive to Highbury every fortnight, sometimes only with me, in which case I would sit with him, or with my mother and me, in which case I would stand with the crowds in the lower tiers. He acquired tickets to several matches in the 1966 World Cup, and I went to one – a boring 0-0 game involving Uruguay (a team that only 16 years previously had been cup winners). I think he got hold of the tickets because of his involvement in selling a highly lucrative World Cup Coins marketing venture to Esso.

More than anything, though, he was particular about his cars. Early on there was an Austin Princess, a Ford Capri, and several BMWs;

later, though, he gravitated to long sleek Jaguars. Two car stories. During the 1960s, Sasha bought a holiday villa in the south of Spain, near Cadiz. It was a newly built estate, and the roads were private. As a family, we went several times. Mostly I remember the small lizards, and the estate swimming pool where I used to compete with Spanish boys over how many chairs in a row we could dive across into the water. In the summer of 1969 – it must have been that year because I'd only just passed my driving test – I begged and badgered Sasha to let me borrow the hired car. He eventually relented, restricting my movement to the estate where the roads were private, and insurance was not a legal issue. I filled the car with friends, including two Spanish girls in the back, and proceeded to show off, driving faster and faster. But then I lost control, the car veered off the road, missing a tree and a telegraph pole by feet, and ended up battered and bruised in a vineyard. No one was hurt; but neither was there any doubt left, not one shred, as to the extent of my stupidity. The road, unfortunately, turned out to be public not private, which in fact obliged Sasha to say he had been driving.

Two or three years later he got his own back – I say this in jest because I'm sure there's no connection between the two events. He must have regained some confidence in me for he agreed to lend me his car, a BMW by this stage, so I could drive myself and friends through France and Spain to the villa for a summer holiday. There were seven of us, four guys in my car, and two girls and a guy in another car. I have no memory of who these friends were, or any other details of the holiday except this one thing that happened. We arrived at the border crossing into Spain, and the officials there demanded to see paperwork for the car. It didn't have a normal British registration plate, but temporary German Z plates. This was a scam my father used so he could park with impunity and not bother with parking fines. We argued and argued, even begged at the border post, but nothing we said would persuade the authorities to let us through. I suddenly felt terribly responsible for my friends' summer holiday. We decided to drive inland, and try a different border crossing in the Pyrenees. The two girls switched to my car, and smiled sweetly through the windows as we tried once again to enter Spain. This time we made it without complications, and the holiday was saved. There was also a problem getting the car back into England at Dover, but I persuaded Sasha to sort it out on the phone.

I think it was the summer of 1970 that Sasha left the Hoddesdon home to remain every night in London, at his office or in a hotel. He was sick of commuting, my mother refused to consider a move back to London (it was she that had pressed for the move out of London in the first place), and the marriage was on very rocky ground.

I recall it as a horrible time. I lived two lives, one dark and miserable in the house, looking after my brother and sister, trying to cope with my mother's depression and constant moaning, and the other bright and lively and colourful, whenever I escaped to be with my friends, or my girlfriend at the time. I mention it here because it was the one time I can recall as a youngster that Sasha gave me something non-material and positive: a bit of respect. He arranged to meet me in a pub in Hoddesdon, and we had an adult discussion about the situation. While his own children were still far too young to comprehend what was happening, he really wanted me to understand the reasons for the crisis, in a genuine, not a manipulative, way – or so it seemed.

Aged 18, I escaped, to university in Cardiff. Because Sasha had never legally adopted me, I was in the unusual position of coming from a well-off middle class family yet being eligible for a full grant. It was not much, but it was enough to live on, especially since I worked in the holidays. I have always been rather proud of the fact that I became financially independent from the age of 18, that I never asked my stepfather for money, nor did I receive any (with one important exception) – not even small amounts (birthdays and Christmas aside). Sasha was not my real father and, I suppose, I wanted to be free of him as soon as possible, and he of me. If anything, the latter – me not wanting him to feel I was a financial burden any more – was more important than my wanting independence.

I have no specific memories of Sasha during my three years at university in Cardiff. My diaries mention him only in the context of arguments with me or my mother, or because he was away somewhere, in the US or Belgium. During this period, he won the battle with my mother over living in London, and they sold the house in Hoddesdon and bought a penthouse suite in Belsize Park. Soon after, he set up his own company, Innovative Marketing International. One of his first big promotions went wrong. He was selling very early digital watches, but lots of them went faulty soon after delivery, and everyone in his office (including temporary staff like me) were involved in repairing the returns – a process which involved opening the watch backs, and replacing the internal module.

After university, and for want of any other life-plan, I ended up living in the Belsize Park apartment. Arguments with both my parents were the norm, and before long I was asked to move out. I like to think this was a calculated move, designed to give me a kick up the backside, not a selfish one. It had profound consequences, in that I soon found myself, by chance, in a flat with Australians who had travelled overland across Asia, and who inspired me to do the same. I was away three years, returning in early spring 1977. By then, my family had moved to a large expensive house (Sasha's business was doing very well) in St John's Wood. Three days – three days! – after returning to the bosom of my family, Sasha, suddenly and without warning, moved out, left my mother, and went to live with a secret mistress – his secretary. My mother was in pieces, and, once again, just as in 1970, I was left to look after her.

Families!

It was a traumatic time, more so for Julian and Melanie than for me. I was preoccupied with myself, reintegrating back into some kind of alternative London society, some kind of normality after so long on the road. I met up with Sasha several times after his leaving, and I was sufficiently adult to understand that, while guilty of betrayal and many other sins, he was not the only person in the relationship, and he was not the only cause of its breakdown. My mother sunk deeper and deeper into a well of despair and martyrdom, and I probably wasn't as sympathetic as I might have been – had I not been through it all before. Time healed things a bit, but my mother never lost the scars, not until Sasha died 20 years later. He gave her a generous settlement at the time they separated, a large house in Golders Green, and a good income. When she died in early 2007, I found correspondence relating to the divorce proceedings, and it tended to show Sasha being helpful and generous in the face of my mother's awkwardness and obstinacy.

After the divorce, my own relationship with Sasha moved into a new phase, one of mutual respect. I made an effort to stay in touch, to meet him for a drink regularly, usually a Sunday lunchtime at a pub near his house, also in St John's Wood. He appreciated me doing so. We would talk about Julian and Melanie, or my mother, and he would tell me how his business was doing. He was full of anecdotes, and could be very charming. As his business became more successful, and he was able to take more holidays and travel widely, I began to sense he was slightly jealous of all the places I'd been; and, as I finally settled into journalism as a career, he seemed mildly impressed with my achievements – at last.

In the early 1980s, he loaned me £15,000. The loan meant I could buy a house, rather than a flat, one big enough for me to rent out rooms to lodgers. His cronies – a property dealer, an accountant and a solicitor – all assisted in the purchase too. Within a few years I was free of the loan: he had decided to gift me £10,000, because he was doing the same for Melanie; and the rest was paid off by an inheritance from his mother. Having that house from the age of 30, made a significant difference to my life.

When I went to Brazil in 1985, Julian moved in, at very low rent, to look after it and my lodgers. I was in Rio for two years (see chapter fourteen), during which time Sasha and I wrote regularly to each other. His letters were warm, attentive and well written. But not so his last one. I wrote to him about my close friend Bel, and how we had decided to have a child together (chapter fifteen). He reverted, in his return letter, to the stepfather that had always considered me stupid, that had always criticised me. Here is my letter, and his response

25 December 1986
Dear Dad . . . I am writing a short letter now to let you know that my friend Bel (whom I think you met just the once when we came to take some carpet off your hands) is pregnant and with luck will have our child in the coming summer, even though we plan neither to marry or live together. I have known Bel for seven or eight years in which time we have enjoyed a strange but rather wonderful relationship: we both have a tremendous caring and loving for each other, sufficient we think to overcome the problems that will inevitably arise. Neither of us have taken this step without thought, and indeed when Bel came out to visit me in November she did so with the idea of becoming pregnant in mind. I have a tremendous respect for Bel's capability but she will also have financial, practical and emotional support from myself and support from Mum with whom she is already close friends, and of course from her own parents. I will now almost certainly return to the UK in March – everything points to me doing so, whereas nothing tempts me to stay here longer. Dad, I'm afraid I've never been very conventional, and, it seems, despite some trappings – like a recognisable profession and house-ownership – I remain a bit of an oddball; nevertheless you have supported me in various ways all these years for which I have been very grateful. I hope this fresh evidence of my waywardness therefore does not upset you too much, on the contrary I hope you will be pleased. . .

11 February 1987
My Dear Paul
Your recent letter concerning your future parental status filled me with mixed emotions. Of course, as you say yourself, you have always been a 'special case' and this already started when you were about twelve and I wanted to send you to a public boarding school, but you refused and preferred to go to a daytime grammar school which, in the event, turned out to be Broxbourne. After heavy pressure from your Mother and myself, you managed to acquire a very respectable university degree but then promptly neutralised this effectively by taking off on a three year (sabbatical) around the world, which you now admit was a mistake as it made it so very difficult for you to decide on your choice of occupation when you returned to England. Certainly in your chosen profession of journalism, you did not need a First in maths and physics – even a Second Class BA in commerce or a BSc Econ would have been more than enough.

Now you and your girlfriend have decided to bring a child into this world: she is clearly under the impression, from what I have heard, that you are to take no further interest in the proceedings having been used, so to speak, as a 'stallion' and will have the child at her parents' home and then bring it up as a single parent. This appears to me to be something of a half-baked idea and reminds me of the 'flower children' ideas that were so prevalent in the sixties. Surely we have all outgrown this? Whilst Society does not frown upon 'bastards' the way it once did, there can be no doubt that a child brought up with a Mother and Father in attendance stands a much better chance in later life. Single parents tend to perpetuate their insecurity through their children and I cannot see that this is fair on a child who never asked to be born anyway. There is an old joke about how to be successful in life and the answer is to choose your parents carefully! What chance do you think your baby will have without the constant guidance of a Mother and Father instead of someone who pops in now and again and could be regarded as a kind of Uncle. Quite frankly, that is where I see your position unless you manage to persuade Bel that the two of you should set up home together. Incidentally, is the child to carry your name or Bel's name? What role do you propose to play in its religious education (if any) and scholastic upbringing. All these questions appear to be totally unresolved from what you say in your letter. In my opinion, emotional and financial support from a distance is simply not enough and it is really not fair to the child.

Anyway, the die is cast and the child is growing in Bel's womb. I cannot honestly say that your letter either pleases or displeases me. What does disturb me, however, is that the whole concept or should I have said conception, appears to me to have been so badly thought out. I would have expected a rather more positive approach and solution from you in this matter because I have always regarded you as a highly intelligent, rational and thoughtful individual.

I very much look forward to welcoming you to England in March and you can rest assured that I will not make your life a misery with any carping criticism. It is just a pity that we didn't have a chance to discuss this situation first.

Your loving Dad (more in sorrow than in anger).

I love the bit where – with galling chutzpah – he takes credit for my achieving a 'respectable' degree!

There isn't much more to tell about Sasha and me. Once I had returned to the UK, and Adam was born, there were no more reversions to the man, the stepfather, that had always been so critical and negative towards me. He proved to be a halfways decent grandfather to Adam: there were presents and cards for his birthday and Christmas, and they met up two or three times a year. One of those occasions would be around Christmas when Sasha's wife, Michele, put on a big meal for all three of her step-children and families. Otherwise, Adam and I, and sometimes Bel, would visit for a few hours on a Sunday, and talk about other family members, or his racehorses, or his recent travels. I would tell him in brief about my own activities, but they didn't occupy him for long. His business had made him wealthy, and he invested in property abroad, and dissipated money on racehorses and betting. His son, Julian, increasingly took charge of the business, which allowed Sasha to spend more time away, travelling – he liked warmer climes than England. He died suddenly of a heart attack, in March 1997, during a visit to friends in Zimbabwe. He was cremated there, but Michele organised for his ashes to be returned to the UK, and to then be scattered at York Racecourse. She also held a small dinner back in London for his family and a few friends.

Given his significant wealth – certainly in the millions – it is rather staggering that he left not a penny to his own two children or to me, or to any of his grandchildren. It transpired that his will had been made 10 years previously, at a time when he was disgruntled with me because of Bel's pregnancy, and angry with both Julian and Melanie for different reasons.

My stepfather may well have given me as much paternal love as he had, in the early days, and his money certainly made a very significant difference to my life, in different ways. Whether these pluses outweigh the negatives of being brought up by a man so incessantly critical and judgemental of me, a top class bonsaier, I don't know. I shall never know.

Top left: Sasha (my stepfather), Barbara, Julian (my brother),
Melanie (my sister), and teenage me; Top right: Roser, Harold
and me; Bottom left: one of Marielle's photos of me; Bottom
right: me performing in the Phantom Captain's *Waiter Service*

Chapter six

UNIVERSITY
THE WONDERFUL WORLD OF WISDOM AND OF FOLLY

'He will be extremely ill-advised to take a full time course of higher education', wrote my form-teacher, as I've noted elsewhere, just months before I headed off to university. Ill-advised in what way? As it turned out, that teacher could not have been more wrong, for university proved to be a wonderful world of wisdom, and of folly. Academically, university gave me nothing, except a piece of paper, but such a good one it helped me land jobs for many years. It would be churlish, thus, to express any resentment for all the time spent in lectures and writing essays and revising for exams.

University found me consorting with new friends, some of whom led me astray, towards folly and fruitless profligacy, but some of whom – Phil in particular – introduced me to interests and pastimes that were absorbing, challenging, invigorating and which would become part of who I was to be. And there was wisdom to be absorbed. It didn't come from the sciences that I studied, but from the impact on me of student culture. Most importantly, wisdom-wise, my student years took me more deeply into Christianity than I had ever been, and, as a consequence, I was able to emerge out the other side, with a right and proper understanding that – of course – god did not exist, other than in the mind and culture of man.

I did not achieve good A-levels. Thanks to the clearing system, I ended up at the downmarket University of Wales Institute of Science and Technology (UWIST), then a part of the University of Wales, which also included the more upmarket and more humanities-oriented sister, University College, on the same site in the middle of Cardiff. The two colleges merged in 1988, and, in 1999, became Cardiff University. If I had managed slightly better A-levels I would have been admitted to Reading to take a degree in cybernetics – and I'm sure my life would have been very different. Instead, I scraped into an Applied Sciences degree. In year one, students took three science modules, but then dropped one, to major in two subjects. Apart from a laboratory project, the BSc Joint Honours in Applied Science was assessed entirely on final year examinations.

I don't have much to say about my academic studies. The diary records with dull regularity the lectures I missed, and those that I attended, often describing them as 'horrible', 'quite a laugh', 'OK', 'quite a good lecture', 'really bad', 'really dragged', 'pretty good'. I started out doing maths (I mention a lecturer called Horner more often than any other), chemistry and physics. At the end of the first year I failed the maths exam and was obliged to re-sit it in Cardiff during the summer of 1971. I must have passed the exam, because I was entered into the second year. I was intent on majoring in maths and physics, and abandoning chemistry. After about a week of the new term, I was advised that I had only been accepted into year two because the chemistry department wanted me, and that I should be dropping maths. I ignored these pleas, and simply continued to attend the maths and physics lectures.

Two academic tit-bits are worth mentioning which illustrate a) how fast, and b) how slow human knowledge/ambitions can advance. In those days, one computer filled a room. It took days to prepare a small programme on a hundred or more punch cards for the giant computer to carry out a mundane logical task. Also at that time, on the physics side, nuclear fusion was all the rage, and it was considered that within a few decades the technology would provide large quantities of cheap safe electricity. Nearly 50 years later, scientists, backed by politicians, are still optimistic about the potential of nuclear fusion to provide large quantities of cheap safe electricity – in a few decades time!

I worked a bit harder in the second year, and entered the third and final year with some hope of actually getting a degree. In fact, I worked more energetically and more enthusiastically for the last six months than I'd thought possible. By this time, although I felt considerable disdain towards the establishment, the system, the powers that be, I realised I would have to play by their rules, with their bits of paper. Having been lucky enough to scrape through for two and a half years, and with the really important exams approaching, I felt I owed it to myself to do the very best I could.

The exams were at the end of May and the first two weeks of June. My five-year diary, as usual, is not very informative. A couple of entries read, 'ballsed the exam', and a couple more say, 'not as bad as all that'. The last exam took place on 14 June, and I then spent a few days hitchhiking in Ireland and a few days at home. A couple of weeks later I am back in Cardiff.

28 June 1973
Most people hanging around, passing on all sorts of rumours, results at 4, or 6, or tomorrow – really quite nerve-racking. . . In pub with the polymer science

crowd and two of their lecturers – they didn't know any results except that Merv and Tony are getting firsts and ME FIRST CLASS HONOURS!

The formal results came out the following day. I was one of only four first class degrees (out of a 100 or so students) and the only one majoring in maths and physics.

There are only the briefest of mentions of this notable result in the diary. On the day of the results, one of my friends is holding me lightly, the diary entry reports, and another friend says, 'Let him go', and to me he says, 'You deserve what you got.' The next day, by chance the maths lecturer, Horner, picked me up hitchhiking, and I recorded that we 'obviously talked about my great success'. The same day my parents are described as being 'overjoyed'. I have no memory of understanding how big an achievement this was; and I suspect it was only in time that I came to appreciate it. Thinking back, I find it very surprising – given my 'great success' – that I chose not to attend the formal degree presentation ceremony (thus obviating any need to hire the appropriate fancy dress). I can't recall my reasons, but it may well have been a symptom of that disdain I felt for the establishment

The moment my exams were over I discarded all the academic learning as effectively as if I'd thrown it straight into landfill. I wasn't interested in science, nor in any job that would have led naturally on from my degree subjects. In retrospect, it's clear that, although I gained general academic skills, I never once – in my whole life long – needed a formula or particle or molecule of the maths or physics or chemistry I'd spent three years learning. But – and it's a huge but – I'm convinced that without the piece of paper that labelled me as being of first class academic ability, I would have settled, and been obliged to settle, for a life with less movement, less colour, less music. (Which is not to say such a life could have been, or might have been, better or worse – just different, definitely different.)

So, on the one hand, the degree did make me feel a bit special, I suppose, and allowed me to believe I ought not to settle for second best. I had no idea what kind of job to do, what kind of career to pursue, but it felt wrong to settle for something ordinary. On the other hand, when I did decide – at three different times in my 20s – to get a serious job, I believe the quality of the degree dazzled each employer, blinding them to my lack of experience for the job on offer. Firstly, a well-known pharmaceutical company took me on in New Zealand as a medical representative, bought me suits and gave me a car, even though I was but a hippie traveller likely to move on in a few months. Secondly, a highly-respected market research company in London appointed me a junior executive despite the fact that I'd done little in the previous years but travel. And, thirdly, after more wayward years, a top industry magazine gave me a job as a reporter (not a trainee) even though I couldn't write, even though I had no knowledge of the industry, and even though I had no training in, or experience of, journalism.

University may be a place of useful career training for some students, but certainly not for all. It is much more than this, though. It's a social growing ground for every student, an arena in which he or she can practice, for better or worse, the trials and joys of adult relationships. And these relationships often have hugely significant impacts on students' lives, more so than the subject of their academic studies. One obvious impact is that friendships made at university often prove highly durable, and last many years, or a lifetime. But away from home for the first time, students fall under the influence, good or bad, of their peers, and are thus exposed to all kinds of new ideas and interests. I certainly think this was true of me.

When I first arrived at Cardiff, I must have felt incredibly free, released from the constraints of a stultifying family and school life. I was anybody's, and anybody proved to be Tony and Gerry, future companions in folly, fun and time wasting. Tony, tall and very long-haired, had hippie tendencies and very little interest in work or study. Gerry, short and stocky, and very blonde, was Somerset-bred and spoken through and through, and was rarely to be found without a pint of cider in his hand, or so it seemed. Together, Tony and Gerry were both slightly anarchic. With them, I managed to drink my way through the first year, becoming rather too-skilled at bar games, such as darts, bar-football and pin-table. I have a photo, intentionally provocative, of Tony standing with one foot on a girl lying on the ground, and he's holding a placard saying 'Keep women down'.

It was thanks to Tony, I suppose, that I gave up socks and shoes. Although my five-year diary does not reveal much about this or either of these characters, there is one entry in which I note that Tony was thrown out of a lab lesson for being bare foot. And in a couple of other entries I comment that 'I wish people would not keep commenting on my feet', and that I am 'wearing sandals at the moment because my feet are going flat'. In a mid-November entry I write, 'getting too cold to walk in bare feet'. Also it might have been with Tony and Gerry that I engaged in a memorable rag week stunt: we scaled the walls of Cardiff Castle and put up a 'For Sale' sign. On reflection, that sounds far too organised for Tony and Gerry, perhaps it was with Jim, a friend much enamoured of climbing and who therefore had ropes and tackle, that I conquered the castle.

I mention Jim because he took me climbing once or twice, until I froze on a sheer rock face, and had to be helped down in a (metaphorical) harness of humiliation. Climbing was one of many activities that I tried and tested during my time at university, but it was not one that stuck. Others did, and almost all of those that did were thanks to one friend – Phil. It was many years later that I realised this, and when the realisation came it stunned me a little. Phil is the only person I still know from my Cardiff days, but my relationship with him – like that with the women who had such influence on me in my 20s – is rather far-removed, one dependant only on very occasional emails. I think Phil came into my life in the second year – he was majoring in maths and chemistry, if my memory serves me right – and we remained friends into the third year. He was handsome, with well-groomed (not like Tony's scraggy) long hair. Girls adored him. Unlike me, he appeared confident socially, but like me (I suspected) he was shy of, or scared of, intimacy.

With Tony and Gerry I'd propped up bars, and fed coins endlessly into bar-game slot holes, but, come the second year, I was wanting more of what Phil had and did. He introduced me to squash, a game I played regularly, if not skilfully, for years thereafter, and to photography. He owned a decent camera and took photographs that he developed in a dark room. I didn't have a camera then, but within a few years, I'd become keen on taking and developing photographs. It was through Phil's photography that we both became involved in the UWIST student magazine, *IMPACT*. We took photographs for it (I borrowing Phil's camera occasionally), we wrote articles, and we spent long hours every couple of months in the editor's lounge planning the latest issue's layout. This was my first encounter – as it were – with journalism, the world I was eventually to decide on for a career.

It was also with Phil that my enduring love of the theatre was born. I don't know if Phil instigated this particular activity or if it was something we decided together but somehow we discovered a small experimental theatre, called Casson Studio, based in the old St Lawrence Mission building. The Welsh Theatre Company had taken over the building in 1963 and used it as an office and rehearsal space for their touring productions, but converted it to a studio theatre in 1968. It was named after the actor Sir Lewis Casson, who died in 1969, with the approval of his actress wife, Lady Sybil Thorndike. We went regularly to see strange and wonderful avant-garde plays that opened up our imaginations. There was one called *Buzz Buzz, Critch Critch* by Ewart Alexander, and another played out on a spider's web (possibly an adaptation of *Hamlet*). When I met up with Phil many years later, he reminded me that we'd seen Orton's *What the Butler Saw*, which had premiered in London a year or two previously, and a play by Caryl Churchill. Max Stafford Clark was among the directors whose work we saw there.

Three years after the end of our undergraduate degree studies, in the autumn of 1976, Phil was still in Cardiff working towards a PhD, and I had stopped travelling temporarily and was living in Viña del Mar in Chile, working at an English school. We had been exchanging warm, almost intimate, letters during my travels, but then I received one that shook me. Here are Phil's exact words.

> This letter must now contain a message of some import. I hoped to speak to you personally but I now feel you will not be home for some time and I do not wish to wait so long. I AM GAY. Now, how does that sound. I suppose in a way it's no surprise, you probably suspected during undergraduate days but maybe did not want to see, as I hid it even from myself. It has taken over six long years of self doubt, questions, answers, retractions, steps in both ways and oh so much stupid pain. Only now can I say it with confidence in my position, with hope, with utter candour. I hope you will not be hurt or wish to forget me. I tell you this and all that follows first, before any other (gay friends apart obviously).

'You probably suspected,' he had written. No, I never had. During our undergraduate years – this is the early 1970s and homosexuality had not long been legal (since 1967) – my friends and I had still talked about 'queers' in a definitely prejudiced way. For example, we had one lecturer who was over-friendly, especially with pretty boys and had a slightly slimy character. As far as we all were concerned he was a joke because he was queer. In my head, not much had changed by 1976, and so Phil's revelation sent me into a spin, prompted me to re-evaluate our student friendliness. I don't think my reply was as accepting as it could have been (I have no copy of my own letters), but I do know it must have been full of questions for Phil's next letter – both generous and informative – provided all kinds of answers and explanations about homosexuality. If I'd had any prejudices about gaydom, Phil banished them.

Some years later, after I'd returned to the UK, and after Phil had completed his PhD in Cardiff, he settled in Suffolk, teaching at a school in Ipswich and living in the small coastal town of Aldeburgh. I went to visit him there several times, and thus fell in love – like he had already done – not only with Aldeburgh itself but with the music of Benjamin Britten, who had, famously or infamously, lived there with the tenor Peter Pears. The love of the town led me, years later, to buy a small cottage which I'd visit every other weekend with Bel and our son,

Adam. And Britten's marvellous operas – *Peter Grimes* of course, but others too – seem to have always found some resonance, musically and thematically, in my own being, just like Lawrence Durrell's novels and T. S. Eliot's poetry.

I saw more of Phil when we both lived in Kilburn, but after I moved to Surrey in the early 1990s, and after he retired early and moved to Italy, we hardly ever met. Yet I remain to this day enormously grateful to the man, not only for his many positive influences on the young me, but also for his friendship during our student days.

It is also possible – although of this I cannot be sure – that I should be grateful to Phil for bringing me to my senses about god. On arriving in Cardiff, I had naturally joined the Christian Union (CU). Other Christians were not my closest friends, but I went regularly to CU gatherings, discussions and prayer meetings. I read the bible a lot, and I certainly prayed every day. Also I remained very close to my Christian group friends in Hoddesdon, and would return home for weekends often to meet up with them.

Many entries in my five-year diary confirm the feeling I have in my own memory that by the second year I was taking Christianity very seriously. I had never felt fully accepted by the CU clique, and saw its members as rather hypocritical. In search of something better – I've no idea what – I would visit different churches, of different denominations, every Sunday. Maybe, I was looking for the perfect congregation, or the perfect preacher, or more likely for people with whom I could feel at one, who would help me towards the emotional experience of god I was craving. Sometimes I would be invited to join a social or youth club after the service, and I was always made very welcome. I never found what I was looking for, though, and rarely went back to the same church. One time, I recall vaguely, after a Sunday evening service at a church I'd never been to before, I was invited to join a social gathering. After some time, with what must have been obnoxious righteousness, I pointed out that no one had mentioned god or Jesus for over an hour.

I think, increasingly, I was trying to intellectualise my belief in god: if I believed in such an all-powerful being, I reasoned, I should be living every minute of every day for him. Yet, he would not tell me what he wanted me to do, and I kept catching my self in hypocrisies. On 25 March 1972, I wrote in the diary: 'A bit worried about my pettiness. It is getting on top of me. Little things, so petty, so unnecessary. How does one control one's thoughts.' On 4 April, I wrote this: 'Haven't read the bible for two days. I wish I could get closer to God.' On 7 June this: 'I pray for a miracle that Graeme or Phil become a Christian. Lord give my life something that's different so that friends will see – and behold there was light.' Indeed, I was often to be found trying to convert my friends, not least Phil, who wasn't shy in trying to unpick my faith.

By autumn 1972, the beginning of my last academic year at UWIST, I had close friends who were both non-Christian (among whom Phil was probably the closest) and Christian, but a large part of my social life was taken up with Christianity. So it is all the more surprising, perhaps, that by January 1973 I had completely abandoned any belief in Christianity or a god. Here are several more entries from the diary.

> 23 November 1972
> I seem very bitter that other people are closer to Jesus than I am.

> 7 January 1973
> Congregational church – communion service – can't remember what the sermon was on – got nowhere near god all day, not at church nor during my three-quarters of an hours prayers.

> 9 January 1973
> Terribly worried about my faith. I don't think I believe there's a god any more.

> 10 January 1973
> Lost my silver cross [which I wore as a pendant] yesterday, coincidence or what?

I did not lose my Christian friends in Hoddesdon or Cardiff overnight. Some, in any case, were only social Christians, so my friendships with them continued regardless, and those that did have a strong belief simply saw me as another challenge to their own faith, as well as an opportunity for a good deed. Besides I could still talk the talk, and was happy to explain and argue from my new standpoint, I could even walk the aisle walk in communion services. I know I did this at least once after losing my faith because my diary records me doing so – I didn't want someone at the service to know about my change of belief at that moment.

I suspect that over time I had subconsciously rejected the values and ways-of-being of my parents, and taken on an alternative belief framework – Christianity. As I eventually matured during those years in Cardiff, it became increasingly hard for my rather rational and logical intellect to accept a world of make-believe. I kept looking for evidence of god, asking him for signs, proof. Why would he not help me out? And then, one day – 9 January it must have been – I woke up and realised, absolutely realised without any doubt, that god did not exist. From that moment, I can say with complete honesty, I have never doubted this, not once. Even when I thought I might die, during the cyclone in Darwin, Christmas 1974, the idea of god or praying never even entered my head.

In the years that followed, especially when I was travelling, whenever I met someone who tried to foist their religion on me I would tell them about my reverse conversion, as dramatic as that of Saul/Paul on the road to Damascus, I would say, and try to undermine their faith. But it wasn't too long before I mellowed a lot in this regard, preferring to avoid challenging others. Indeed, these days I find myself utterly opposed to the anti-religious proclamations taken by Richard Dawkins et al. Inter-society friction, distress and war are not caused by religion per se but by human nature. Conversely, though, religion has been of great importance to human societies, helping them work together, evolve; and it is still important because it provides solace for the fragile conscious mind: hope.

Our student days, how full of folly they were, but how wonderful. For most, university is a relatively safe place to grow and to grow up; but perhaps I had more growing to do than many. Once I'd escaped from the bonsaiers of adolescence, my roots and branches flourished, shooting outward in every direction, creating perhaps a tangled mat of strengths and weaknesses, hopes and fears, beliefs and disbeliefs, emotions and controls. Yet, better a tangled thicket full of opportunities and possibilities, requiring but a bit of self-pruning, than a future clipped and trimmed before it's begun. And as for hope, I had no more need of the religious kind, not with all my new interests, my piece of paper, and a wide wide world to explore.

Chapter seven

THE HIPPIE TRAIL
FINDING ONESELF, AND WHAT I FOUND

Emerging from the cloistered environment of student life into the harsh reality of adulthood, I didn't feel very comfortable or happy. I had no purpose. I went home for a little while, working temporary jobs, until Sasha kicked me out. Good decision. I ended up in an Earl's Court flat with an ever-changing cast of Antipodeans, many of whom had come overland from the far side of the globe. One, a young woman no older than me, had done so alone. If a girl can do that, I thought in my cocky boyish way, so can I – a thought which fitted in neatly with the following question I kept asking myself: how can I live on this earth and not know what's on it? I carried on doing odd jobs but now I was earning money with a purpose. I was going to travel round the world.

This was the mid-1970s, by which time many were already taking the hippie trail to or from Australia with India at the mid-point serving as a kind of experience-climax. There were no guide books for the Asian countries in 1974, no Lonely Planets, *no* Rough Guides, *indeed their originators were individuals like me who took the hippie trail more or less at this time. What we did all use was a guide produced by the alternative BIT Information & Help Service, located in West London in a shabby office next to the editors of IT (*International Times*) magazine. Put together from travellers' letters and information, it was about 100 typed foolscap pages, photocopied and stapled.*

I still have my copy. The front page, light blue paper, had lots of information about BIT, such as: 'BIT's main purpose is to help with the emergence of alternatives to the present repressive aspects of western society.' And near the bottom it explains: 'The point of telling you the above is to encourage one or two among you, once you've returned to this country, wise from the east, full of energy, enlightenment and a distaste for western consumer society, to consider coming to join the BIT collective.'

'Wise from the east' and 'full of enlightenment' – these were definitely not tongue-in-cheek perceptions then, as they might be today, nor was the idea that hippies were travelling to 'find themselves'. It is also true that many travellers conjoined a search for wisdom, enlightenment and 'finding themselves' with an interest in taking drugs, a combination

that had already been popularised by leading writers and intellectuals, not least Aldous Huxley. Personally, I was not very interested in drugs, although I did partake out of curiosity, there being so much talk on the road about such things. And I was also fairly clear that I was NOT trying to 'find myself'. When people asked about my purpose in travelling, I always repeated the same mantra: how can I live on this earth and not know what's on it?

As with so much of my life, I do not have solid, real memories of my travelling times. But I do have a diary which records what I did every single day. The front cover says: 'London to Christchurch, New Zealand or bust (the new game for life seekers)'. I call it Diary 1 even though, in fact, I do also have the five-year diary which contains many (much shorter) entries from the years 1963 to 1974. Diary 1 is actually a desk diary, which allowed me half a page for each day (though many entries are extended with continuations on blank pages in other parts of the book). The hand-writing is cramped, and nearly illegible at times, and the writing itself shows little attention to grammar or structure, and certainly has no literary quality. Nevertheless, I feel these entries, more than anything I could write afresh now, give the best taste of my life on the hippie trail. The following are basically verbatim extracts, whittled down to no more than 5,000 words from 80,000 in the diary. I have tidied up the grammar, and occasionally I've altered the vocabulary or reorganised the order of sentences.

My journey to Australia took me through these countries: Belgium, Germany, Yugoslavia, Greece, Turkey, Syria, Jordan, Saudi Arabia, Kuwait, Iran, Afghanistan, Pakistan, India (and Tibet), Burma, Thailand, Laos, Malaya, Singapore, Indonesia. And these are a few of the experiences I found in this, the first part of my round-the-world adventure: seeing Nureyev perform in Swan Lake; driving a truck across sand-rutted desert; witnessing a car accident in the waters of the Tigris!; discovering deserted ancient cities; walking hand-in-hand with Arab boys; selling blood; feeling hash-induced paranoia in the middle of tribal Afghanistan; having cave-dwelling Bedouin hosts eat scraps from my own plate; watching four Pakistanis fully occupied in operating a domestic lawnmower; seeing dead people burn; losing and finding my diary; meeting godless priests in a remote Himalayan monastery; viewing the largest book in the world; window-gazing girls in Bangkok; learning to swim against the current in crocodile-infested rivers; finding the largest flower in the world; being stoned by children; fearing moonlight sacrifices; working in a power station; being nearly wiped out by a cyclone.

18 June 1974
Total funds: £150 in envelope, £85 in wallet, $240 in traveller cheques, £150 in Singapore.

24 June 1974
Vienna, Austria. What a hassle finding somewhere to sleep last night. I was wandering around this park up by the Sud Bahnhof, and strange men kept following. Turned out to be the local gay playground, so I stormed off and slept very well in the gardens of some college. . . . At 4, I join the queue for the ballet. A mad rush to bag a place – so many people pushing and shoving, but, for one act, I had a seat. Nureyev and Carol Cain in *Swan Lake* – magnificent. There were 10 encores after the 3rd act!

6 July 1974
Istanbul, Turkey. I wash, which is nice. WOW WOW WOW Istanbul. I walk around the Sultanahmet Mosque, and the grand bazaar – endless arcades of shops selling leather, rope, shoes, carpets, souvenirs, clothes, fruit, water, cigarettes, sweets, shoe cleaning services, bread rings. The owners sit on little stools, while everywhere there are boys and men selling chai and porters carrying fruit or packets of paper on their backs (like walking right angles). It is a dirty city; the drivers are really mad; and there are mosques everywhere. I catch a boat day-tripping up the Bosphorous – three hours nearly to the Black Sea and four hours back.

10 July 1974
Nevsehir, Turkey. At about 11, I start wandering out of town. A short lift in a lorry whose driver wants me to do some work, then a long lift to Kaman (with apricots) – the land gently undulating and getting harsher and more arid. In Kaman, children swarm around, bring me apples and smiles. One woman shows me some French writing and is disappointed that I can't read it to her. Two Turks in a German car take me to Kirsehin; a friendly guy on a motorbike takes me 20km; and then a family bring me to Nevsehir. Women wear white scarves around their heads and across their faces, and very baggy slacks. The rock in this area is so soft that, since a long time ago, people have hacked their homes out of it; doors and windows in the rockfaces can be seen all over the place. I hitch out of Nevsehir past Goreme, a town with an outcrop of rock in which people still live.

13 July 1974
Damascus, Syria. I hitch and take a bus to Damascus. On the bus, Khalid befriends me. Once in Damascus, he takes me to his flat which he shares with a brother and a friend. In the evening, we stroll slowly around the town, stopping to talk to friends. Many boys walk together holding hands or arm in arm, very strange.

14 July 1974
Damascus, Syria. I visit the Omayyad Mosque. This is the most beautiful place I have yet seen. As you enter through the arches of a large courtyard, there are the most fantastic mosaics of bright colours far above, with enchanting pictures of villages. To one side, there is a vast edifice with two beautiful altars of mother-of-pearl in wood and very detailed wood carving. People come here

for cool and rest and prayer. In the middle is the tomb of the Prophet Yehia (John the Baptist) with a velvet cloth covering. So beautiful. . . In the evening, Khalid goes to the cinema with his girl, while I walk in a pleasant garden in a mosque. I play chess with someone who claims to be the fifth best player in Syria. Khalid is happy; but sad that I am going.

15 July 1974

Amman, Jordan. It takes a long walk, a free bus ride, and several lifts to get to the Syrian border (past many soldiers). Here in Jordan, the soldiers are hand-somely dressed in red and blue berets. From Ramtha I get a lift to Jerash – an unbelievable place. It's a remarkably preserved Roman-Greco town with pil-lars, arenas, forums, temples – the stone roads still have the ruts of chariot wheels. I make up a chorus which I sing to myself over and over again: 'Have you seen, have you seen, this old old city.'. . . In Amman, I learn that it is im-possible to get a visa for Iraq – so, either I must go back to Turkey, or travel to Iran via Saudi Arabia and Kuwait.

19 July 1974

Petra, Jordan. At Shawbak – 30km from Petra – I am besieged for about three hours with groups of boys from the agricultural college. First they take me in for water, then a teacher gives me shai. One boy finds me a Pepsi and another wants to take me home. After a couple of lifts and a lot of walking, I reach the Siq of Petra, a long narrow winding canyon – the rock is sheer, sometimes to 300ft and wow, suddenly the Treasury, the face of a temple carved in the rock. . . Then I come across the caves, many hundreds of them, in some of which the Bedouin still live. Petra is very touristy. I am so exhausted I collapse on the sand somewhere. A Bedouin child finds me and takes me to his cave/home where I am received with Arab hospitality. First, I'm given a mattress to sit on, then the father joins me. Shai is brewed – it is difficult to make them under-stand when I've had enough. I talk and then write a little. Later, I am brought freshly made bread with eggs, meat and tomatoes – my first real food for two days. All the time the man and I sit and never move – the wife or children bring the water to wash our hands, the shai, and the food. The wife and chil-dren eat my leftovers.

21 July 1974

Rafha, Saudi Arabia. There are 100 lorries this night, all going in convoy across the desert as far as the Jordanian border – 120km of no man's land. My Lebanese driver, in an empty gravel truck, is the ring leader for six others, and he keeps racing across the sand to round his colleagues up – he finds them by following trails of dust. This is a really rough ride – the roughest in my life (I have to use the full force of my hands to protect my head from hitting the cab-in roof) – but ten times better than anything at a funfair. At one point, my driver lets me have a go at the wheel, but I can't double declutch properly so I don't get very far.

23 July 1974

Kuwait City, Kuwait. I sleep well but still have diarrhoea. Astonishingly, this is a FREE hostel with air conditioning and cold water! Good to see my friends from Amman here. . . Three of us go to the blood bank, and after only one hour, an orange juice and biscuits, we are £14 better off.

25 July 1974

Persian Gulf. We manage to get to the harbour just after 7:00 – the haggling starts all over again. . . We buy food, and play cards until the tide comes in. . . Finally, our dhow – and a whole group of other others – are Persian Gulf bound. Only I am still onshore and so have to clamber across several moored dhows and swim – I am happy to be in the water, because I've been sweating so much. Once on board, though, the sailors tell me there are sharks in the water. The sailors on our boat seem very friendly, they give us fish and rice. . . The toilet is a metal bucket with a hole roped onto the back of the boat.

26 July 1974

Tigris. The sailors ask us to hide clothes in our packs while they themselves wear several pairs of new jeans and jackets – to get them past the customs. The dhows dawdle all morning in the estuary, occasionally police come and search them. At one point they take some things away in a sealed sack – I think it's shoes. Now it is middle afternoon. I sit on the cabin roof as we motor up the Tigris river – the sun is beating down on my white body. We are nearest the Iran side of the river and there are endless orchards of palm trees and wide irrigation channels. I see a few big tankers. We are still motoring in a group with many dhows – the sailors occasionally shout at each other or pass watermelons between them. It is so peaceful cruising up the Tigris, only a purring engine and a little swishing of water – the palms are beautiful. The red, green and white Iran flag now flies from all the dhows. Around dusk we stop for more police – this doesn't take long but once they've gone, all the dhows start racing each other. Then there's a collision. The bows of two dhows and a westerner's vehicle on a third dhow are all damaged. On ours, everyone is laughing! While we wait for the others to sort this out, we take baths in the refreshing river water and play solo whist. When the sun disappears, the many lights of the Abadan refinery are visible. For a second night, we sleep on board.

7 August 1974

Mashad, Iran. At the Afghani consulate there are a hundred people, half collecting passports and half filling in forms. A visa costs £5 – what a rip off. But mind-blowing, there, in the queue, is the guy I met at the Tournament Pub in Earl's Court, several months ago. He has come from England in three weeks – super express. His first words are 'you're slow'.

12 August 1974

Qala-i-Nau, Afghanistan. Our crowded truck stops at an all night chai shop, which is very welcome. A man here gives us some hash, and Bernard wants to smoke it so he crumbles a large bit and reforms a cigarette. I smoke most of it. About half an hour later, I suddenly realise the whole thing is a trap. There is no one I recognise in the chai house, just Bernard and me and laughing Afghanis. They encourage us to sleep, give us more tea. I feel I can't walk straight. I struggle to the door and grope my way to the bus but there are bodies everywhere inside – I climb onto the roof. I'm frightened because I'm sure Bernard is going to be robbed. I'm struggling to think what to do. One by one, people come out of the chai house, take their snuff stuff, and look up at me on the roof. I don't see Bernard come out. Next, a whole band of men suddenly arrive at the chai house. A man greets them and there is some sort of roll call. One by one they climb up onto the roof of the bus, around me – they all have swords! I am thinking: this is not happening, the hash is doing this, this can't

65

really be happening. A man tells me to go down from the roof, and then it occurs to me that this is not about robbing Bernard and me, but that we are caught up in a gang of bandits which has some other purpose. I stumble down and into the bus – and there is Bernard smiling. And I see the other familiar faces. The bus departs – but this is not the end of my paranoia, I continue to imagine we are going to be robbed.

17 August 1974
Mazar-i-Sharif, Afghanistan. I have one sore by the eye, two sores around the nose, two on one arm, and two on my feet. My nose is always running, but I can't blow it because it starts to bleed. I put socks on so flies won't find the sores on my feet, but the socks stick to the sores and when I pull the socks off they rip open the sores. For four or five hours the truck crosses desert, almost the same as Saudi Arabia, tracks everywhere with deep ruts signalling the route. We have to walk a kilometre or so and, foolishly, I do this in my bare feet – I now have a huge blister as well.

22 August 1974
Peshawar, Pakistan. I smoke a last cigarette. I am just about to put out the light when smoke seems to be coming from the fan. The manager comes running in and looks really scared. Immediately, he notices the mattress smouldering away – lit by my cigarette! The commotion dies down and he starts demanding money from me. We talk slowly (long periods of silence). I say I'll give him my sheet for the damage, and that I'll tell other travellers this is a good hotel. But he wants money – 200 rupees. His demand comes down to 90 rupees, and then 40 rupees. I say I can buy a mattress cheaper than that. Then someone calls his 'honour' to join us. He fixes a price of 30 rupees. I insist I am poor and can pay no more than 20 rupees. Stalemate. The manager gets angry, I get angry. Finally, I offer him one English pound and my sheet. His 'honour' accepts immediately, and then finally we all go to sleep. What a laugh – I'd only put the mattress on the floor because it was so dirty and old and full of bugs.

25 August 1974
Lahore, Pakistan. An unbelievable sight at the red fort: one man pushing an ordinary lawn mower which is also being pulled by a water buffalo controlled by three men.

30 August 1974
Sonamarg, India. This beautiful valley has four glaciers – one is enormous, just rolling over the mountain like a steam roller – and three frozen snow drifts. I make for the nearest one, it looks walkable but takes longer than I think to approach. I pass several tents, sheep and cows, and a funny-looking red/brown animal like a beaver. I stumble over rocks and make it to within 100 metres of a narrow snow-covered crevice through which water is falling.

1 September 1974
Leh, India. On the road to Leh (little Tibet): many army camps, pretty villages in the valleys, box-shaped white-washed houses stepped up the mountainside with small windows un-geometrically set in the walls, people wearing velvet top hats, a yak, a Buddha carved in stone, mantra walls a metre thick – Buddhists are supposed to recite these as they pass. In Leh, there are two main streets and a market where they meet, three bread-makers, two banks,

general stores (which sell a lot of army goods too), three hotels, one power station going from 7-11:30.

2 September 1974
Homes, India. Two young monks guide me around the Homes monastery, but persist in asking for pens. I am shown the room where the head lama used to sit – highly decorated and painted and carpeted with pictures of Buddha. One of them takes me to his room, makes me chai and Ladhaki chai (salty, I don't like it). Later a man rings a gong around the temple, and my boy holds a big piece of wood and bangs it against another at an ever-quicker rate. Seven or eight monks arrive. They are dressed in dark red blanket robes and yellow shawls (although one has an orange shawl). They bow to Buddha and sit down in the temple along two lines, cross-legged. They begin to chant. I sit behind. The monk in orange has a drum. The others use symbols or a bell or blow on horns. Ladhaki chai is brought around three times, and ordinary chai twice and, each time, the monks slurp away for five minutes. Some monks do a lot of bows to Buddha. They chant for two hours. The whole set up is much like any religion. I mean there's no religion left – it's surely purposeless when chanting the same words so repetitively for so long.

10 September 1974
Delhi, India. Sleeping on the grass is tolerable – I wake up damp with mosquito bites. I am smoking and eating too much, and I have a habit of licking the left side of my moustache. I walk down to the main Old Delhi post office, past the big Friday Mosque and Red Fort. It's a long walk but joy of joys there are ten letters waiting for me.

16 September 1974
Varanasi, India. So many people thronging to the Ganges – crazy. I'm sure there are hundreds of thousands, rich and poor, with little bowls to collect water, occasionally sprinkling some on the cows. Early in the morning I go out of town to the Benares Hindu University. I talk to an old guy – very friendly. He tells me this is a special day when everyone goes from one temple to the next. For much of the day I sit in the main library reading up about Hinduism and Buddhism. Both religions believe in the wheel of existence and the reincarnation of the spirit into some sort of animal – you live and die until you can get out of the system. Buddha found a way by reaching enlightenment.

17 September 1974
Varanasi/Siliguri train, India. Here on the bank of the Ganges is where they burn bodies, neatly arranged and draped in cloth, on piles of wood. I'm not shocked or horrified but pensive. It is strange watching the flames grow larger and eat the once living forms – maybe I am a little shocked. Long narrow alleys and many steps lead to the Ghats where people are washing and boatmen canvassing. Walking along a tiny busy narrow street I find the milk and curd sellers.

27 September 1974
Rangoon, Burma. At the YMCA I suddenly realise I've left my duty free bag on the bus – with my diary in! I take a scooter taxi the wrong way – it's pouring but really pouring with rain and I am totally soaked when I get to the station. There I find my friends (who I knew were heading for Mandalay) but they haven't seen my bag. Then I'm running, running to the tourist office (I don't

know what I would have done without a map that an American had left lying about in Calcutta airport). I'm nearly crying for my diary. It's 20 minutes before they help me sort out that I must have been on a UBA bus. Running, running to the UBA office. There I make enquiries – a bus driver comes in the door and gives me my bag with the diary, but minus the duty free. I am so happy.

29 September 1974
Mandalay, Burma. All the men wear a cylinder of cloth from their waste to ankles with the loose bit at the top tied forming a large knot; only the rich ones wear trousers. The women wear blouses and long bright coloured material tied lightly to one side. They look clean and smart, neat and tidy, and there's no pushing, no hassling in the streets. It's so different from India. . . To Mandalay Hill. There are 1,729 steps to the top. The Buddhas are of various types: small, big, standing, sitting, gold-plated, marble-handed, crossed-hands-on-leg. On the way down we get a fine view of the 730 pagodas which constitute the largest book in the world – the Buddhist holy words are inscribed on marble plates and housed in the little pagodas.

6 October 1974
Bangkok, Thailand. The National Museum is full of royal regalia such as enormous cremation chariots, and exquisite mother-of-pearl boxes and sword cases. I am totally overwhelmed by the vast intricate beautiful murals of palaces and country scenes. The temple of the Emerald Buddha is magnificent – one of the most beautiful places. . . In a theatre I watch a traditional play enacted, the story of how one of two royal brothers escape from a sea giantess – lovely glittering costumes and tall gold hats, very slow dancing, hands and head moving in time with music from a horseshoe of small metal drums. . . The sex scene here is unbelievable – whole areas of night clubs where the hostesses come and caress you before you've even sat down; countless massage parlours/brothels with little Thai girls in school uniforms wriggling their bodies behind huge panes of one-way glass (mirrors for them) waiting to be a customer's choice.

13 October 1974
Luan Prabang, Laos. I'm up early, but still weak, and find a friendly cafe by the market. I'm into two fried eggs for breakfast plus an Ovaltine and cake. There is not so much of this town – at one crossroads are three travel agents all doing tours to the big waterfall, the caves and the Meo villages. The Sunshine Hotel keeps a couple of monkeys and a bear on a string all day. I talk to the young men here, the students who like to play the guitar and sing Western music. They don't know much English but they know enough to ask me if I have any LSD and, when the monkey climbs on the back of the bear, to say 'monkey fuck the bear'. Nice boys. I sit in the most Western restaurant in town talking to a German who's been travelling for a year. We eat Vietnamese food – rice with mint and cress leaves, meat and nuts. I discover that I can fly out tomorrow or Wednesday – and, dear diary, is it possible I've mentioned before my troubles in getting a flight to Darwin and into Australia by 31 December [after when a law change will require me to have a work visa]. People say the flights from Bali are booked up for three months! From Timor it's OK, but it will be the monsoons and it takes six weeks to get through from Bali to Timor in the dry season. So, so I'm rushing a bit to get to Kuala Lumpur where I can find out more definite information about flights.

19 October 1974
Sadau, Thailand. I catch a bus to Sadau, the border town (where I stuff myself with some very nice local pastries and no one asks me to pay, and where a young lady sews up the seams on my yellow trousers for nothing). I could make Malaya tonight except that I remember I have two unused Thai airmail letters. So I write two letters, then fill out the immigration forms but I'm told the Malay border is closed. I need to look for food and shelter so I ask a young guy where the Buddhist Wat is – he takes me on his bike to a temple. The head monk is sneaky-looking and sits on a throne and cross-questions me. He is drinking a coke, smoking cigars, having the odd chat with his mates, and farting.

27 October 1974
Singapore. Tao Payah, where Eddy lives, is a satellite town with hundreds of tower blocks of 2, 3, and 5 room flats. It's a terrifying place – only five years old but supposedly with a life span of 99. Eddy is only 18 but has some mature ideas – he's chairman of a teenage movement trying to help young people. I go to a meeting with him where everybody gives a little speech. Eddy himself praises Tao Payah, and says it is a luxurious life compared with that in India. A guest speaker talks about the government's fear of youth problems it sees in other countries, but says it is trying to prevent them in the wrong way. For example, bars have been shut down because it is thought they provoke drugs and hippie ways of life. There are many community centres, yes, but who caters for the problems of the mind?

28 October 1974
Singapore. I'm hungry. I am wandering up and down a market lane looking at all the stalls deciding what to eat when an old Chinese old lady comes up to me, opens her bag and gives me a tissue. When I look inside – I'm expecting a spider – I find a S$10 note. I think it must be a forged one – I look round to give it back, but the lady has disappeared. I am astounded.

1 November 1974
Kuanton, Malaya. So, there is Yappy (who I met hitching a couple of days ago), Francis and Steve. They are turning a job – putting up advertising boards in petrol stations – into a two-day holiday and taking me with them to the east coast. . . Driving a few miles north to a deserted beach, it is so very dark, yet I see one of the most beautiful sights of my life – distant forks of lightning lighting up whole scenes, as if by magic, of the still sea, islands and beaches lined with palm trees. . . We camp at a really nice spot under some trees next to still water cutting us off from the beach – the sound of the surf, the misty moon, mosquitoes buzzing (despite Yappy's efforts with mosquito coils).

2 November 1974
Kuala Lumpur, Malaya. Yappy turns off the main road into the jungle to find a large river for Francis to do some more fishing – we all end up swimming from a sandy beach. I panic when I first get in the water because it's deep and the current is so strong – the others, of course, are all laughing, and as the water sweeps me down, I panic more. Yappy shouts for me to swim not against the current but diagonally across it. Which works. Afterwards, Yappy tells me there are crocodiles in the river further down.

9 November 1974

Tomok, Indonesia. The local tribe – Batak – who live around the lake have their own language and weird-shaped houses. These are built on wooden supports with plenty of bamboo and bamboo weaving, and branch-thatch roofs. Mongoloy, my host, does a super meal in the evening for 11 – vegetable stew, crabs, fried fish, soya bean curd, buffalo milk curd, aubergine, tomatoes and cucumber rice.

13 November 1974

Bukkitingi, Indonesia. I catch a bus 15km to see the largest flower in the world. I sit in a teashop waiting for the rain to stop – it doesn't so I take off my shoes and shirt and run and walk. It's quite a way up a hill where there is a fenced-off forest. I climb over the fence. I find a chart showing the position of the flowers but they are difficult to spot. Finally, there, sitting on the wet jungly earth, is a pink jellyfish – 25 inches in diameter – a solid flower with its petals tightly packed. It's the only one I see, so I hit the muddy path to return. I'm frightened – of leeches. Very prickly palm leaves catch me, and I must tear myself away from each one. I slip on the sloping surfaces, and there is an incessant dripping of leaves, movement and sounds of dark misery. I hitch back to Bukkitingi on a wood lorry.

17 November 1974

Padang/Djarkata boat. The Indonesians are cramped under the canvas, they spew and spit and throw all their rubbish on the floor – it is disgusting, enough to make me vomit as I try to thread my way through with bare feet. My policeman friend, the one I met in Padang, has changed character completely – he's become one of these humble cowardly creatures. He begged bread from us for his child. The crew each have a long rope with a double hook trailing from the back of the boat to catch fish. The toilets are filthy. The best times are sitting on the deck when it's cloudy but not raining, or at night, or in the captain's quarters where it is comfy and cool. My foot is throbbing.

19 November 1974

Djarkata, Indonesia. The sandals I bought in Amman have finally gone to the place for sandals in the sky. A pilot comes out to the boat very quickly and we dock before eight. I limp and bus to the nearest hospital – five or six doctors prod at my dirty swollen foot. They give me a prescription and take 500 rp off me which is not OK.

25 November 1974

Potollingo, Indonesia. When nobody is looking I climb a wall and bed down for the night – within one hour, though, kids are shining torches and throwing stones at me. One of the boys carries a whip. They continue to pester me until I pack up and start on the road again.

27 November 1974

Denpassar, Bali, Indonesia. The hotel owner takes me to a cockfight. Three or four different gambling games are going on at once (dice, betting on cards, betting on numbered balls). Boys are selling oranges and ices, and an old man is selling palm wine and beadie-like roll-ups. Before a fight, the owners carry their cocks around the crowd, showing them off, and ruffling their plumages to make them angry. Each one has a three inch razor secured to a claw. After five minutes of parading, the crowd reaches a pitch of excitement – men are shouting out their offers and bets louder and louder – and the cocks are set loose in a marked-out square. They fight with their mouths, jumping on each other and chewing at each other's neck. A fight lasts less than a minute before one cock just lays down bleeding and dies.

28 November 1974
Batur, Bali, Indonesia. From Penloken there is a marvellous view of Mt Batur (although the crater is covered in mist). It's a long descent to Lake Batur, a quiet water stretching round the volcano's base. I want to get to the other side of the lake where there's some hot springs and a full moon festival, but all the men and boys quote me 2,000 rp for the journey – far too much. I decide to walk, but it's across black lava rock with gullies a few feet wide, sometimes hidden by shrubs. I reach a small village after about 20 minutes but the headman refuses to give me directions unless I pay 2,000 rp. I press on but it's getting dark and I begin to lose hope. So, when I reach a deserted temple area I decide to stay the night. I write poems by moonlight – I'm feeling pretty sad. I move under the shelter of an open temple which has a roof but no sides, and tuck into my sleeping bag. I watch the clouds dance with the moon, which is full and quite high in the sky. Suddenly I see several men walk into the temple area on the other side – the two leaders are all in white. Immediately I think of witches and sacrifices (I'm so glad I'm not smoking any Afghani hash). The men have a lamp and torches. They stop and start unpacking some bags. I'm scared they will find me; but they turn out to be friendly, and we talk a little around the fire. I sleep for two hours while they perform rituals. Tomorrow they go to the festival, and they say I can go with them for 50 rp!

29 November 1974
Ubud, Indonesia. Up at 5:00. We march down to a landing point at the lake side – a boatman is waiting. But, even my new friends cannot persuade the boatman to take me for less then 2,000 rp. This is the most closed-shop tourist rip-off I've ever encountered: 50 rp for the locals, and 2,000 rp for me. I feel very depressed about not getting to the hot springs and festival.

6 December 1974
Darwin. We leave Bali with some fine views of the islands all ringed with yellow. The plane travels through air pockets which is quite scary. Not long after 6:00 we land in Darwin airport. The whole of the plane is sprayed before we get off. I'm given a permit to stay for 12 months. There are white men in shorts everywhere. A guy called Peter the Dutchman is doing the Asian trick of hustling people to come and stay at his house. There are great showers, and a crowd of people for dinner.

12 December 1974
Darwin. I start work at the power station. It's fucking hard – removing great long tubes from a boiler house, I get an hour lunch and two smokos of 15 minutes.

23 December 1974
Darwin. Gerry is being generous with his grass and we have a few joints most nights. A spaced-out chick arrives at the house. She's alive and sexy but hung

up on dope. We go to a party and I talk to her for hours, but it's Wayne who takes her home. I go for a swim (last night Wayne and I found the back entrance to the local swimming pool) – it's gorgeous swimming at night in the nude. I am a bit troubled – torn again between thinking that sex of such temporary nature is emotionally disturbing and the knowledge that I have yet to know what I'm talking about. Wayne thinks I'm a crank for passing up the opportunity of going with her.

24-28 December 1974

Darwin. There's a work social at the Rugby Union club. I am really pissed. I've no idea how I get home. Later, Gus tells me I shouted 'the cyclone's really coming' and passed out, and that all attempts to wake me for dinner were in vain. I wake later in the evening and go upstairs with a splitting headache. I fall asleep again and wake up absolutely soaking – rain is howling in through the window and the floor is flooded. I join the others downstairs. The wind is getting pretty heavy. Wayne is drunk and jolly. We make expeditions outside – the first one, just after midnight, is to see why a car has stopped. It is virtually impossible to walk, the wind is so strong. Inside again, I go to fetch my money, passport and diary and put them in a plastic bag. When the eye comes, between 2 and 3, it is a chance to sleep undisturbed. But then the wind comes back with a vengeance in the other direction. Gus is still half asleep, I wake him and he jumps in the cupboard with Wayne. Gerry and I have drawers over our heads and we crouch behind the bed. We can't get out of the room, the door won't open. The whole wall is going to go – Jesus – I reach up over the bed for my plastic bag and pull it down to my body – just in time before the house explodes.

I remember shouting and swearing and somersaulting through the air and landing on rubbish – I may have been unconscious for a while. The next thing I know is that thousands of pieces of glass are hitting my back. I lie flat and grope with my hand for some cover. I find a board just big enough to cover me and feel lucky. I hold onto it with my life to stop the wind blowing it away. I think through what I'll do if the board does fly off, and I decide that I would make a run for it. I am lying on my side on glass and wood in two inches of water. I dare not move my left leg because I think it's slit open or broken. I can't see much. I think I'm facing away from the house. It is cold. I find a plastic mac by me and wrap myself in it but the wind keeps blowing it off. I am shivering. I can't decide if I'm going to live or die. When I think I see lights through the dark and swirling mist I shout but my voice can't rise up above the roar of the storm. I am sure all the others are dead. I can't see how they can be alive. I feel so lucky that I'm not in pain and that I've found the board to protect me.

Later, as visibility improves, I see lights and a house nearby – I shout more often as the dense mistiness begins to lift. More than two hours later, dawn is approaching and the wind is abating to nothing more than a strong gale. I look around a little more and discover that my board has only remained in place because it's wedged down by the bed that I'd been hiding behind. Then I hear voices behind. There are people alive! There is a light and I can see Peter and the van. I make an effort to turn over. There is no cut artery in my leg, or anything seriously wrong with it, but I still have to hobble when I walk. I go to the van where I find several of my friends. We are really worried that the rest of us are under the pile of debris where Peter's house once stood.

Long after it is light and the wind has fallen still more, we find that the rest of our friends are next door in a house still standing. I am crying with joy. Incredible. We all have little wounds but nobody is seriously hurt. Several of us – not me – search the piles of rubble around and are taking people to the hospital. I really want to be part of this operation, I even try to join in at one point but my knee is really crook. The whole town is completely devastated – steel telegraph poles are bent to the ground, palm trees completely uprooted, roofs lying around everywhere except on the tops of houses. All that is left of Peter's house is a bathroom on stilts and one of the long walls at a 45 degree angle. I take a ride down to the hospital – a wire fence has been put up around the entrance to stop hoards of people. I am seen within 15 minutes but the doctor isn't interested in my problem. I'm not surprised – all around are people bleeding, crying, nursing wounded children; all around is tragedy, tragedy tragedy.

We are ferried to Darwin High School in little groups with blankets as our only spare clothes. I have real trouble bending my leg and it takes time to get in and out of the purloined Volkswagen. We are among the first to arrive at the school. Everywhere is under water but there's not too much damage. We annex a dryish room for ourselves. Peter is alternating between fits of crying and fits of bossing everyone around. He's lost all his money. It was stored in cash in an attaché case. I have a little cry at the thought of my family sitting down excitedly for Christmas Day breakfast and turning on the radio and hearing about Darwin. We all manage to send a telegram off home for free, and, a day later, we get a free telephone call. I am emotionally distraught hearing all my family's voices after so long.

People begin to pour into the school – there are almost 800 here – and it becomes a main centre where all goods (food, clothes, cigarettes) are brought before distribution. There is a small team of dedicated cooks – so we have good food. My knee doubles in size. I am so incapacitated that it is as much as I can do to go to the toilet. We work consistently – Susie and I do a little work in the kitchen – I prefer to wash dishes for two hours and get my meal immediately then queue for half an hour. The evacuation programme continues and is going better than expected. Peter has gone, disappeared, somebody says he's driving south in his van.

29 December 1974

Darwin airport. The radio informs us that single men can now be evacuated. I decide to go to Sydney, and so spend the next day in the airport watching coach loads of women and children being evacuated; we are given food and drink by the Salvation Army. Early evening the Starlifter we'd been promised arrives. It is going to take us all away. I am horrified at the way the Americans are squeezing every last person in. We have to sit cross-legged in about 1 sq ft – from front to back nobody is going to be able to move. I still can't bend my leg properly and so decide to get off – I'm not that desperate. The following morning I take the first plane – a Hercules to Brisbane. We sit on actual seats and are allowed in the cockpit to have a smoke – it's a beautiful serene sight, floating above the clouds. The journey takes five hours. We are shuttled across a boring-looking town to an evacuation centre – an empty bus garage with clothes, social services, Sally Army, airline officials. We register, are given $62, and then booked onto a flight to Sydney. We eat, and then I put on some new underpants.

31 December 1974

Sydney. A flight at 6:30 to Sydney – comfort, less than an hour. Gees, Sydney is a big place. After landing we are given a meal, registered, and then handed some more money from the Red Cross. I am sent to the Quarantine Station in Manly – it's a long ride over Sydney Harbour Bridge to North Head. There's a fine view of the harbour, lights everywhere. I'm given a salad meal and shown to a hut-type room. I find a telly lounge, and inside is Gerry!

It was my good fortune that I escaped any serious illness or trouble in my half year of travelling across Asia. The travelling wasn't fun, it was often hard work, and my diary reveals that I was often weak from low level illness, and tired from walking so much, often in search of the cheapest bed or food in town. Also, I was often frustrated at all kinds of things: lack of information; being unable to go somewhere or do something; waiting for visas, transport, or friends. But, wow, what an incredible amazing journey, geographically and metaphorically, to have taken.

Some years later, I wondered if, in fact, I really had been a classic case of a mixed-up young person trying to find himself. Perhaps, I argued to myself, that I'd misunderstood the meaning of the phrase, and taken it too literally. Perhaps, I HAD been trying to 'find myself', but in a much broader, less direct way than through chanting, new philosophies or drugs. When I came to think about it again, though, a simpler explanation seemed obvious: I hadn't gone off travelling to discover myself but I had truly, simply gone off to discover what else there was in this world, outside of myself. And I found a lot.

Chapter eight

New Zealand/Chile
New pastures, deeper places

I like to talk about New Zealand and Chile as my two favourite countries on earth, yet I cannot justify these choices by any objective criteria. I've probably been to over 60 countries – having collected them in Asia and the Middle East on the hippie trail as if they were tourist sights in a city to be ticked off; I've also been at least once, if only for a few days, to most Western European and South American states. I've clearly chosen to live my life in Britain; and by chance, I suppose, I've taken more holidays in Spain than anywhere else. Moreover, I've never elected to revisit either New Zealand or Chile. So why do I continue to feel such reverence towards them both?

I have three answers to this: nostalgia, sex and swagger. To take them in reverse order. Geographically, they are very far away from my home; they are both full of wild and beautiful scenery; and they emanate a sense of physical adventure. I imagine, therefore, my highlighting them as I do is a little bit of swagger, an attempt to characterise myself with their excitements. But of course, there is more to it, not least that in both places I stopped travelling – for a year in New Zealand, and for three months in Chile – and discovered all kinds of new pastures in which to graze, and many a deeper place to explore. Indeed, these were serendipitous times in which interesting jobs, sparkling friends, and fine places to live came my way with little or no effort. It is no wonder then, that nostalgia – or saudade as the Portuguese say – colours my memory of these past times. And if I was to pick up on one aspect of this colouring, it would be sex, for aged 23, in New Zealand, I finally lost my virginity. It would be a further year, and not until I was in Chile, before I found out a bit more about adult relationships.

All of which is by way of introducing the latter, more substantial part of my three year round-the-world adventure.

Having escaped Cyclone Tracy relatively unscathed, and been evacuated to Sydney, I was housed by the Australian government in, what was then, Manly Quarantine Station for a month. Much as I admired Sydney Harbour and the new Opera House, it was too hot, and there were too many flies. I evacuated myself further south, to Christchurch, New Zealand, my wallet having been fattened, first by working in the Darwin power station before the tragedy, and then by an Australian government emergency hand-out. On arriving in New Zealand, I began a second diary.

> 13 March 1975
> Christchurch. Here beginneth the 2nd book of the travels of Paul Lyons. Having reached New Zealand without busting our hero has settled for a while there to catch his breath and some money. He has South America as his next goal and is currently engaged in learning Spanish. He has planted himself in a flat with two students and is slowly making acquaintances, is reading very much but at present is finding it hard to obtain a position.

I hitchhiked around the North Island for two weeks, before returning to Christchurch. In an effort to improve myself and meet people, I joined a debating club. When I was moaning, to friends at the club, about not being able to get a job, an older man suggested I try to find work as a salesman. I reacted by saying I thought that would be like giving my soul to the devil. Nevertheless, within days I was looking at the classified ads with new purpose, and by mid-April I'd secured an interview for a job with a pharmaceutical company, Sandoz.

> 17 April 1975
> BIG DAY. First I go into town to buy some trousers for my 11:15 interview. In the library, I read up a little more about salesmanship. I have to choose a shirt – first I iron my blue one with short sleeves, then try my grey one, but both have lousy collars for my type of tie knot. I feel untidily dressed as I walk around to the motel where the managing director and sales director are waiting for me. I am bombarded with questions for one hour – it seems to go pretty well [. . .]. After I can't settle to do anything at home, I'm just thinking about the job. My letter about a bike accident is printed in the paper – this makes me happy even though the registration number of the car has been edited out.
> I am just dossing about in my hovel of a flat when the two smart Sandoz men arrive unexpectedly at the front door. I am in my shorts (thank god I wasn't wearing my kaftan). The managing director is a smooth bugger, he's got a look about him. They don't seem to mind my dress but they want a snap decision. I have to say YES, so they welcome me to Sandoz. These two suited men in my dirty flat, shaking hands with me in my shorts – it's worth a picture. Afterwards, one thing sticks in my mind: the sales director looking very pleased with himself and muttering about how we should make a good team. The job is in Dunedin! I am to spend two weeks in Auckland and then move to Dunedin. I will have a salary of five and half thousand pounds, plus car. Well baby!

Thus, within weeks of arriving in New Zealand I had, what turned out to be, a perfect job – medical representative. I possessed a new car (red Toyota), a decent salary (far more than I would have earned with a typical traveller's job of barman or waiter), and the requirement to travel all around the South Island visiting doctors in every town. Moreover, I wasn't even going to have to sell anything, all the work entailed was talking to doctors and advising them in medical detail why Sandoz drugs should be prescribed.

In Dunedin, I quickly found a room in a flat. It was owned, and dominated, by Jan, a vivacious young woman confined to a wheelchair having suffered terribly in a motorbike accident. The flat was across the road from a beach (would I ever be happy living away from the sea again?) and Dunedin's lively centre was not too far in the other direction. I soon signed up for the local folk club, run by Pete Graham (who I would run into again in London some years later), joined my flatmates as a regular at various pubs, and generally profited hugely from the city's student social life. I also acquired a bicycle and a beautiful ginger and white kitten. I called her Ginquin. She rode around with me at the weekend – whether on the bike or hitchhiking – in a woollen shoulder bag, her cute little head poking out.

My Dunedin year was full of adventures, exploration and discovery, more Enid Blyton it has to be said than Ranulph Fiennes. But, at last, this insecure boy from the suburbs was starting to mature, to blossom even. He could not have been further away on earth from his home, but also he could not have been in a place more stunningly beautiful. A near-empty paradise of rolling green hills, pastured and forested; of craggy snow and/or glacier-capped mountains with adjacent ski fields; a myriad of picturesque beaches and coves – all close by Dunedin, or at least within half a day's car ride. It's true what they say about this place, that you can ski in the mountains and swim from a beach on the same day.

Dunedin itself held various secret places. There was the old wooden house I discovered, deserted, dilapidated. I described it as 'weird' from the outside, and inside it 'was as though somebody had just left the place in a hurry'. I found 'beetroot on the floor, an old encyclopaedia, collars and ties, pictures, letters, paints, bottle-tops, an old gramophone with 78 records'. I saved a couple of items from further dilapidation: 28 volumes of the 1911 edition of *Encyclopaedia Britannica* (which I had shipped back to England) and an old framed photograph of the most beautiful Maori girl which I still have hanging on my wall today.

And there was Cargill's Castle, a ruin on the cliff top overlooking the sea, not open to the public, but all the more romantic for being so secluded.

15 November
Did damn all today as well – went to a few jumble sales – read on the beach for hours – was really feeling depressed, wasn't sure what I was going to do tonight – just moping around when lo and behold a girl named Pam stood at

the door – remember I met her ages and ages ago and told her to come round – So we sat talking for a while then I took her to 4 Elbe Street – the old house from whence I have the *Encyclopaedia Britannica* – she loved it – searched the place more thoroughly than I ever did – Feeling good to have somebody to be with – I thought it must have been rather brave of Pam to come around out of the blue like that. She has a bit of life in her – Then she took me to Cargill's Castle, over the rocks and up the hill – very romantic – watching the sun set – crumbling old castle – a mess of a place but quiet and peaceful, watching Dunedin one way and the sea and the cliffs the other way.

Beyond Dunedin, my favourites places included Lake Tekapo, Milford Sound, the Routebourn Track, Nelson and Picton, Stewart Island. Sometimes, when driving through this picture-book land, usually heading for a small town's surgery to chat to the local doctor, I'd pass or cross a river with such crystal clear clean waters that I couldn't help but stop, strip off my work suit, and dive in for a swim. Cold, but exhilarating.

Our lives and exploits, I should say, were often fuelled by beer – bought by the jug. Two embarrassing incidents stand out. Early in November, a crowd of us drove a few miles east of Dunedin, past Port Chalmers, to beautiful Long Beach, with its large cave, to have a fireworks night party. I drank a lot. Even in my diary written within a few days, I confess to not remembering much. I woke up in the cave around four in the morning, totally alone, and with no way of getting back to Dunedin. I couldn't understand what had happened, and was furious with my friends for having left me all alone. Only when I'd finally been collected by a flatmate, did I discover the truth: I'd insisted strenuously on spending the night on the beach, and hadn't let anyone help me to a car and take me home.

An even worse case of memory loss occurred one night at a ski chalet in Queenstown. It was owned by Maxine's family, Maxine being the girlfriend of my flatmate, Ross. Here is an edited version of my diary entry for that day.

30 August 1975
Saturday night was one Hell of a Night – we zipped down to Arthur's Point pub [. . .] and though it was slow starting we got some drinking games going and Thumpers hit the roof – the moment any strangers came near us and were not doing anything, I ordered them to join us, we had a massive crowd playing and it was going really fast [. . .]. Neat night – fell asleep in front of the fire. In my half-pissed stupor sleep I went to the toilet to have a pee but – so I found out later – I peed in the doorway of the girls' bedroom – apparently Ross told me it wasn't the toilet but I said it was – I remember only climbing into my sleeping bag and curling up into the foetus position. Later on, Maxine's Mum came in – we had a chat and a cup of coffee. It was only in the morning that Ross told me what I'd done – I felt so crushed when the

girls got up – I apologised to Maxine in the car and we had a laugh about it which made me feel better.

A few months later I would contract hepatitis, and this would put a serious brake on any drinking, and, consequently, on the acquisition of any further memory-loss anecdotes.

It may have been drink that helped me, finally, to lose my virginity. In November 1975, a friend invited me along to a party. There I ran into a girl called Chris with whom I'd played silly games some weeks earlier. As people were drifting away from the party, my diary reveals, '[I] asked her if she'd like to sleep with me – as easy as that – for the first time in my life I was with a girl in bed making love for quite some hours.' I have a vague memory of Chris giving me three marks out of five (for I had confessed my inexperience) which wasn't bad given the rather cold and calculated way I'd approached her. A couple of further one-night encounters followed before I went steady for two months with a young American girl who had inherited money and bought a house in Dunedin. What I recall best about that first affair was a party we gave in her garden, and how we cooked the food in the traditional Maori way, with a Hangi. This involves digging a pit in the ground, and then using it to make a fire to heat river boulders. Once the fire is burned out, and while the boulders are still very hot, baskets of food are placed on top – containing, perhaps, a side of lamb, whole fish, vegetables etc. – and covered in wet sacks. Water is poured in, and the pit filled with earth and left for several hours. Since we'd never laid a Hangi before, and there was a crowd of hungry people, it proved a stressful process waiting long enough before digging the food out. But when we did, it was all succulent, steamed and unbelievably tasty.

My plan had always been to stay in New Zealand for a year, and to then cross the Pacific to continue my travels in South America. By early 1976, I was sweating with travel fever. A three week tour around the North Island, when I fell in love with the warmer climes of the Coromandel and Northland peninsulas, flared rather than cured the fever. I was on the road again, hitching, exploring, a free man in the wind, and I didn't want to stop. I researched my options for getting to South America, and a liner to Panama seemed the most economical. But then I had a remarkable encounter. Sitting in a pub in Port Chalmers one night, I was with some friends and we got talking to a German, older than us, who was taking great pleasure in trying to puncture our naive and youthful views of the world. When he suggested we go back to his boat to try some proper (German) beer, we imagined he had a large yacht. Not so, his 'boat' turned out to be a huge container ship. We drank his beer, and his Schnapps and defended our student ideals. But I also discovered that he was going to Panama, and that he – and captains of other ships owned by his company, Hamburg Süd – would take on board one or two extras to work their passage! This was unbelievable. I had had no idea that it was still possible to work one's passage like in the old days. He told me what to do, and gave me contact names and numbers.

Thus, within a few weeks I was on board *Columbus America*, sailing first for Australia, and then Panama – and it wasn't costing me a penny. There was one other, so-called, work-a-way – Edgar. We each had our own private cabin, and private shower room. We also had delicious German food: three hot meals a day, plus German bread and sausage and cheese, lemon tea and excellent coffee whenever we wanted. The work was light cleaning and greasing of turnbolts mostly, but the key requirement was that we didn't make a nuisance of ourselves. In my spare time, I read, wrote letters, and continued learning Spanish. I also played cribbage, backgammon and Scrabble with Edgar. He had brought a little grass with him on board, and this also helped the time go by.

Excited I was, tremendously, to be travelling again, but I was also parting – somewhat coldheartedly – from my girlfriend, other good friends, and the happy, busy new life that I'd made for myself. So there were tears too. On seeing the lights of New Zealand fade into the blackness of night as *Columbus America* sailed away from Wellington, I made up this refrain.

> Lights of a land
> Quickly slipping into a dream
> Into stars that are a wheel
> Leaving days of gold
> Leaving days of cold
> Leaving my spit upon centuries of spit
> Leaving my tears on these shores

My knowledge of what I did during the last days in New Zealand, the journey across the Pacific, and the early months in South America is very sketchy. This is the only period in my adult life for which I do not have a diary – it was stolen with a bag of mine in Huancayo, Peru. It was extraordinarily distressing to lose that diary, and I remained in Huancayo for some days solely in the forlorn hope of recovering it. Thus, many a detail about my adventures in this period – late February 1975 to early July 1976 – have been long lost. I do have, though, a few of my own letters, those I sent to family which were returned to me many years later.

It was not a good beginning to my new adventure. The first days in Panama proved among the worst I ever had travelling. We left the ship in Panama City, and made our way to Colon, the port at the eastern end of the canal. There, not only was I robbed of much money (the first time despite all my travelling in Asia), but I had the worst bedbug experience of my life, and I contracted hepatitis. I know that I was infected with hepatitis in Colon because it was there that Edgar and I parted, and I found out later that he, too, had suffered from hepatitis about three months after our parting. His letter outlined a series of other mishaps, in Columbia, and then back through Panama, Mexico, the US and eventually to Calgary, most of them money, visa, or drug related.

From Colon, I boat-hopped through the beautiful (and then completely unspoilt) San Blas islands, with white sand beaches and friendly indigenous people wearing the most colourful clothes and brilliant gold rings in their noses. The last boat link across the Caribbean Sea – to Columbia – was the most to difficult to find, and when I was offered passage it was on a small smuggler's boat, with all kinds of goods roped up and filling the hold and deck area. It was a rough voyage, and I was scared at times the vessel would go under. I was no less fearful when we landed on a deserted Columbian beach, because, I realised, I'd entered the country illegally. I was already well aware of Columbia's reputation as a dangerous destination for travellers, not least because some police were known to extort money from foreigners, even if it meant planting drugs on them. In fact, I came to see how it was only in cities and in areas much frequented by tourists that danger lurked so ominously, and that – as everywhere in the world I suppose – off the beaten track local people could not have been friendlier. I had my passport stamped without any problems at a nearby police station. Then, anxious to be in the safer haven of Ecuador, raced across the country – through Medellin, not yet dubbed the most dangerous city in the world, and Bogota, where the smiles of pretty girls seemed so enticing, but where paranoia filled the city centre streets after dark.

I made for Otavalo, in Ecuador, to visit the indigenous peoples' market famous for its weavings. There, I bought several pieces of old material, beautifully woven with many different coloured stripes; later, as I travelled south through the Andes, I would buy more weavings. The most beautiful of all, though, was a full-sized poncho, tightly woven from heavy cotton in scores of colours, red being the most dominant. I'm ashamed to say, I bought this from an Indian on the shores of Lake Titicaca, who was wearing it. Attracted by the rainbow colours and simple striped design from afar, I approached the stranger, and bargained a price from him. Back in England, I would wear this poncho on winter days, and feel special, regal. Occasionally, since then, it has hung on a wall as decoration, but at present it's sadly in a drawer, looked at and enjoyed all too infrequently. A few other of my Andean weavings have been used for cushions which continue to decorate our lounge.

After Otavalo, my next target – as a traveller intent on visiting the most interesting, the most exotic, the most extraordinary places – was the Galapagos Islands. I had sailed through them on *Columbus America*, but getting to visit them, it turned out, was an expensive proposition – air tickets being more than twice as expensive for non-Ecuadorians than for nationals. Too much for my budget. From pleasant Quito, I journeyed south to the unpleasant coastal city of Guayaquil in search of a cheap passage. I tried cargo boats, cruises, the navy, the air force, but without any luck. In a last desperate attempt, I traipsed the streets visiting many ordinary travel agents in the vague hope of finding one so unfamiliar with foreign tourists – there not being many in Guayaquil – that they would sell me an air ticket at the Ecuadorian price. Bingo. I managed to find a return ticket for $65 instead of $145.

As I say, I have no diary to help my memory, but I do have a letter I sent to my family (from Lima, dated 10 June) and its contents are all I know about my time on the Galapagos.

Both going and returning I had frightening moments as my ticket was checked (thinking the mismatch between the ticket and my obvious appearance as a tourist would get me into trouble), but it was fine.

It's expensive on the islands too. To get the best deal one has to hire a boat, to cruise round the island, and fill it with eight people. It is a very touristy scene, but nothing can be done about it. I spent one week in the main settlement (it's full of characters from all over the world) waiting for people to fill a boat, and the other week travelling around the islands. They are all tips of volcanoes, sticking out of the sea, some old, and some new just 100 years old (a mass of cracked black lava). There is a lot of beautiful emptiness, but of course the main attraction is the wildlife that is not so wild.

Sitting in the little port of the main village I saw the following: a pelican or two sitting on a post fishing, a heron (a giant blue one) doing nothing, lots of 2-3ft long marine iguanas crawling around the rocks, thousands of little lizards, mocking birds that will land on you, lots of beautiful fish in the clear water, and a seal. Around the islands, I saw: thousands of sea lions and seals all without fear of humans (one can swim with them), penguins, fearless land iguanas up to 4ft long (landing on their island these enormous lizards come trundling down to meet you), hawks and doves that come within two feet of you, and flamingos. On the boat trip we ate only fresh meat killed the same day: goat, tuna, durado (white fish), lobster and crab. And, of course there are the giant tortoises – enormous things. They are threatened by the introduced animals like the rat and goat, and are therefore being cared for and protected by the research stations where one can see them at all stages of their life.

Hey, I'm 24, how about that. I've never been 24 before. We had a little celebration in the Galapagos. The islands had run out of beer so we got drunk on rum.

Once back on the Ecuadorian mainland, I began to suffer from unexplained bouts of tiredness. Orange pee and yellow eye-whites eventually indicated hepatitis, and I decided to make straight for Lima. There, the British embassy directed me to a clean but expensive hospital. The diagnosis was confirmed, and the cure: no walking, no alcohol, no chocolate, little grease, lots and lots of rest. And where should I go for such recuperation, I asked naively, and was answered with a shrug of the shoulders. I wrote home about how this was 'terribly depressing', for, in effect, I'd been told to stop travelling, i.e. to give up the raison d'être of my hours, days, weeks and months. What to do? where to go? Of course, it occurred to me to fly home, but I dismissed the idea out-right. I was far from ready to give up. What would I be going home to? A further complication was that I had no idea how much – if any – of the costs of not-travelling would eventually be paid out by my modest travel insurance. This was probably the single biggest challenge of my travels.

I stumbled on a small, clean hotel – significantly better than I was used to allowing myself – with a snack bar on the ground floor, and there I holed up for a month. A month! Every morning I would make my way slowly downstairs to the café, and there I would stay all day before returning to my small room, where I had a television. After a week or so, I allowed myself a daily walk, very slow and sedate. It was on one of these walks that I met a gentle Frenchman, Didier, with whom I was to have something akin to a platonic love affair – certainly it was the closest relationship I had ever had with a man (though, clearly, my friendships with Colin at school, and Philip at university, had similarities). Didier decided to wait in Lima until I was ready to travel, so we could head for Cuzco together. His companionship brightened up the latter part of my self-imposed convalescence, and then our growing intimacy added joy and laughter and emotional warmth to the highs and lows of travelling.

Going south from Lima, through Huancayo where I lost my diary, we stopped for days in Ayacucho, a sleepy town only a few years from becoming infamous as the base for Shining Path. There we competed with each other for the affections of two local girls. I recall feeling jealous because I thought Didier had got further with his than I had with mine. Here we teamed up with a lovely Canadian man, Jim, and his temporary travelling companion, a cool, attractive English woman by the name of Annabel, and continued south.

One of the most abiding of my travelling memories is of the four of us sitting atop Peruvian lorries, all wrapped up in our ponchos against the biting cold, but in ecstasy at the glory of riding through the snow-capped Andes. Every now and then I'd sing out: 'Onwards, onwards, upwards through Peroooooo, through Peroooooo.'

Annabel and I fell into bed for a while, but I remained closest to Didier. The four of us stayed together exploring the wonders of Cuzco and Machu Picchu, travelling round Lake Tititaca and into Bolivia. In La Paz, Annabel received the most terrible news: her brother had been killed in a farming accident. I accompanied her to the airport for her flight home, and the loudspeaker system was blaring out Paul Simon's *Fifty Ways to Leave Your Lover*. The following year, once I'd returned to London, we tried to revive our relationship but there was little more than Peru we had in common.

My friendship with Didier would survive longer, for several years. In the late 1970s, I would regularly find myself in Paris for one reason or another, and we'd always make time for each other. However, one afternoon, when still together in central Bolivia, our intimacy broke down dramatically – at least for me. We had descended from the high Andes and were enjoying the colonial pleasures of old Sucre before heading on to the 17th century silver boom town of Potosi. Some 10 days earlier we had made a pact to give up smoking, on forfeit of a massive $50, to be paid to a beggar. One day, when we had separated for a few hours, I chanced on him sitting on a bench in a square, smoking. I wrote in my diary: 'Such a little thing, but such a great bond broken – the money has nothing to do with it – D was trying to pretend he would give up – trying to be something he couldn't be – I have spent the whole day alone – not finding it easy to talk to him or join in our mutual commentary of the passing days.' Such was the emotional closeness I felt between us that this seemed no less than a betrayal. We continued to travel together as far as Santiago, but the betrayal seeded a growing resentment I felt towards him – directed at his lack of initiative, his easy, uncritical way of being. It was simpler, I decided, to be alone again.

And so into Chile, a very strange country geographically. It is more than two and a half thousand kilometres long, from the arid Atacama desert in the north to the cold wet mountains and fjords in the southern Patagonian region, but averaging only a little over 100 miles in width. From Santiago, I aimed to hitchhike south to Puerto Montt from where I would take a boat to Punta Arenas, Patagonia, then cross into Argentina to travel north again towards Buenos Aires. The journey south was a pleasure, with the rolling Chilean countryside reminding me at times of Britain. I wrote in my diary: 'Sheep and cows graze peacefully between the trees and bushes and barbed wire fences, the land rolls gently greenly, rivers, streams, pools are abundant. It is like England. People are surprised when I tell them.' And everywhere I went people were friendly, generous. I felt safe, almost at home. Sometimes, it took a while to hitch a ride, and I would sing over and over again, like a mantra, 'Apples and bread and cheese, spring and south and me.'

It rained a lot in the south, and I was soaked by the side of the road many times. One time, when I was feeling particularly cold, damp and fed up, I recall thinking that it was only because I was prepared to be cold, damp and fed up that I was actually visiting such fascinating places. I arrived in Puerto Montt having just missed the boat, and was told the next one was not for two weeks. I hitched across the border into Argentina for a few days, to visit Bariloche with its beautiful lakes and mountain scenery, its fancy hotels and chocolate shops. My diary records me reading Hermann Hesse, and meeting lots of interesting people.

I returned to Puerto Montt. The rain was too depressing, and I decided to head north again, to the sun, preferably near a beach, to wait out the time before returning for the boat to Patagonia. A 22 hour train ride carried me back to Santiago, from where I took a short trip west to the chic coastal resort of Viña del Mar, and its port neighbour, Valparaiso. 'Buzz, buzz, buzz, buzz, buzz, buzz,' I wrote in my diary, 'on Monday I fell in love with Valparaiso – its thin curling streets, its dark green and old hills, the street characters, the port and port life – the old English banks and companies, the life, the plazas, the slippery fish, the hill trains, the pretty girls at the side of wretched beggars – and with Viña so close.'

The next day, chancing my luck, I went to the British Institute enquiring about work, and was directed towards a British school, slightly north along the coast at Reñaca. Amazingly, I was instantly offered a job until mid-December. Despite my traveller's rags, the headmaster, who spoke impeccable English, said, 'I can see you are a gentleman.' I'm sure he meant Englishman more than gentleman, since my diary records how I was convinced that I was being employed for being British and nothing else. As an Inspector, my job was no more or less than a super-prefect, monitoring uniform compliance and behaviour in the playground. But so what, I'd fallen in love with a place and, against all the odds, found a job enabling me to live there for a while.

After returning to the British Consulate to check if there were any restrictions on my working, I met a young man in the street, Diego, and he suggested I try the residential homes on Cerro Castillo (Castle Hill) overlooking the sea and all of Viña, for a place to live. I did, and I found one, a room in a courtyard pension, with a kitchen I could use. It turned out to be right next door to a large residence housing a leather workshop, run by the Morel brothers, where I would spend a lot of time in the next months, and where I would make myself a pair of tyre-soled sandals.

And, as if serendipity had not already shined on me enough that week . . . With nothing much to do at the weekend, I chose to hitchhike – rather aimlessly – north along the coast. Walking down towards a small fishing village called Horcón, I met – and immediately fell for – a girl in the street. We got talking. Nene was a young music teacher, and her parents had a holiday house close by. She invited me in, and then to stay. The village proved to be a very special place with beautiful beaches, and a character that was part hippie and part secret hideaway for the Santiago rich. From then on, most Friday afternoons, Nene would bus from Santiago to Viña and together we would hitch to Horcón for the weekend. Her parents disapproved of me – I could understand why. Once, they surprised us in bed, arriving unexpectedly from the city, and we had but minutes to dress and hide evidence of our sinfulness. We were also caught in my courtyard room on Cerro Castillo. My landlady told me with some anger that I was not allowed to have guests, and that hers was a respectable house. We skulked out together, near midnight, with Nene almost in tears, to seek refuge with friends.

With Didier and now with Nene, I was journeying – hitchhiking perhaps – into a new and richer emotional landscape, with higher mountains of joyful emotions and deeper valleys of unsettling ones. I may have been to the land of love with Myra (more of which shortly), but that relationship was innocent and uncomplicated, childish. I was becoming far more aware of the feelings in me, wanting to be more conscious of happy ones, but, more significantly, needing to cope with the disturbing ones, to understand where they had came from, why I was feeling them, and whether their triggers were in me or others.

For the first time, traces of self-analysis and angst appear in my diary, starting with the disappointments I felt in the relationship with Didier. Once we had parted, and a good few weeks after Annabel had flown out of my life, there is this: 'MONDAY BLUES – The solution is easy – I need someone to hold me tight for a while – to warm my disappointments – meet my fears – someone to take my hand.' Once Nene had walked into my life, or more accurately, once I had walked into hers, the self-analysis only worsened for, in truth, I had no idea how to be in a loving relationship. I wanted more sex than Nene could give for practical, emotional and physical reasons, and I had no idea – if my diary is reliable – how to deal with this and my own unfathomable resentments. Nene was giving me so much, in truth, and I just kept on wanting more. The tensions this caused in me and our relationship left me struggling for self-explanation.

25 November 1976
I wrote a message to Nene – sexual relations have turned into a shambles – but she did not understand. Here is the message: 'Sometimes one can see in the future. One sees things, one tries to change what will happen. The magician is a wise man and a fool, he knows and doesn't know too much. He has a wand, he uses it. When it works it is splendid for the heart mind ego – when it doesn't work well he doesn't look for reasons in the wand but everywhere else.'

It is no wonder she didn't understand! At the time, I thought it was me teaching Nene about life and relationships, and even today I have a sense of cloying guilt over my arrogance. In hindsight, I suspect, I was learning far more about myself and relationships from her, than she was from me.

I think it was through Diego that I met Christian, an architect student. We became very good friends. He had a real passion, a zest for life, I remember, and took me one evening along the coast to a beach of dunes where many other students were camping out. We were all there for a 12 hour through-the-night reading of Dante's *Divine Comedy*.

Through me, Christian and Nene became friends, and decided to travel together in Brazil during their summer holidays, from December. They wanted me to come too, but I had declined believing I needed to be on the road again, alone. Nene and I had a very emotional Christmas – I was staying in Santiago with her large family who had, eventually, come to like me – for I was to be leaving on the morning of the 26th, and we would never be seeing each other again.

It turned out to be a very special end to a very special time. During the day on Christmas Eve, Christian, Nene and I went to Diego's large rich house, and then for a ride in Diego's brand new Mini. In early evening, I was privileged to take part in Nene's family Christmas meal with many relations. There was turkey, a Christmas tree with flashing lights, and presents for everyone.

Afterwards, Nene and I headed out again because this night, for the first time in three years since Augusto Pinochet's coup had ousted and killed Salvador Allende and formed a dictatorship, there was no curfew sending people scurrying home at an early hour.

26 December 1976
Santiago. There is no toque de queda [curfew] this night. That is far more worth celebrating than Christmas. We hit the plaza, dance and swim and play and act like liberated prisoners. It is not crowded at 4 in the morning, neither

is it empty. [. . .] Nene's cork shoes go floating off in the pond towards London; we are returned by dawn. [. . .]

Little incident with the police: Christian going round a roundabout was going to leave by an exit but saw the police and changed his mind – two minutes later a giant car (black and white) with giant siren (red) overtakes and overshadows the tiny little Mini, and puts fear into everyone's hearts, as they arrive with their nasty sub-machine guns. Felipe [Nene's brother] and Christian fumble changing places in the front of the Mini (Christian doesn't have a licence) – Nene was confident, clever and childish. Felipe insisted that he was driving but Christian told the truth as it was obvious the police had seen him. Between smiles and threats and games of justice, the policemen let them off on the pretext of Christmas, but he realised also that there was no harm in these people, just frightened schoolboys.

What my memory, as opposed to my diary, remembers more acutely is experiencing the fear emanating from my friends, the kind of fear of corrupt authority that I had never known, but which my friends had been living through for years. I was a political naïf, and there is little about the political climate of Chile in my diary. I had been in Santiago for the third anniversary of the Pronunciamiento Militar, and watched many thousands of people parade past Pinochet.

11 September 1976
Banks, schools, faculties, corporations, ministries made floats – people were jubilant – smiles, singing, young and old – smart, scruffy, bearded and non-bearded, slowly moved with the procession to parade along Avenida Benardo O'Higgins Libertador, past the infamous Pinochet and his scandalous rogues.

Once I had settled in Viña, the people around me were always extremely cautious about expressing political views – though not in the Morel leather workshop. Tens of thousands of artistic and left-wing minded people had fled the country, thousands more had been arrested, tortured, imprisoned, and the rest were learning to live by the dictator's repressive rules. I had hardly noticed, and the suffering of a whole country, a whole people, largely passed me by. I was, though, to have a further – and far more frightening – experience with the police, a few weeks later in Brazil.

On Christmas day, Nene took me up into the hills to a river where we could bathe naked, and we had one of our most romantic days. I wrote in my diary about the absurdity of this: 'Nene is very happy. I am very happy and yet in 12 hours time we are totally separated, more or less for the rest of eternity. FOR EVER. On Christmas Day in the afternoon we are Adam and Eve. On Boxing Day we are separated for ever. How and why is it possible. The answer is very simple – because I have chosen this course.'

I, in my arrogance. But I was to pay. I took the bus on Boxing Day to Mendoza, Argentina, starting my travels once again, and there in a cheap hotel room I wrote the following:

26 December 1976

Since I awoke this morning just before 6 there have been tears in my eyes. Sometimes they stay within sometimes they dribble down my face, and my nose runs too, and sometimes when there is nobody near I sob and sob screwing up my chin. Now I want to sob, my eyes are like an overfull teaspoon that doesn't quite run over the side due to surface tension.

I woke N with two kisses hoping she would fall back to sleep and remember it all as a dream, but she came and watched me, sling my mochila over my back, take her hand and say goodbye. I remember now she did not say a word, or smile, or cry or anything, much like in a trance, and I walked away from her with whispers on my lips, but ice, ice cold retreating from her life. And she must have seen me, exactly as she first saw me [in the lane in Horcon] before I turned my head and said 'hola'.

If I am like this constantly crying, I cannot imagine how terrible she feels. Perhaps she can sleep and she has the family around to occupy her – her piano – and I feel so terribly alone. Perhaps it is the strongest relation I have ever had. The last few days we were like infatuated lovers, forever kissing and embracing. And the days were so long, nights only there because somebody said so. I go over in my mind the weekends together, the meetings, the partings, the smiles and the tears. How can I do that: from such a deep relationship and then walk out as though it never existed. Maybe after all it is a very ugly thing to do. Now I feel very ugly. I want to see her on the other side of the street. I want the bell of my pension to ring on Friday afternoon. I feel totally lost and empty.

Very quickly, I changed my mind, and decided I did want to travel in Brazil for a month with Nene and Christian. I wrote proposing we meet in Buenos Aires. Once in B.A. myself, I contacted Arturo, a friend I'd made in Bariloche, and he invited me to stay. His was a rich family, but the atmosphere inside the large house, even during the New Year festivities, was cold if not frozen. Only after a few days had passed was I told that Arturo's student brother was missing, had disappeared. I did not stay in touch with Arturo, so I never found out if his brother returned or remained one of the 'desaparecidos'.

In early January, I raced off to Uruguay to explore for a bit (I still have a well-used mate gourd and bombilla) before returning to B.A. to wait for my Chilean friends. But I waited and waited, increasingly frustrated; eventually, it transpired they had been in the city some time before bothering to contact me. I was (absurdly) angry, and it took a few days before we were friends again, and ready to travel. We headed off to Paraguay, though our first attempt at crossing the border failed. Having already been shocked to find in Argentina that men were not allowed to travel on trains in shorts, we now discovered, even more shockingly, that Paraguay prohibited anyone with a backpack from entering the country. We returned to the nearest Argentinian town, put on our smartest clothes, and purchased string shopping bags to hold our rucksacks and their contents. We found Paraguay a very poor, sleepy country, where everything seemed to be named Guarani, and which was ruled like a private estate by its dictator Alfredo Stroessner.

We headed for Brazil via the fabulous Iguazu Falls, and soon after found ourselves in jail! One minute we were walking in the streets of Curitiba, and the next several policeman were obliging us to accompany them. Here's how I recorded the frightening incident in my diary.

> 29 January 1977
> We are a little insulted but don't cause trouble. In the police station, we are body searched and removed of all our possessions. We are placed in semi-cells. I start to ask to phone the British consulate. Laboriously long forms are filled out and every personal item is listed. The money is counted scrupulously. They are friendly. We are suspects. We think we can go when they have finished, but no we have to wait while they phone headquarters. In time, more policemen arrive and are curious. Two police cars arrive. We are told to get in them; they have armoured back seats. I am afraid for us. I start to protest that I want to phone the consulate. They will not let me. Finally, I am forced in the car by two policemen. I have in mind untold horrible things that I know are possible. I am afraid for Nene. We are taken to the Centre of Investigations. There the same forms are filled out again. They are so long. So many policemen come and go. There are some very ugly greedy faces. After the forms are filled out, we are locked in a room. We are suspects. The policemen were making jokes about how we looked like terrorists. It seems one policeman was killed by three Paraguayans yesterday. When we spoke Spanish to the two cops in the Plaza they became suspicious. It is obvious to them we are not anything more than tourists, but sometimes vengeance is very unreasonable. I am still afraid for us, not physically afraid but aware of the possibilities. [. . .] I sleep and have nightmares, and wake with a very bad headache. After three hours we are taken upstairs. Upstairs are secretaries, and people coming and going and people in suits. I am very relieved. Somebody gives me a pill for my headache. In 20 minutes we are out in the wild and very very relieved.

Brazil continued to prove a difficult place to enjoy, especially with three of us travelling together, but the country left such an impression on me – its size, geographical diversity, the extraordinary mix of people, and a culture more colourful, vital and dynamic than anything in Europe I knew of – that for years after I would talk to friends about wanting to go back there, maybe to live for a while.

The parting from Nene and Christian this time was less intense, less emotional. I would never see Christian again, though, we would continue to write to each other for more than a decade, and I always looked forward to his exquisitely written letters. Nene, I did see a few years later, in Holland, where she had gone to live and work as a nanny.

We had both moved on, and were little more than strangers. I fear, though I cannot remember exactly, that I was not kind. The meeting served, in fact, to end a correspondence in which we had allowed ourselves to use language that continued to kindle the embers of our affair despite all the reality of time and distance.

I owe Nene very much, for taking me into her world so generously for a short few months, for her love and friendship. But writing this has given me the new thought, the understanding that my love of Chile, my lifetime of avowing it as one of my two favourite places on earth (away, of course, from this great Britain of ours) is thanks to Nene, rather than anything about the country per se.

Before closing this chapter, I wish to revisit its theme, and how changes or the maturing – if that is the right word – in my psyche were reflected by changes in my writing and the way I wrote. In New Zealand, I had begun to include poems in my diary, and then in Peru and Chile I had become more emotionally self-analytical. But in South America, I also began to include short fictional stories, fables really, shorter than a page, always inspired by characters or events around me. It is clear, looking back at that diary, how I must have been intent on recording my experiences in a more original, imaginative or colourful way than hitherto. A dead cat on the side of the road is no longer just a dead cat, but the focus of varied reactions by passers-by. A young waiter in the city who spills a pile of napkins onto the floor is suddenly longing for his family and rural home far away. An old lady who serves breakfast to the market sellers, and has done for half a century, remembers her apprenticeship as a child. A hungry boy beggar can no longer stand the sight of rich people eating inside a restaurant so rushes in to steal a steak. And so on.

These stories were surely also influenced by the books I was reading. I had always carried several, or more than several, in my otherwise light, frameless rucksack, but whereas through Asia and the early months in South America, their additional weight was a purely physical burden, by this time their weight was also meta-physical. I have already mentioned Hesse, but three other titles from my backpack will suffice to demonstrate this: *The Doors of Perception* by Aldous Huxley, *Labyrinths* by Luis Borges, and *Zen and the Art of Motorcycle Maintenance* by Robert Pirsig.

Borges opened up for me a style of writing, intellectual, a little surreal, a little mathematical, which suited my bent, but Pirsig gave me a key that unlocked a puzzle I had never thought to question. Throughout my schooling, I had failed miserably at English (witness my crying over essay homeworks), and, as I've said, I gravitated towards maths and science which required little writing skill. Pirsig, in his now classic book, explains how he had a student who was unable to write a 500 word essay about the United States. He asked her to write about her own town, and when she couldn't do that, he suggested she try the high street, and still the subject proved too difficult. It was only when he narrowed the subject down to the Opera House, and told her to start with the upper left hand brick did she turn in a 5,000 word essay. This example is the core of a sustained and passionate bit of theorising from Pirsig about how creativity in individuals can be stunted (or 'bonsaied' as I have called it) by the habits and expectations of the teaching around them. I wrote in my diary: 'Pirsig says the problem was not that she didn't have anything to say, but that amongst all the information she had, she couldn't think of anything original or new to say. This was my problem. [. . .] The system pulled me to conform in my essays, but my mind told me that this was no good, to write an ordinary essay was pointless.'

I cannot claim – however neat it would be – that this understanding from Pirsig banished any fear of expressive writing from my mind and allowed me to start experimenting with fiction again nearly a decade, possibly, after my last school English lesson, yet it certainly must have fuelled an internal pressure towards writing more creatively. Composing the fictional fables in my diary had come to seem a more interesting, a richer way of recording experiences than simply listing what I'd done, where I'd been and who I'd met. Moreover, the fables allowed me to use my imagination to explore an enhanced interest and knowledge of my own emotions.

I returned to Buenos Aires, hoping to work my passage back to Europe on another of Hamburg Süd's container ships. Having decided to head home, though, I was too impatient to trek north again to a Brazilian port (where they docked), and wait weeks without knowing when a vessel might take me on board. I thought about flying – I had the money – but decided that I didn't want a too rapid journey towards my old life either, and so I paid for passage on a liner, the *Marconi*. I had been away from England for nearly three years.

Chapter nine

THE THREE MS
THREE EXPERIENCES OF LOVE

How does one write honestly about one's past lovers? How does one write honestly about love? As a reader I want the rawest, truest material. As a writer I might be able to expose myself and feelings in that way, but what about those I am writing of, what do they think? And what do you think? Some of my love affairs have been amazing, beautiful, wonderful. But do you want to read about them? Or do you prefer your real life tales to be dark and as miserable as possible? Would you prefer your exposure to romance confined to novels and fairy tales? I don't know; but I do know that romantic love, in its various forms, has been such a vital part of my life that I could not pass the subject by in consideration of what you do or do not want.

With apologies to those involved I have decided to concertina three stories into one, into a single chapter, to cut each short, but to try and weave them together. Conveniently for me, these three stories involve three women, each extraordinary in their own right, whose names all begin with M, all of whom I met in the 1970s and with whom I still exchange very occasional emails. After much reflection, I decided against asking for permission, so have no idea if any or all three would object to me using their proper names. Instead, I've given each a pseudonym. And – for this is what writers like to do – I have tagged each woman, each love in some way. First there was enchanting Myra, the hippie from Yugoslavia, with whom I experienced innocent love. Then there was the stunningly beautiful M, a South American singer with whom I experienced what I shall call blood love. And, not necessarily in a different time, there was the fascinating Marielle, the Scottish lover, with whom I experienced poetic love.

I fell in love for the first time when I was about 20. It was the summer of 1972, before finishing university and travelling. I was working at a Butlin's holiday camp in Minehead. Chris, my friend from school (he of the CW consortium), and I had applied earlier in the year, and driven down to Devon in an old A35 van, called Jogger, I'd bought some time after Samantha had finally fallen to pieces. She was called Jogger partly because of the suspension, or lack of, and partly because its number plate started with the letters JOG.

We began our Butlin's lives as kitchen skivvies, washing up, but then managed to wangle better jobs as waiters, serving tables. I have scars on my hand and knee, however, where I slipped and fell on an already broken jar of jam. Despite bleeding profusely, I was led far away from the scene of the accident to another distant part of the compound to sign a disclaimer form before being given any first aid. That was one mini-disaster. Another, which could have been far more serious, and was no one's fault but my own, stemmed from the fact that Jogger's brakes weren't too effective. In fact, they ceased working one day when we happened to be above Lynmouth, on the Devon coast, about to coast down one of the steepest roads in the country. I managed to bring the old jalopy to a standstill with the handbrake – only yards before the crest of a hill.

Those were the days. Most memorably, though, I met Myra. One evening, many of us were sitting at a large table eating and drinking. She and I had not seen each other before. We were both dressed rather scruffily, like hippies, but crucially – for this bonded us instantly – we were both barefooted. Before long, Myra asked if I wanted to go for a run on the beach, and I did. We had two weeks together before Myra's contract finished and she left to go travelling before returning home. I recall almost nothing except that I was in love, and that, although not quite platonic, she and I never did more than kiss (I was still a Christian that summer, and a virgin). A first letter from her, addressed to Kent Dining Hall, Butlin's Holiday Camp, Minehead, Somerset, and dated 7 September 1972 has only five words: 'Paul, I love you. [Myra]'. Many, many letters followed but it was not until I left England in 1974 to travel that we met up again. I found her in Ljubljana, and then she took me to her home town in the mountains. Here are two diary entries which are more reliable than my memory.

31 June 1974
Today is Sunday – we see the cloud leave the valley and it is so fine. We go walking – an old lady comes to talk and then leads us through the forest to a house she wants to sell – she makes us tea and shows us around. It has an enormous oven for warming the main room, with beautiful tiles; the plastered walls have line designs rollered on; there is a slivovitz cellar complete with old barrels; and a working spinning jenny. We walk back a different way. For hours we laze in the sun eating bilberries and walnuts, and talking about the future and people, being silly and having fun. We go back to our hut in the forest, make a fire and cook steak and eggs. Eventually we tidy and lock up before heading back to the city. Once there, we drink a beer and watch each other climbing trees.

1 July 1974
Yesterday was like those days at Butlin's, [Myra] and me playing as children and talking of wise things. Today is like the last day at Butlin's, we walk and talk all the morning. She tells me more about her lonely days and happy ones. She said she wants to come to Australia [where I am headed] in February but I will have left by then.

After leaving to travel towards Turkey, and thereafter across Asia and to Australia and New Zealand, I constantly yearned after her – nothing gave me more pleasure than receiving her letters. Here's a diary entry from 1975 when I was in New Zealand, and two from 1977.

30 September 1975
Can you imagine dear diary how I felt today when I got three letters from [Myra] . . . I went to the beach for two hours to read all those words – am I a fool – I could go to her tomorrow if I wanted to . . . but I am afraid. I say in a letter 'when we are old we will meet again and maybe something is still there.' It is surprising I did not cry, I usually do.

11 April 1977
5:30 – feeling down and sad, thinking about [Myra], reading over some letters. How beautiful to find her in them . . . But more than a year has passed without news. Almost tears come to my eyes when I think of her. Such a strange dense beautiful romance. I will probably never see her again, and the few days I knew her will remain so prevalent in my memory as a most beautiful thing. . . [her name written large].

12 April 1977
A letter from [Myra] lies on the doormat. How strange, a year has passed, I have thought about her often but never written about those thoughts. On the other page, there is her name, it does not exist in any other books of mine in letters so large. And there on the mat is a letter from her!

In time, of course, I fell in love with other women, and had other relationships; and Myra married and had two children. But I never stopped loving her in an innocent fairy-tale kind of way, the memory of our childish love being secreted into some corner of my mind, only to be brought into focus occasionally for emotional comfort and pleasure. We didn't meet again until 1982. I was on a trip to Vienna, and it suddenly seemed like a good idea to travel across the border to see my first love.

January 1982
So, here I am in [Myra's] house. . . And I wonder why I am here and if I should have come. I came, I'm sure, just as an old friend, but there is more there hidden in our histories. Already we have stolen kisses and I have desired to love her. Wanted her. I have never known her as a man before. She comes to me in the morning, after her husband has left, and holds and touches me; we are silent innocent lovers. We tell each other we love, still, after all these years. I am frightened that our kisses will go too far. The spirit of [Myra] lives on despite

the trappings of husband, children, house, all of which weigh heavily on her flighty spirit. . . Perhaps I am a symbol of a freedom she once had, a reminder of her childish past and still present.

I only stayed three days, and Myra and I stole kisses whenever her husband and children were out of the house (or sometimes just out of the room). I didn't feel Myra was being disloyal to her husband, only that we were finishing something we'd started before she'd even met him, and we were finishing it simply, easily and – true to the whole nature of our relationship – innocently. I think Myra writes about it best in her letter sent to me a few days later.

January 1982
It is Sunday evening, perhaps you are home again, not so far as you used to be a week ago. . . What about you after so many letters and such a long time. I touch you. Paul in the shell, away from himself, away from people, away from the earth, sky and stars, away from this world. Away from me. Wrapped in his scarf. I want to dishevel your hair. It's funny, I hadn't even thought about you as a man, and me as a woman. Any way you are a man, and I accepted it quite easily. I don't want to be an esoteric and romantic being. Maybe you needed just a dream of someone like that, like Don Quixote, and I had profaned myself by being like I was. I found the papers with your name on, I made a fire with the matches you brought from the shop, I found the apple in your bed . . . so many little signs of you – empty house. I have your face in my hands.

After this meeting, there were few letters, and I knew little about Myra's life until in 1991 when she found herself in London twice. We met once in January at Victoria station for about 90 minutes. My diary says she stared at me intensely and with amazement, while I felt quite distant. And then in July, she came with her daughter, and they stayed with me for a couple of days – we took her daughter and my son to Regent's Park and the zoo one day, and to Hampstead Heath the other. We hardly referred to the past at all.

It was to be another long time before I saw her again. She came to visit for a couple of days in March 2002. We debated environmental issues, and talked about our children. I wrote that it was 'a treat, a real treat' to see her again. And when she emailed with a thank you, I replied back saying I had felt some echoes of the old sadness. Which was true, amazingly enough, I did. I may even have shed a tear. She was, after all, my first love, my first experience of love.

It is difficult to avoid using the metaphor of the heart when writing about love. It is so very useful a metaphor – the intangible 'love' turned into a physical object 'the heart', which somehow, through the immense power and flexibility of language, manages to be both re-moved from medical reality and yet still symbolise the tangible core of our emotional bodies and souls. And – crucially – because it's tangible, the heart can be written about with more symbolism, with more of a descriptive narrative, than can the far less tangible thing called 'love'.

I mean, I want to think about the heart as a dwelling. Myra was responsible for finding the door; but it was me who invited Nene in for a dance or two. When M arrived in my life, though, she marched right up to the door, didn't knock, and came right on in. And in so doing, she stomped around, made the place her own, as if I wasn't there, redecorated in her own style – and in her own colour – largely blood red! Until M, my heart had been an unsophisticated place, largely unexplored. M transformed it into an opera house of grand passions. The sweet innocence of emotions experienced with and for Myra, and the slightly deeper joys and sadnesses with Nene, were gone. Instead, my life with M was all agony and ecstasy – uncontrollable emotions, love for fucking real. Bloody fucking love.

It was March 1976. After three years away from England, I was on the *Marconi*, a passenger liner, heading back from South America towards Europe. I was expecting to spend the ten days rather alone, reading and writing, trying my best not to dwell on the sweet memories of Nene and my time in Chile, but thinking about the future, preparing myself, if at all possible, to settle down to some kind of normal life again. The boat hadn't long left Buenos Aires, when I met M. I'd found a hideaway, on deck, where I thought no one could disturb me, and was trying to whistle out a tune on a wooden recorder. As if by magic, but in fact drawn by the sounds I was making, M appeared from nowhere. She was probably the most exotic-looking, the most beautiful woman I'd ever met. She could have materialised from the pages of a fashion magazine, with her ultra-slim sexy body, long jet black hair, dark sultry eyes, huge, that swallowed me up whole. It turned out, she was an actress and singer; her confidence, her womanliness, her sexiness, scared the hell out of me – but she didn't seem to mind. Within an hour, she had asked if I wanted to take a shower with her. A shower!

This is the way I've remembered the story for the last 40 years, there's not much evidence for or against it in my diary, and so I've no reason to alter it now. We agreed on which shower room to meet in, and went back to our separate cabins to collect towels etc. I arrived at the shower room first, entered, locked the door behind me, and began to undress. Whether I was in a state of heightened sexual excitement at the thought of soon being naked with such a beautiful woman, or rather in a state of nervous agitation over whether I'd be able to perform adequately, I have no idea. A knock came on the door soon enough, though, but it was accompanied by a man's voice: 'Is there anyone in there?' I didn't answer; and then the man tried to open the door, and repeated the question. 'This is a ladies' shower room,' he added. It was. And I was a man. But I was not man enough. Stupidly, I gave in all too quickly, put on my shirt, or whatever, and emerged sheepishly, long before there was any sign of M, and retreated to my cabin.

I hardly saw her again, despite searching all day and every day. And when I did catch up with her, she wouldn't tell me where she'd been or what she'd been doing. Subsequently, I found out she'd befriended the captain who'd given her access to the first class facilities. Months later, she showed up in London, wanted nothing from me (she'd found a place to live and a job), except my friendship, and we soon became lovers, and more. We decided to live together. All we could afford was a small bedsitting room in Chelsea where we had separate single beds. I worked in an office during the day, she in an Argentinian restaurant at night. I desired her constantly, but couldn't satisfy her, so we would only have sex on Sundays, as a favour to me. She was so cool and grown-up, and I was immature, at least sexually, or so I felt. Here is a diary entry that gives some feel for our ridiculous life together.

1 December 1977
So this morning we didn't speak, sometimes there is silence in the morning. It is not a pleasant silence, it is a sort of I-don't-want-to-talk-to-you silence. Last night, we were in someone else's room listening to Led Zeppelin and were good together, drinking, smoking, and so when we came back to our room, I wanted to sleep with [M]. She said I couldn't sleep in her bed and so I was upset; some five minutes later I called over asking her again very gently; and then five minutes later she called out to me somewhat antagonistically; 20 minutes later I screamed. It was good, I really wanted to scream, and [M] went hysterical with anger.

We did talk about it sometimes. I tried to suggest that sex was like everything else, it could be worked at, we could get better. But this idea was outside her experience. To her credit, though, she wrote home to her mother asking if this might be true. After months of tension in the bedsit, we moved, not long before Christmas, to a delightful garden flat in Kilburn, one that I'd taken over, at low rent, from family friends, Peter the Girl and Tony. I assumed this would be an end to all our problems. It wasn't. There were one or two nights when M didn't come home at all. The ecstasy I'd experienced of adoring and having that adoration acknowledged and allowed and satisfied occasionally, was more than outweighed by the agonies of jealousy and rage and confusion. Within three weeks, she was gone, for good. She had not looked after my heart at all, she hadn't known how. She'd moved in, refurbished, and then moved out leaving behind only chaos.

And yet, our relationship transformed quickly into a kind of incestuous brother-sister friendship: we had other relationships, but would often come together as friends and end up making love (or occasionally fighting). I don't think I adapted to her sexually, rather I think she learned to take pleasure from being softer, gentler – perhaps her mother had said it was OK. We made love on LSD once which was excruciatingly pleasurable and a very special experience, as was another time, on her birthday, when, because my nose bled and she was in the middle of her period, both our bodies ended up smeared, painted in fact, all over with blood. It wasn't a kinky or weird love we'd finally learned to show each other, just rather beautiful.

We enjoyed this liaison for a couple of years until M finally decided, in 1979, to return to her home country. Apart from a rendezvous in New York in 1981 we haven't seen each other again. We stopped writing, possibly as a result of the Falklands/Malvinas conflict, and I later established that we'd both been living in Rio de Janeiro at the same time without realising it. We are still vaguely in touch, a short warm email once a year. As far as I can tell, she has had a rich, fulfilling life, with a husband and two sons, now grown-up. Here is a note I sent her in 2001.

> '[M], I'm having a nostalgic moment – forgive me. I'm typing up a diary from 1979, which is difficult enough, but then by chance I find – somewhere it should not have been – a letter from you from that time – I still have your letters – but this one was somewhere else. And suddenly I am so very happy to know I still know you. We are living such different lives, in such different places, in such different ways; and, if and when we meet again, of course, we will be almost strangers I suppose, but never mind, just to know, to remember the friendship of those times, and to know that we are still in touch touches me deeply. Now. So, thank you, just thank you.'

Marielle also waltzed into my heart barely stopping to knock at the door, but whereas M redecorated with uncontrolled and extreme combinations of her own, with brilliant highs and lows, with blood and sweat and tears, Marielle – astonishingly – put a paintbrush in my hand, taught me how to take some control of love, to love creatively, to make it conscious, to embrace and describe it in words, to turn love and loving into poetry. In short, she transformed my heart from a place where only base and primitive colours could be experienced, to a more refined dwelling where I could display emotions in subtle shades and tones of my own choosing, in photos and pictures, and above all in words.

She was a Scot, red haired and deeply freckled, living in Greece as part of a small commune with a dozen others, mostly Austrians. We met at a theatre festival in Amsterdam, the summer of 1978, and she came back to London, to stay in my Kilburn flat for several glorious, exciting weeks. It was she who persuaded me to shave off the ragged beard I'd had ever since hair first grew on my face. It was she who found handsome lines, and took artistic photographs in black and white, the first cool pictures of myself I'd ever seen. It was she who wrote me poetry from morning till night, and received it too. It was she, who like no one ever before, read me just like a poem. And it was she who taught me how to fly.

Here is a fairly typical entry from my diary at the time.

8 July 1978
My poems are a fuzzle of words squeezed out of my head. A lot of things pass by, some wonderful moments with [Marielle]. The freedom of our sexuality, mounting desires rising together, with the touch of lips or a glance across the room. The freedom of children, the desire of adults satisfied. We inside our own sexuality, on top of it, we drops of juices. Exploring the essence of poetry in our lovemaking, erotic fantasising, fairy tales come true – the boy with the lyre and the epic erotica of the clitoral sigh. Beautiful whisperings.

This commune of hers, near Pyrgos, in the Western Peloponnese, was an extraordinary venture. I went there once for a week. The 12 members had, when still in Vienna, built a bed large enough for all of them, but they'd now moved on from such prescriptive behaviour. Having decamped to a large house by the sea in Greece, every member would move in and out of encounters with each other, never restrained by sexual inhibitions. Alliances formed and unformed on a daily or weekly basis, but they all had such confidence in, and love for, each other that sex was as easy and enjoyable as cooking a meal. The group accepted that hierarchies were natural, and Marielle, slightly older than the others, had long been accepted as one of two leaders. In some ways, it was the idyll they wanted it to be. Empty beaches only minutes away, a positive and warm atmosphere in which individuals could flourish and express themselves, whether physically, intellectually or artistically. I didn't believe in it all, nor was I seduced, but – wow – Marielle and her friends had certainly created something wonderful, even if it couldn't last.

There was never any question of commitment between she and I, other than when we were physically together. Yet, I'm sure I felt she was the most important woman in my life for a couple of years. When she came to Kilburn – which she did on at least two more occasions – I naively informed any girlfriend at the time that I couldn't see her for the duration, with ultimately disastrous consequences for that relationship. Between times, we wrote to one another constantly. Our letters, mostly in the form of poems or poetical prose, were full of colourful, exotic and playful expressions of love and passion. Yet, they were hardly real. It was as though Marielle had introduced me into an imaginary world, one without real or concrete consequences, where every wonderful emotion was possible. We only had to say it, or write it, and fairy tales would come true. This is why I say she taught me to fly, to feel and express emotions fearlessly.

As with Myra and M, I cannot really do justice to Marielle, or the arc of our relationship in a few paragraphs. But in summary, I would say, like some people have a skill for playing the cello, or for growing things, or making money, Marielle had a talent for loving, and through loving for bringing the very best out of who she was with. I have none of my letters to Marielle, except for occasional extracts in my diary, but I do have scores of her letters to me. I would love to reproduce many of them for she wrote so beautifully, so poetically, but I am going to limit myself to extracts from two, in autumn 1978.

> I remember a secret garden
> I remember time stopping as I lay in his arms whispering words of eternal love, secretly so the birds would not hear and hold me to them
> I remember the bluest of eyes and a background of sky, beckoning me to come closer, stay forever in that moment
> I remember I wanted to make him laugh and fall in love with me again and again
> I remember how I missed him before I left him for moments like now
> I remember doubting my own name, my own game, giving him the blame for being too sane
> I remember the echo he didn't hear and the fear that madness was near
> I remember how he touched, how he loved very much
> I remember a tongue in my mouth and the path he took down south
> I remember him as a teacher, as a preacher, as a reacher
> I remember his street, his defeat, his retreat
> I remember his pride, his stride, his ride
> I remember his grace, his face, his place
> I remember what I felt as I knelt before him, above him
> I remember what I knew in a man

> Paul, this Sunday you are not alone, my love. I am tingling in you. I find you so warm, so wanting and wanted, taken and taking. Heart-breaking the longing now. You are wrapped up in me now, my love, the firefly is burning brightly. She would fly with you.

And here are two extracts from my diary:

3 December 1978
Where is [Marielle]? How do I dare live in such confusion until my love for her is burnt. Maybe it is unburnable. How dare I live without her? How dare I not be with her? How dare I not – I find words so mundane, so banal. It is impossible to say just what I mean.

26 July 1979
Letter to [Marielle]: The married ones – time and time again they repair to the photo albums to find out quite what it was they had. I sweated gallantly last night, charitably donating my odours to the airs, that would not, could not, move to cool me. You can make me sweat in Amsterdam. In Vienna I'm sure I'd sneeze. In London I probably fart too much. In Greece you can hear me sing. This side of midsummer's day I feel old. Most of summer's joys are found in silence. I read about the sadness, madness, gladness the other day. It contained more love and passion than three-quarters of the poems in a book of love poetry. That magic still haunts me. That magic still haunts me.

In 1990, after several years of silence, I received a long letter: 'Dear Paul, what a struggle to find words to start this letter. It used to flow so so so, you know, easily. . .' She had fallen pregnant and decided to make a go of it as a family with the father. A second daughter came along, and then they went to New Zealand for a holiday, and stayed, living in a camper van for a year, before settling down in a rural community. A few years after the letter, she and her daughters came to stay with me in Kilburn. There was little of the old magic, and after she'd gone, I went back into my diaries and thought and wrote about her.

18 July 1993
'[Marielle] opened up a dreamworld of ideal romance and I just followed her lead. I could do it without fear because it was such a strange land – it was obviously not real. But for her this was never a clear division and she journeyed in a landscape where people were the paths and emotions the weather. . . I remember the many letters we wrote declaring the most intense of loves, but mine were invented, not felt.'

I see that I used the word 'invented' but, in hindsight, I don't think that was right or fair to myself. Perhaps, if I had been clearer, I might have written that my declarations were more literary than felt, more poetical flights of exaggeration than true deep emotions.

Love is many things, and indeed so many more than that which I felt with Myra, M or Marielle. Yet how can I not celebrate, not shout about the love and romance that each one of them found for me and in me, and gave me – innocent sweet love; blood love, with passion, sweat and tears; and magical love, the love found in potions and dreams and poetry.

Chapter ten

THEATRE
ON AND OFF STAGE

OFF stage is the place for me. I dislike the limelight or spotlights or attention of any kind where a group of other human beings expect me to perform in some way. This is no surprise given my childhood during which, generally speaking, any attention towards me or what I was doing was likely to be negative or critical. I can imagine a child whose personality is so charming and entertaining that he or she grows up expecting to be looked at; and I can imagine parents who believe so strongly in positive reinforcement that their children are clapped as if on centre stage from an early age and thus yearn desperately for it the rest of their lives.

As a young man, though, I had little understanding of my own psychology, and so I did venture, somewhat experimentally, ON stage. A passion for the theatre seeded at university led me, in my 20s, to become involved with the alternative theatre world. This pathway culminated for me in the acquisition of an Equity card and a performing role at the Edinburgh Fringe Festival. But, now, I see this naive and playful foray into alternative theatre as a more or less wilful excursion into quasiphobia territory – an effort to impel change into my life.

I suspect that writing has been a way for me to seek admiration, but secretly, furtively, without being looked at. Given my enthusiasm for the theatre then it is no wonder that I also tried to write for the stage. I felt – and I was clearly mistaken – that I had a good ear, as they say, for dialogue, and that I had the kind of imagination required by a playwright. A critical moment in the story of my life as a writer came about as a result of one particular stage production, a modern ballet in fact, by Ballet Rambert. Years later, by an amazing coincidence, I met the man who had written the book which inspired the ballet.

I had been away for nearly three years. I have already written about how my parents separated a few days after my return, leaving my mother in near-hysterics. About how the beautiful M tried to seduce me on the boat from South America to Europe, and how we ended up living together for a few short months in Chelsea and then in Kilburn. My first priority, on re-settling in London, was to get work, which I did, in a market research business, and about this I will write in the next chapter.

Much else was happening to me in my spare time. Did M have any influence over my be-suited self-esteem? While I was playing the businessman, she was working at a new Argentinean restaurant in Covent Garden. Whenever we socialised with her friends, I always felt inadequate, grey, as if the business suit had become a part of me. It had been an exciting, colourful, ever-changing life on the road with a pack on my back, but I was not adjusting well to an ordinary, nine-to-five existence.

One day, when standing on an underground train, I had this overwhelming feeling of impotence, simply because I was unable to shout something, anything, out loud. I was afraid to; but why? Intellectually, I knew there would be no consequences, other than a strange look or two. There was no external reason hindering me, only an internal one. The remedy I prescribed myself was acting classes, at the City Lit. I did not fit well into them, and soon switched to a mime class at (the very alternative) Action Space. This suited me better, at least those parts of me that imagined being in the spotlight might bring excitement into my life.

That mime class changed my life. As we can never go back and re-live any part of time passed, it is normally a redundant calculation to try and imagine what might have been, or what might not have been. Nevertheless, individuals have made a very significant difference to my life, and I can say with certainty that the chances of meeting them would not have happened without that mime class. It is one fact that I had a brief and rather pleasant affair with the mime teacher, Pam. It is another that before long I was able, without excessive embarrassment or fear, to mime – short sketches of passion for a silver hand rail on a tube train, for example – and thus draw attention to myself. But in terms of life changing, I am thinking mostly of Harold, a charismatic, effete, and very theatrical South African with long dark curly hair and eyes that latched onto one as though he had just fallen in love. Harold, more than any night class learning, gave me the confidence to become extrovert, and through being extrovert my city life got moving at last; I was travelling again, not geographically across countries, but metaphorically into social worlds.

Harold was proud of his bisexuality, and with endless charm and good humour kept trying to seduce me. I never felt threatened, quite the reverse. For the first time since being home, I felt friendship was living up to what I expected of it. He had this gift for making people feel special, and confident; and, together, it seemed we could do anything, not least clowning about in parks. He soon invited himself to live in one of my spare rooms (I had moved into the Kilburn flat with M some months earlier, and, as I've explained, she had moved out within weeks), and life got even better. We were clowns, artists, writers, and we would soon be famous, with homes in Paris and New York as well as London. We rarely went out without returning to the Kilburn flat with fresh friends, a boyfriend for Harold, and sometimes a girlfriend for me. I had never felt so attractive, so charming, so self-possessed as I did then, in Harold's company.

Also, I was exploring London's cultural offerings, especially its theatre. Two companies blew my mind, as they used to say: Shared Experience and Phantom Captain. I first saw Shared Experience perform *Arabian Nights* at the King's Head in April 1977. Four or five actors using no sets and very few props, or possibly none, told a series of tales so vividly, so brilliantly that I was left stunned by the power of theatre. I tried to see every one of their performances for years to come, an undertaking that was helped when a good friend of mine, Luke Dixon, coincidentally, became the company's administrator, working with Mike Alfreds, the director.

In November that year I was first wowed by the Phantom Captain, at Action Space (which had become a second home, I even worked in the cafe there for a while), performing its surreal and interactive show, *At Your Service*. Seated in the restaurant, formally-dressed waiters and waitresses came to the tables offering menus of experiences. Initially, I chose a tea dance, and the waitress brought a tape recorder and we danced. Other items on the menu included: a blow job, i.e. a waiter playing the harmonica; and auto-eroticism, i.e. a waiter moving a toy car over a person's body.

And the following April I was stunned by a Japanese company Tenjō Sajiki performing a show – *Directions to Servants* – at Riverside studios. The avant-garde director, Shūji Terayama, had based his remarkable theatre, involving a large troupe of acrobatic actors and various mechanical contrivances, on Jonathan's Swift's satire of the same name. I wrote in my diary: 'This performance was amazing, the precision of movement, the flexibility of body, the symbolism, the structure. . . Across the stage different things happen endlessly – absurdly . . . my head buzzed around and around the theatre trying to absorb the totality of the thing.' This was probably more performance art than theatre but if I were asked to name the best show I've ever seen, or the one stand-out performance of any performing arts I've witnessed in my life, this would be it.

Theatre was fast becoming the most important focus in my world. Taking part in mime classes at Action Space and going to see so much breathtaking and inspiring drama were having a strong influence on my hopes and plans. Moreover, having Harold – who never stopped performing – in my life was giving me the confidence (albeit, as it turned out, falsely) to act on these hopes, to want to be a performer, to be a performer.

One experience from the time is worth quoting from my diary.

22 May 1977
Hitching back from Oxford yesterday I was picked up by a cameraman named Oliver who invited me to be a film extra in an avant-garde movie about Russian repression! We did various warm-up workshops and I met interesting people. The scene I was in concerned Natalie, a Russian poetess, whose small room is invaded by a crowd of people infested with morbid interest in her. Yesterday, they filmed a trial scene, as if it were a game of cards, and the judge was biased against the defence. It was a really nice feeling in the workshop, very smooth, although some people were always trying to get attention. A guy called Norman Coates works for Inter-Action and said there might be a job going with the Almost Free Theatre. Oddly, one of the other film extras, a fat guy, had picked me up earlier, on the way to Oxford.

I went on to apply for the job at Inter-Action but nothing came of my application. Decades later, in 2005, Coates contacted me by email, having found the above paragraph in my diaries online. He told me he had remained in theatre design all his life, and Oliver had gone on to become a well known cinematographer.

Another experience was travelling to the Fool's Festival in Amsterdam twice, in 1978 and 1979. The first time I went, with Harold of course, I met Marielle, about whom I have already written. She lived for theatre too, though in a very different way from Harold. Simply put, Harold adored attention, loved performing and did so all day long, in the street, in shops, to every Tom, Dick and Larry. Marielle, by contrast, who had worked in professional theatre, had become more choosy about her stages and her audiences, preferring to perform within the private lives of, and for, her friends. This had led her to live in a commune in Greece, where she and her friends re-imagined – as though part of an uncontrolled drama – rules for living and loving. Marielle, in particular, had a gift for catalysing emotional development from others, she certainly encouraged me to flap my wings. So it was the combination, I would say, of Harold and Marielle who were responsible for leading me into thinking, believing, I should be a performer. Help.

As an aside, I should mention the second trip to Amsterdam, for that time Rosy came along too. Had I not gone to that mime class at Action Space, and had I not met Harold and then Marielle and taken to the idea of clowning, I would not have become friends with Rosy Gibb (and her husband Andy), nor others I met through her. Soon after meeting Rosy, I suggested she should try clowning too, she had the face for it! Rosy took to the idea immediately, and became involved in all kinds of alternative theatre events – not least as Miss Piss in the 1978

Alternative Miss World, which was made into a film by one of her friends, Richard Gayor. She worked hard, and with purpose trans-formed herself into a professional clown, becoming successful; later on, she matched that success as a magician too. Over the years, she made me feel like one of her family, and I was always welcome in her home where she introduced me to any number of visitors as the one who had got her into clowning. Even some of her obituaries – she died tragically young in her 50s – mention 'a friend' who changed her life. I have no doubt, though, that Rosy would have found clowning without my intervention, for she – like Harold – had this inner need to be noticed, to spark a smile, to be liked and loved by everyone.

I was not very good at the technical aspects of mime, and I gravitated towards a combination of performance art and clowning. I was encouraged – in workshops and classes – to find my inner clown. And my inner clown, who I called Pici (Harold was Poco), was a rather timid creature. I might have been able to act out some private drama – on the tube, and in parks etc. – in a way I could never have done before this change in my life, but I only did so by acting privately, as though no one were watching. I recorded a few of my 'performances' in the diary.

> 7 June 1979
> WHAT DID PICI DO TODAY? Starting slowly he found plastic spoons – knives or forks wouldn't do. He collected them and cleaned them impeccably with a cloth bag attached to a cloth sun. He visited every bin on the site. He stole some too. He found some string. He went everywhere cleaning his spoons, hoping that everyone would see him. He stopped sometimes to count them. When all was prepared he chose his spot and emptied the bag of its spoons and string and replaced them with the sun. Placing the bag in the middle, he formed a fence of the large spoons, an outer circle, and with the little spoons an inner circle. People started to watch. He wanted them to watch, but then got scared. He paced around the outer circle. He should have made it into a full blown ritual but didn't. He should have been one spoon short and got someone to fetch one for him. He should have waited until the sun was about to break through the clouds, he should have got some of the spectators to dance around and shout a little. It was all an anticlimax. He slowly revealed the sun from the cloth bag. Did they realise it was a sun?

My love of street theatre led me, in the autumn of 1978, to become involved with a group calling itself the Demolition Decorators (DDs). They had squatted a large building in Covent Garden, and, in my diary, I called them 'the Revolutionaries'. They had a strong link with the radical *International Times* (IT) and its information centre (BIT), and also claimed to have 'single-handedly' won buskers the right to play in the London Underground system. Many years later, one of the group put out a CD of DDs performance material he had saved. The accompanying publicity material stated: 'Audiences could not be neutral and many outdoor performances involved an appearance by the police. At one gig, some of the audience were so incensed, they firebombed the hall. Although very political, they were never fanatical or bitter. There was a mystical quality about them.'

My involvement with the DDs was fairly short-lived, and very non-committal. I think I found the whole thing vaguely amusing or entertaining, and I failed to absorb how seriously others in the group felt about certain issues.

24 September 1978

These Revolutionaries are infiltrating the crowds and selling back copies (and front copies) of the magazine for 20p. Half of the money will go to IT and half to the Demolition Decorators; [. . .] The socialist, the rockers against racism, the backers against fascism, conglomerate in Brockwell Park having walked from Hyde (who was cornered in the) Park policed, trafficked and toed. And now here are they, they who are infiltrated. Here are the black-faced and leather capped; here are the green-haired and paper-clipped ear, here are the dying Dylans, and the sons of their friends; here are the music ones, the rock and roll and reggae drones; the pumping bands and the trendy dance hall lambs; here are the violently colourful tightly cossetted and the hanging weekend dollies; the strong in faith and poison dither here and there, reflecting, selling, telling who and what. So they jangle through this cloudy crowd, dressed close to the ghosts of Ku Klux Klan, in white raincoat and underpant headcovers covered in dark seedy-appearing sunglasses, selling IT to the best of ability.

6 November 1978

Surely, a whole play, or a novel, could be written entitled 'The rise and fall of the Demolition Decorators'. Another Monday meeting passed by. The group and its members are more interesting than the actual gigs they perform. To-night, for example, we had a sharp-but-dulled-by-drugs couple from BIT who took up our time and space. They wanted to hold their tenth anniversary in our squat. The mob, our mob were patient with them. I find myself willing and practical but often defeated by the criss-cross mutterings that cut under and fly over me. I walk out into the street to collect some boxes. I am in bare feet. I return and crush them beneath my feet and feel the fire of my impatience. I tramp around avoiding eyes, the quick and supple. I catch the crossfires but have no effect on them.

15 November 1978

The Demolition Decorators Monday meeting. Notes twang through the cold buildings from a solo electric guitar. The ex-coach seat that I sit upon is held upright by breeze blocks; others sit on bottle crates; a board covers a hole in the floor caused by the fire in the grate spreading too far. Mary wanders around, sober calm. She's pretty tonight, hoping to do something, anything. There is a rumour that the police are going to raid us because of the wood fire, so Mary has been cleaning out the ashes. 'Upstairs at Ronnies' is scribbled on the wall with orange paint behind a makeshift counter. Next door Willy shows the visitors from BIT his cubbyhole, the IT office. Pages and articles and pho-tos are still strewn across the table. The magazine was due at the printers on

Friday, but one person's perfection is cauterised by another's ideals, and the pages get changed and cut, cut and changed. Meanwhile, revenue from advertising is awaited to pay the printing costs. Single notes still twang. A lady has been and gone with the electricity money, but a small donation from BIT has upped our finances slightly. It's nine o'clock, still no one else has arrived, so the Monday meeting finally starts – and my gut rumbles.

3 December 1978
Poor old IT was gutted; poor old BIT was definitely unlucky. They invited guests from everywhere, and from anywhere they came. A 10th anniversary and all that. How many bands were to come? 9 or 10, 20 or 30. It was all friends and grooves, smokers and abortion campaigners, squatters and the rest. What a shame. Poor old IT, its thousand files, its million prints, its two typewriters, its five cabinets, its three desks – who was to blame after all? Those two friends, the best of friends, too keen, too overworked, who let the paint dry, and the wallpaper dry, and then catch fire, with flames licking up the wall, up the wall, out the window, the side of the house. I hear Paul went squeak at 2am and saved a life or two, but neither an office nor a bed was saved.

The huge fire at the Covent Garden squat was a backward step for the DDs; another was the police prosecution that took place the following February. I reported in my diary a visit to Wells St. Magistrate's Court where four of the DDs were being charged for highway obstruction. Thereafter, I appear to have left the DDs behind, or they me. However, I cannot resist quoting one further diary entry from five years later, evidence if you like that at least one person had been moved by me performing as a street clown.

10 August 1984
I was at R's last night, talking to a girl called Sara about my clownish past. She mentioned a house full of parties in Covent Garden, five or six years ago, so I tried the name 'Demolition Decorators' on her. She recognised it immediately. She said she had thought we were all magic, being only 14 at the time. I told her about the evening I had mimed and clowned the building of a room with rubble and rubbish, oblivious to the party going on around me, and she actually and vividly remembered me and my act. Amazing. What is more – I have to say this to someone – I remember that I impressed myself that Friday evening. It was an improvisation lasting a couple of hours and I really acted, really built a room and really possessed it, despite the party. But I felt at the time nobody had appreciated my invention, my playing, my art. And when Sara remembered me, it was as though I'd been waiting all these years to hear her applause.

I have mentioned Luke Dixon briefly already, but before he became the administrator for Shared Experience he was acting as the administrator for the Phantom Captain theatre group. I have no memory of how we met exactly, nor is there anything about this in my diary. But, by the summer of 1979, he had managed to secure me a temporary position with the company, along with a required Equity card, for the duration of the Edinburgh Fringe Festival. The Phantom Captain had rented a large hall, with kitchen and extra rooms, and used the spaces not only for its own productions (Peter Godfrey's *Marbles*) but for a popular, and hopefully money-spinning, one-man show by Quentin Crisp called *A Cure for Freedom*.

It had been an ambition of mine, since first seeing the company at Action Space, to work with the Phantom Captain, to be a waiter offering experiences, and this I had become, alongside other, more mundane duties as a stage manager, sweeper-upper. It was the apex of my theatre career, and yet – poor me – it was a profoundly unsettling experience for a dream come true. I felt insecure constantly; never confident with the core group of main characters, all of whom seemed to have presences and auras that tingled and sparkled together socially leaving me very much on the outside, inadequate, unknowing. These, after all, were creatures that shone in the spotlight, could magically transform themselves to more exciting beings, while all I could do – I was fast learning – was cower and long for the shadows.

Here is a single example, the thought of which still leaves me squirming psychologically, despite the passing of many decades of spotlightlessness. One night, when performing *At Your Service*, I was waiting on a middle-aged feisty woman (I later knew to be Fran Landesman, an American poet) who looked at my menu and asked for a 'Rakish Angle'. Unfortunately – and this does seem ridiculous now – I didn't actually know what 'rakish' meant, and so simply contorted my body to create angles. I cannot recall Fran's specific reaction, but whatever she said or however she looked cut me to the quick, and left me deeply embarrassed at my failure as a performer.

Perhaps I am painting too dark a picture of my time in Edinburgh, since there were certainly excitements, one of which was seeing part of *The Warp*, written by Neil Oram, directed by Ken Campbell and billed as the longest play in the world, 20 hours or more. Another was straying into social gatherings more misty and mysterious with sensual and sexual nuances than I'd ever been aware of before. There is little in my diary about this peak in my theatrical career, but a brief, edited, extract gives some flavour of my thoughts.

13 September 1979
Should I say something of Edinburgh as if in conclusion. [. . .] With the experience of three weeks hard work that achieved a well run disaster. Blah. I saw bits of Edinburgh, discovered some of its secrets. One night in the Traverse, a woman propositioned me, right out of the blue, she had large fat eyes and had

had plenty to drink. I was impressed by the chutzpah of the suggestion and I would have gone with her of course but in the confusion of leaving I lost her. All the booze and fag ends, the swilling of pints, the standing in jostled crowds, the ugliness of the scene. All these actors, Berkoff, Cunningham, Crisp etc. swarming together . . . At least at the students' fringe club could be found entertainment. [. . .] but no one seduced me – did I seduce anyone? I think I just stood around looking pretty. Patrick, Gill and Stewart of the Traverse decided I was a Tease – this was indeed news to me – I had never considered myself that before. I think they were attracted to me and yet I showed no signs of return. Gill explained that my gestures and body language were sensual/sexual giving the impression that I was very open. I thought that was a good thing, but perhaps not. And it certainly didn't get me into bed up there. Nice to be talked to though.

My theatrical involvement with the Phantom Captain went no further, though I did help out with a second hand bookshop the company had decided to open to raise funds. The shop premises were somewhere in Camden Town, I believe, and it cannot have lasted very long, or made very much money. However, I mention this because of the most remarkable coincidence that happened on my first day. I decided to check the prices of the books. The first two I picked out at random had no prices written in them. Then, I picked out a third book from a different shelf. There, on the inside cover, I saw the price, 10p, and an inscription: 'Presented to Paul Lyons, for obtaining third highest marks, King's Own Camp, August 1965.' At that time, in 1965, I'd been living outside London, some 20 miles north of Camden.

Also thanks to Luke, I became marginally involved with a (now iconic) magazine called *Performance*, contributing brief theatre and performance art reviews. The magazine (founding editor Rob La Frenais) continued through to 1992; and since 2017 all 66 issues have been made available online. The list of contributors reads as a veritable who's who of alternative theatre in the period. The very first issue, as it happens, included a review of Phantom Captain, a report on the Demolition Decorators, and an interview with Ken Campbell. And the second issue included an article by Angela Carter and a review of Shared Experience.

By 1979, I had begun to shift my ambitions in the theatre away from performing (for obvious reasons) towards writing. I had abandoned my market research career, and the regular pay that went with it, for the far more superficially attractive label of 'writer', and more specifically, to write a stage play about Aleister Crowley. I first read his autohagiography in the autumn of 1977 and the man fascinated me, partly because he came across as so literate, but also because of the charismatic power he seemed to have possessed. I had managed to gain access to Crowley's papers at the Warburg Institute, and this fuelled my hopes of being able to produce something well researched, solid and original. Somehow, I also got hold of Gerald Yorke, in his late 70s then but a friend of Crowley's from the past. He generously gave me an interview, though I'd done so little research I didn't know the first thing about him, or how closely, in fact, he had been involved with Crowley.

I worked hard on the play, typing every day using a neat Remington typewriter (given me by an old woman I'd volunteered to help in Belsize Park a couple of times), and, in a few months, produced a substantial, full-length play. I based the action at Crowley's Abbey of Thelema, a house in Sicily he had turned into a spiritual centre. Here is one diary entry about my research, the writing, and Crowley himself.

22 February 1979

Fascinated and aloof and wallowing in the garlic and sapphire of Crowley's life. Pushing myself to get two or three pages written each day. Clickety clack of the typewriter, seems to be the secondary effect that I do between the cleaning and the cooking and the talking or playing with R. My imagination is scarred. The translation of my imagination into scenes on paper is the most difficult. Creating characters, working within them, showing them up through conversations. There is the swamp of stage directions that are the length of a novel in themselves. In capital letters they stand out bold. And now with a new ribbon in the clickety-clack machine, the blackness is overpowering. How can I will myself to work eight-ten hours a day when the ideas run out; I have to search all the books for the next scene or spark of talk. I resort to a cigarette or cup of coffee or leave the house. [. . . I] spend two hours submerging myself in AC in Therion in The Beast 666, in the Great Hand of Boleskine. I handle some typed manuscripts by Leah Hirsig – 'Record of the Abbey of Thelema'. She describes in detail the incidents relating to Betty May's expulsion from the Abbey, it's perfect. There is a folder with letters written to and from AC, some about blackmail, money and debts; and I touch with care the magical record or the drug record of one Aleister Crowley for a period of two weeks at Fontainebleu in March 1922. In intricate detail he records the times and amounts of cocaine and heroin he took. He records the conversations he has with himself, justifying his next dose, and how he is going to exterminate his need for the drugs, and how he figures he should be able to use them forever but without becoming addicted. How he excuses himself because of his illnesses, especially his asthma, the symptoms of which are immediately alleviated by heroin – this allows him to take doses outside his fixed regime, without admitting it to himself. He continues to fascinate me, and I would like to get access to more papers.

Could I find any theatres to be interested in my play? No, of course not. I do still have the densely-typed manuscript, and can see how flawed parts of it are. But who knows what could have become of it with the kind of professional scrutiny and manipulation most play scripts undergo, or so I've always said to myself.

Among the most important producers of new plays at the time in London outside of the West End, was the Bush Theatre, one of the very best of London's fringe theatres and my best – but forlorn – hope for a positive response to an unsolicited submission. Less than three years later, the Bush did present a play about Aleister Crowley, by Snoo Wilson. The play had been commissioned by the Royal Shakespeare Company back in 1974, I discovered, but was then extensively rewritten for the Bush in 1982 to become less of a farce, as in the original, and with far more of the action at the Abbey of Thelema. 'On entering the theatre,' I wrote in my diary, 'I was agreeably surprised to see a set much as one I had imagined for my own play.' And, since then, it has been a conceit of mine to think – unfounded I am sure – that the Bush and/or Wilson were sparked into their revival by my unsolicited manuscript, and that some of my ideas might have found their way, by literary osmosis if nothing else, into Wilson's re-imagined script.

Having tried to interest theatres in the Crowley play and realising the difficulties of such a process, I turned my attention to radio plays, thinking at least that I would get a fair reading from the BBC, given its insatiable appetite for drama. Four such plays followed – all destined for the dusty drawer. I have already mentioned (in the introduction) the one I wrote during my cathartic time on Corsica. Then there was *Eddie's Eggies*, a humorous-yet-serious portrait of a man so obsessed with birds' eggs that he stole them from the Natural History Museum in Tring. Two others: one about a couple's visit to a commune in Greece (based on my experiences with Marielle), and the other about an auction of secretly-grown vegetables in some future police state.

A decade later, I would return to the radio play form to write *Scarlett's Magic Computer*. This was an adult homage to the children's story *Sparky's Magic Piano*, and was set in the fast-paced world of oil trading and journalism. It featured a computer which talked to its owner when no one could else could hear it (long before such computer abilities were as common as kettles). Around the same time, and inspired by my five year old son, I would write a last stage play, this one for children – *King Top-of-the-World*. It starred a boy, his gran, a bicycle, a chimney spider, a bat, all battling against three nasty men – Axlegrease, Chopperbone and Papershredder – trying to chop down a forest. Both plays now seem dated, to say the least.

Through my vain and inglorious attempts at performing I certainly got closer to the spotlight, if never comfortable there, than I ever did through writing drama. Yet it was fun trying, and it was another small step on my never-ending writer's journey. However, before closing this chapter on theatre, I want to go back to June 1978, to another mind-boggling performance that I witnessed, but one that I associate directly with wanting to write and be a writer, and thus to leaving market research, to writing the Crowley play, and then to going to Corsica to hide away to write in the winter of 1979/1980. The performance, *Cruel Garden*, was choreographed by Christopher Bruce in collaboration with Lindsay Kemp, and danced by Ballet Rambert at Sadler's Well. It told, in a thrillingly dramatic way, of the life of Federico García Lorca, the Spanish poet and dramatist who was murdered by Franco's forces in 1936, drawing on his most famous play, *Blood Wedding*.

On returning home, I got out the Remington, and proceeded to write my first ever substantial piece of prose fiction (i.e. far longer than any of the fable-type shorts I'd been including in my diary), and I called it *Cruel Garden*. My *Cruel Garden* – a sustained and somewhat fabular piece of stream of consciousness writing – had nothing to do with Lorca nor did it bear any similarity to the Rambert production. Looking at the piece today, I can see far more about my subconscious state of mind than I realised at the time. But this was the moment when I decided that writing was what I wanted to do. Further similar bizarre, symbol-strewn and poetical stories followed, all of them consciously, pretentiously and incompetently influenced by the likes of John Fowles (*The Magus*), or Nietzsche ('I would believe only in a God that knows how to Dance') or T. S. Elliot (*Four Quartets*).

The astounding thing about Rambert's *Cruel Garden* and its pivotal impact on my life is that nearly two decades later I met the man – Ian Gibson – who wrote the book (*The Death of Lorca*) which had inspired Lindsay Kemp to devise the ballet. I was in Spain, near Granada, staying with Rosy (the clown). She mentioned that her cousin lived nearby, in Restabal, and that we'd been invited to a party at his house. The cousin turned out to be Gibson, who was then already working on his now-famous biography of Salvador Dali. He was somewhat taken aback, not at my tale of literary inspiration, but of the gushing manner in which I told it.

Unfortunately for me, the stage no longer holds the same magic it did back then, in my youth, and though I still enjoy a visit to the theatre, it is for entertainment rather than insight into the world or inspiration for my own creative self. I am sure this is much to do with my age and a concomitant jadedness, but I can't help thinking that the state of British drama has become jaded too, decadent, that it's lost its purpose, its innovative edge – the one that drew me to it in the first place.

Top left:
13 Aldershot
Road, Kilburn

Top right:
Sasha Lyons

Left:
Fred Goldsmith

Bottom left:
Vera Caspary

Chapter eleven

WORK
A REAL PLACE IN THE REAL WORLD

Almost everyone born into this world needs to work to live. Pre-civilisation, Homo sapiens foraged or hunted for food, then he learned to tend plants and domesticate animals. For most humans through history this was their work. Barter allowed some to do other jobs and exchange their labour for food. Systems of money developed to make such exchanges far simpler, releasing many to concentrate on trades, crafts and services. In most places of the world today, the vast majority of people do work which has no connection with food production, though a large share of their income – how large depends on their and their nation's wealth – remains dedicated to food consumption. For a long time, income has been required for other needs, especially shelter but also clothing, transport, health and leisure. Generally speaking, an individual cannot survive without an income, and, generally speaking, an income depends on that individual having work.

This practical and fundamental need to work has been codified by middle class culture into something called a career. Many young men and women study and train for one career or another, whether it be a trade, such as builder, mechanic, lorry driver, or in a sector such as catering or health or manufacturing or in a profession such as lawyer, architect, or engineer. A career, in coded terms, means a long-term prospect for income; without it, the coded subtext implies, money will always be far harder to acquire, and it may be a struggle to buy food, to live, to be happy. Of course, this is a highly simplified view, especially in the Western world, where vast numbers of individuals manage alternative ways of staying alive, by relying on the state or family members, for example, or by dropping out and working only intermittently or switching types of jobs.

The important fact remains, though, that for practical and psychological reasons most of us need to work to live and to feel OK about ourselves within our social surroundings, i.e. to have status. I was no different, even if I had thought I was.

Going back to my childhood and home life, I don't recall doing chores at home or any associated pocket money I might have earned. There is, though, a record in my five-year diary, from when I was 10, of pocket money, and of being given a few shillings for washing windows and cleaning brass. But I do have two work-related memories from this same period, when we were still living in Hampstead.

I belonged to a Cub Scout pack that met every week behind the Everyman cinema for various life-skill activities and games – bulldog was one. Once a year, we would join in with the Scout movement's Bob-a-Job week ('bob' being the slang word for a shilling which is probably equivalent to a pound today), offering our services to friends and neighbours to do small chores in exchange for a shilling or more, thus raising funds for the movement. It's my childish memory that I sought out Bob-a-Job opportunities with great fervour, and earned more, at least one year, than any other Cub. None of these earnings of course went into my pocket.

However, I did have a regular job too. For a few hours every Saturday, I helped our local milkman on his round, delivering milk and other sundry produce to more or less every household on his route. He always gave me a tub of double cream for my efforts, which I handed on to my mother. Would that have been all? Surely, he would have given me a bob or two, too.

Later, after moving to live in Hoddesdon, Hertfordshire, I had a regular Saturday morning job in a supermarket, working with the fruit and veg. Aged 17 or 18, a laundry employed me on to drive its delivery van. I must have done this all too efficiently because I have a sense of the other driver, an old-timer, getting into trouble for being more leisurely than me on his rounds. During my university years, I took on freelance market research, knocking on doors and asking strangers to fill out questionnaires. The most fun I had working, though, before the end of my student days, was at a Butlin's holiday camp in Minehead. I've already mentioned this for it is where and when I met Myra.

I am sure I had other jobs, but the most important thing I learned about work in my child and teen years was to be thrifty, to spend less than I earned, to underspend so as to add to my savings, not draw on them. I don't know how I learned this trick of life, whether it was inculcated into me by my mother, who had come from a relatively poor and working class background, or from a more innate element in my character. I certainly did not learn to be a saver of money from Sasha, for he was a spender, a money show-off. Part of my carefulness with money may have come from wanting very much to be independent of my family, i.e. Sasha.

I had no idea what to do when I left university. One fuddy-duddy physics lecturer had tried to persuade me to go into the world of pneumatics; and a career adviser could think of nothing more worthwhile to suggest to me than becoming a career adviser. For the best part of a year, I worked for a temporary agency doing all manner of short-term jobs, the best of which were at the Arts Council and the Chelsea Flower Show. As with the laundry van job, I found myself anxious to work well and efficiently, whether to please my bosses, to avoid criticism, or to satisfy myself I'm not sure, perhaps all three. In Darwin, before Cyclone Tracy, I did manual work at the power station to earn dollars; and, in New Zealand, the job I fluked at Sandoz as a medical rep gave me a first sense of professional work, of wearing a suit and tie, of business.

On returning to London, after my travels, and seeking a decent job, I turned to market research, for which I had some relevant experience. Remarkably, unsolicited letters to a few companies landed me a couple of interviews, and a position with Market & Opinion Research International (MORI) as a junior executive. MORI had been set up in 1969 by an American, Robert Worcester, and later became part of Ipsos MORI, one of the most respected market research companies in the country.

I wore a suit and tie every day, and shared an office with Stewart, another junior executive. We had a lot of laughs, but I was incapable of treating the job as seriously as Stewart. For example, I recall using the photocopier to take surprisingly interesting images of my hands and head. I worked on the research and preparation of questionnaires; I wrote reports on the results; and I became involved in discussions with clients. One project required me to prepare and organise a survey of public opinion on potential slogans for a poster advertising the film *Midnight Express* due to come out later in the year. But the survey, apparently, was redundant, for the producer disregarded our expert results choosing instead his own favourite slogan. For someone with so little experience, I was given plenty of responsibility, yet I found most of the work dull. I liked one of my senior colleagues a lot, and he had been with MORI since its launch, but I saw how his day-to-day work was not that dissimilar from my own. Could I go on doing the same thing for years and years? No, I couldn't – not with the bright and enticing worlds of theatre, art and literature yet to be discovered. It is worth noting, however, that I remained on good terms with MORI, occasionally undertaking freelance projects for the company, even abroad.

And so, having dropped out of the mainstream once when I went travelling for three years, I now dropped out again, to live on make-believe. But all the exploring, whether geographical or social, led me, inevitably and unsparingly, towards an existential crisis, a nervous breakdown, a complete and utter loss of faith in myself, and my self's place in the world. This started happening in 1980, not long after my winter on Corsica, when I began to acknowledge my own inadequacies, especially with regard to 'being a writer'. Half a dozen brief extracts from my diary serve to show my state of mind.

24 April 1980
These really are depressing times for me. I feel incapable and very small. I continue to visit people who are not in. I go away and the fates conspire against me. My restlessness eats away at me. I am directionless and very nearly friendless. I treat life too playfully. I cannot take it seriously. [. . .] This constant self-perspective is fucking hard to live with. There are tears in my eyes and sadness and loneliness tonight.

I drink too much whisky (for the first time I perceive the possibility of turning to drink, in the same way that I perceive the possibility of a nervous breakdown) and listen to *Peter Grimes*. The light is dim, the curtain drawn, all contact with the world is shut off. But I don't want this, I want to be at a party, in bed with a woman, on a boat across oceans, dancing, something, tonight. My hold on reality is very light.

28 April 1980
This morning I cried and cried and I cried. I truly wept. And Roser comforted me. Why did I weep? What depths of depression? Where did such reserves of tears appear from? And Roser made love to my tears. I don't think I've let anyone be so sweet and kind to me. And more that night, it occurred to me that I had never cried in someone's arms. [. . .] A very heavy day for the cold hard Paul, the independent one. Roser, these pages are for you. Love, Love, Kisses. No te vayas. And, And, And. Gratitude, Gratitude. Thanks.

6 May 1980
Preposterous tears again. Repeating over and over again that I must have a plan, an alternative plan. [. . .] But the hollowness continues. I feel as though I am broken into four pieces and each of the pieces is being cracked and strained to breaking point. I am weak to take so much comfort from R.

12 May 1980
Hot and almost humid. No real progression out of this depressive cycle. Early Monday morning, Rachmaninov *Piano Concerto 2*, but none of that drive, ambition and lust for life in me.

14 May 1980
My guts are so empty and tears roll down my cheeks AGAIN.

I cannot conceive what will happen to me next. Roser will leave, Colin will return, and I will go on living in this small room for 30 years moaning about not being able to pull myself together. To be relying on my own efforts in these times is absurd. I couldn't make it worse, could I? But I can't go on moaning, but what the fuck can I do?

I am super-glued to a whirlpool.

19 May 1980
Go back down to the bottom and start again
    Go back down to the bottom and start again

Go back down to the bottom and start again

A feeling that I should take the lowest job and befriend anyone who will have me. Start all over again. Bleach the piece of shit.

20 May 1980

The room looked like this.

[I had strung red metal tape across the room in dozens of different ways, until it looked like a 3D spider web. There is a diagrammatic picture of this in the diary. The only way I could move in the room was by climbing in and out, under and above, round and through the tape.]

On the record player a double bass concerto plays. The needle gets stuck in a groove [the music repeating endlessly]. The most perfect of moments.

Last night I danced away the ugliness of the weekend through the interstices of the web I wove. It was the exact portrayal of my mind.

The crux of this crisis was that I had no work, no pathway for the future, no career by which to define myself. I sought neither medical (pills) nor psychological (counselling) help for the depression simply because it never occurred to me to do so. I don't think I ever doubted that I had sunk myself into this pit of despondency, and therefore only I could get myself out of it.

A year earlier, I had lost the lovely (and cheap) garden flat in Fordwych Road, Kilburn, because a developer had bought the property and evicted us. Harold had found another place for us to live, but it was far away, in Leyton. I hated our new home, which we had christened the 'Black Cafe', and even more so on returning from Corsica. Although Harold had gone to live in Paris, Roser was still in residence, and a great comfort, yet being stuck in Leyton aggravated my gloom.

In the summer of 1980, my efforts to secure a short-term (and thus cheap) housing association property back in the Kilburn area succeeded. During the summer, Roser and I moved into a 1st floor flat at 21 Iverson Road, and set about decorating. It felt like a new beginning. As chance would have it, the innovative Tricycle (now Kiln) Theatre was just about to open up round the corner on the Kilburn High Road. It was created out of the old Foresters' Hall to a design by architect Tim Foster. I helped with the final stage of painting red the scaffolding that supported the two-tier three-side seating; and, for the next couple of years, I felt very involved with the theatre, spending many an evening working with the front of house staff, manning the bar and/or ushering.

In August 1980, I drove with Harvey (an Australian friend) and Roser to the north of England. I had some MORI freelance work to do, but we also wanted to visit a sculptor friend of Harvey's and a potter friend of Roser's. While driving I talked about my career troubles, about my wants and needs and my capabilities. Harvey suggested I become a journalist. I said, what a good idea, yes I think I'll be a journalist. This conversation proved pivotal.

By way of a pause in this narrative, I have a little to say about Harvey, Harvey Shields. He was – and still is as far as I know – an Australian sculptor. He had come to Britain, like many Antipodeans, to see the Old World for himself. He had lived for a while in my Fordwych Road flat with his girlfriend Noelene, who made and played ocarinas, and then they had moved into a flat in West Hampstead. While I still felt little more than a child much of the time, Harvey seemed a grown-up. He had an artistic career, but while in London was working to earn money in a printing shop. The job also gave him the opportunity of producing a glossy paperback combining photos of his sculptures with a text about the theory behind them. He called it *Place Meant*, and though I could never say so, I didn't understand a word, nor did I 'get' anything from his welded pieces of sculpture.

But I had a lot of time for Harvey, and we stayed friends long after he returned to Australia. I now see my past relationship with him as part of a trend in me of seeking out people who lived more seriously and productively in the real world. Luke was one of these friends. Though he worked in alternative theatre, his role was as a skilled and real-world administrator, finding funds, organising venues etc. And Raoul (who I had met through Rosy) was another important friend in my life, a fully fledged medical consultant; and to this day I've never quite got over my envy of his real-world status.

A shocking thing happened to Harvey. The owner of the house wherein he rented a garden flat (in Sumatra Road) used an agent to collect money from the tenants. Harvey, by socialising with the other tenants, found out the agent was charging the tenants far more rent than he forwarded to the owner. The owner, a diamond merchant, sacked the agent, and asked Harvey to take on the responsibility of collecting the (reduced) rents. The resentful agent physically attacked Harvey, beating him up. Harvey reported the assault, and the police were ready to prosecute.

Then, one day, Harvey came to visit me. He told me that the agent had offered him £1,000 (worth three times as much in today's money) to drop the assault charges. I suggested he talk to the police, and he said he would, but I don't know if he did. Instead, he persuaded the owner of the house to join him, and the two went together to visit the agent and collect the offered £1,000. As the money was being handed over, several policeman sprung out of hiding places. Harvey and the owner both were then charged with blackmail. Harvey had to move out of his flat, so as not to be in contact with potential witnesses, and he was forbidden from even entering a geographical area around the house, one which included where I lived.

It took a while for the case to come to court, to the Old Bailey. For months beforehand my own future plans were restricted by needing to be available as a witness. Only in the days preceding the trial did the defending barrister decide not to call me. I wrote in the diary about attending the trial.

25 September 1981
All day Thursday I spent at the Old Bailey in the public gallery of Court Four. For there Reginald Harvey Shields and [the property owner] were under trial on four counts: two of blackmail, one of conspiracy to prevent the course of justice and one of deceit. The two defendants had taken the stand in their own defence. I watched the end of Harvey's evidence and almost all of the owner's. [...] How serious it all is, how much money is being spent, how many people's time being taken up. Both of them could be imprisoned for up to three years. Harvey's throat dries up as he is cross-examined in the witness box. The prosecutor's job is to trick the witness into admission or error. But Harvey thinks carefully before answering each question. He is a good witness. When he is allowed to step down he returns to the dock to put his feet up. He reveals different coloured socks, quite out of line with his fawn-coloured suit.

[The owner] is more spontaneous in the witness box. His first instinct is to let fly at [the agent]. He has been listening to the bastard lie for days in the box and has had his entire life screwed up by the man for almost a year. This is his first chance to say anything of import and be listened to. He alternates between bitter anger and a resignation born of a sad disbelief. He appears genuine.

It is difficult to understand how the police were taken in by [the agent]. How would a diamond merchant lend himself to petty crime to screw £1,000 out of somebody he had been giving money to for years. The only real evidence and some of it did seem damning, was on the tape of the meeting (the meeting organised by [the owner] with four policemen in cupboards etc). A lot of what was said was very open to different interpretations which defence and prosecution clearly tailored to their own cases.

[A man nearby] leaned over and asked me whether I thought the witness was telling the truth. I said 'yes' and he replied: 'He's lying through his teeth.' Of course it was [the agent], younger and more solid looking than I had imagined. He had sat there every day lapping up the whole trial. He is untouchable, the police have dropped the assault charge against him, and however innocent they find the defendants, there is nothing that can be done to [him]. [...]

Harvey and [the owner] were acquitted on a majority of 10 after the jury had been out three times for a total of four hours. The judge had summed-up in favour of the prosecution.

Soon after Harvey had been arrested and made to leave his flat, he took up with a friend, Judy, who happened to live in Belsize Park with an elderly woman, Eva. Bizarrely, Eva was the second wife and widow of Sasha's grandfather, my Uncle Fietje who had been around throughout my childhood. With the trial over, Harvey left the UK – who could blame him – to live in the US. There, once, he sought out my real father, Fred, and his wife, the sculptress Gail. To this day, one of Gail's exhibition catalogues sits right next to *Place Meant* on my shelf with books by, or connected to, friends and family.

Would I have come to journalism without Harvey's timely suggestion. It's fanciful to imagine I wouldn't have, but it's impossible to know. The idea of being a journalist had never occurred to me before, it had been beyond the scope of my vision. This was true even though I had been lightly exposed to the business of producing arty magazines: at university when I regularly collaborated on the student newspaper, and when I wrote, sometimes with Luke, a few reviews for *Performance* magazine, which was trying to document the new performance art movement. The brilliance of this new idea – me becoming a journalist – was linked, I think, mostly to it providing a means for me to develop the craft of writing. During the previous year I had become acutely aware of how impoverished my writing and writing ability really were. Journalism, I realised, would not only allow me to keep the dream (of being a writer) alive and work towards it, but give me a career (i.e. money to live and a modicum of the real world status I felt so needy for).

I borrowed *Journalism Made Simple* and *Practical Newspaper Reporting* from the library, and wrote to the *Ham & High*, a local and highly respected weekly. Its editor, Gerald Isaaman, generously granted me an interview, even though he had no job to offer, so he could give me – a would-be hack on his patch – advice. More importantly, I hooked up with a freelance journalist by the name of David Paul. I managed this by placing a classified ad: 'Researcher, writer, journalist. Do you need a non-secretarial assistant?' David haunted law courts and County Hall knowing what kind of stories to look for and how to sell them to radio stations and local papers. I tagged along with him for a week or two, and produced a small amount of copy, but the relationship did not last long. Crucially, though, it allowed me to strengthen (legitimately but not accurately) my CV text: I now had journalistic experience – experience being the most valuable of all job-seeking qualities.

I applied for many jobs over the next few months, ever hopeful, and became accustomed to receiving rejections. Early in 1981, my luck changed, and I secured a position as a fully-fledged journalist on a top industry magazine called *European Chemical News*. Weekly, it had a full-time staff of around eight, and was published by IPC along with a multitude of other specialised trade and consumer magazines out of a large modern building right next to Sutton station. I must have talked a good talk in the interview, or, more likely, my degree and science background blinded the editor, for I had neither writing ability nor the reporting experience/training the job required.

Consequently, I soon found myself struggling, on various different levels. I didn't get on well with the rest of the staff, I didn't try very hard. There was far too much going on in my private life, and though I'd accepted the need to work in the real world, I saw no reason why work should extend beyond working hours. Consequently, I suspect my colleagues found me aloof, strange and possibly arrogant. It didn't help that I was a year or two older than several of them who had far more experience than I: in the scheme of things I should have been showing newbie humility, and I wasn't. In my first monthly report, I was described as 'truculent and brusque', and a diary entry from the time confirms my poor attitude.

> 28 April 1981
> It is undoubtedly true that I have been a little too carefree in my attitude. I did rather waltz around in my first weeks at ECN. Tonight I condescended to go for a drink with the other journalists, but they still managed to make me feel guilty when I left after half an hour to catch a train. One forgets the pressures that exist to make one conform. They are afraid I find them uninteresting or that I am rejecting them, so they respond instinctively in counter-aggressive ways. Since Tony [Cox, the editor] gave me that rather obvious warning I have endeavoured to make myself super nice and work super hard. They'll get used to me eventually as long as I don't get the sack.

My efforts to be 'super nice' came too late or were considered insufficient for the editor, Cox, because the next month I was given an official warning that I might be sacked at the end of my three month probationary period. I was given several specific and difficult journalistic projects over the next four weeks to gauge whether or not I was up to the job. I believe Cox – who had taken a great dislike to me – devised these tasks in the hope I would fail them. I didn't. Having survived the trial, I certainly relaxed and my colleagues attitude to me also softened. I'm not sure Cox ever quite got over feeling he had made a mistake in employing me. He was a terrible editor, and an awful people-manager. He had no tact, or manners, and, in my opinion, had risen to the role of editor primarily through his knowledge of, and links with, the chemical industry. The fact that his Russian wife worked on the magazine didn't help my situation.

One time he came back from lunch drunk, and was told that I had taken a phone message for him. He came to my desk demanding the message, but I explained that I'd left a note on his desk. After looking for it, he stormed back shouting, demanding I find it. I made a show of looking for it on my desk, and elsewhere, insisting all the while I had left the note on his desk. His behaviour was that of a school yard bully, and was intolerable. Under normal circumstances, I suppose, someone else might have given in, resigned – just what he wanted – preferring unemployment to having such a bastard for a boss. However, I was all too keenly aware of my vulnerability, and need for work, a career. I understood that there were costs associated with being on the bottom rung of the ladder, and more so because I was starting late. I'd been given a lucky break, and I wasn't going to give in. Later that afternoon Cox found the note I'd written – in his pocket. He offered me an apology, albeit a very grudging one.

I can honestly say this was the worst working experience of my life. It was a trial by fire, I suppose, and, to use another cliché, I survived by the skin of my teeth. Cox kept me on probation for nine months, and even towards the end of this period I still thought I might get the sack.

9 September 1981

Am I an idiot? To pursue a career that is so obviously against the grain of my abilities? But is that why I'm doing it? Surely I chose to write because it would be tough and because it was the only career that I felt I could justify my life with. Did I ever expect it to be easy? But will I get better? And what will happen if I get the sack at ECN. I really will be left in the shit. I'd never get another job as a journalist [. . .]. On the other hand might it not knock me into an entirely different direction where I could be more successful. That is difficult to imagine. Also it's very difficult to face the world with yet another unprogressive period of my life. What the fuck else would I do?

Cox never stopped shouting at me, hassling me, being obnoxious, even after I'd been taken on as a fully fledged member of the *European Chemical News* staff, and I never stopped looking for another position. By the end of my ECN time, after about two years, I had become a decent reporter: I knew how to dig out a story from an interview, a press release or annual report, and I could type it up in a classic journalistic way. I also learned how to proof read – in those days we still travelled to the printing company's premises to check proofs – and to go for drinks with my colleagues after work.

Despite the many low points, there were a few high notes too. I made a real success out of the probation task I'd been given, to write a monthly report on the chemical shipping market, demand, rates etc. I don't believe this had been done before, and I had to start from scratch making contacts, and encouraging them to swap information in, what was, a very closed market. Once it was up and running regularly, and something of a success, my colleagues affectionately called my *Shipping Monitor* page(s) 'Boys at Sea'.

On one occasion the 'Boys at Sea' column got me into serious trouble. I'd been fed, by a broker, the idea that the Norwegian partners in a chemical shipping joint venture were at loggerheads, and I mentioned this 'friction' in print as the cause of some individuals leaving one of the partners and setting up a rival firm. The owners of the companies in question were furious, though I didn't know this at first. They organised a press conference in New York, and enticed me to attend, offering to pay my expenses. Cox wouldn't let me go, thankfully, since, I later discovered, there was humiliation awaiting – the conference had been planned, essentially, to denounce my article. I did travel to Oslo and Bergen a few months later to research articles, not least with the partners in the joint venture. Once comfortably ensconced in a meeting room, the two chief executives turned on me. I wrote in my diary about how I sat quietly for a while, absorbing the anger, but when I felt the tirade going on too long, I found myself arguing back, thus wasting the whole interview. A lesson learned, I wrote to myself.

More amusingly, I was given a taste of life at the top of the business ladder, and of the joy of press trips.

7 June 1981

What a day out with Hoechst U.K. ECN sent me on a freebie to cover the opening of some new laboratories at Stainsland near Halifax. I was going to fly the shuttle to Manchester but because of an air traffic controllers strike, Heathrow was virtually closed. The PR director picked me up at the start of the M1 and drove me to Luton where the rest of the Hoechst executives had grouped at the McAlpine air centre. They hired a private jet – no less than £920/hour – to Yeadon airport midway between Bradford and Leeds. The sensation of flying in a small plane is more real, the lift off, the action of movement through the sky makes more sense, the control of the aircraft can be understood. Most of the short journey was above the clouds. Still, with the sun streaming in and smoked salmon sandwiches to eat, I didn't mind too much. [. . .] The return flight was a farce [. . .]. All the directors got drunk out of their minds and played children's games: I played a mock game of chess using pieces of sandwiches, while champagne was splashed about over people's heads. The chairman himself (or rather his chauffeur) gave me a lift back to Kilburn in the chairman's Merc!

By November 1982, I had secured the promise of another job, at Platt's, based in central London, not like ECN stuck in the suburbs, and with a significantly higher salary. This gave me confidence to stand up to Cox more, and, indeed, I shouted back at him once – the only time in my working life I've ever lost my rag with a colleague. It took months for the job move to be finalised, and occasionally I relapsed into paranoia that it wasn't going to happen, and thinking that I'd have to leave any way, and be jobless. As if getting away from *European Chemical News* wasn't enough of a miracle change in my life, I also left behind short-term housing and the rental market to become a property owner: a four-bedroomed terraced property in a Kilburn back street. This step up in my fortunes was partially enabled by my stepfather Sasha (as I've already explained in chapter five).

I started working for Platt's, a part of McGraw-Hill, an American publisher, with extensive news operations in Europe, in March 1983 within weeks of moving in to my new house, 13 Aldershot Road. The stress of it all affected me physically. I became chronically tired, unable to bring myself to proper fitness and health. McGraw-Hill paid for a full medical, but this didn't uncover any cause, leaving me insecure, fearful of my new workmates and boss thinking I was flaky, lightweight, and not up to the job. I had spent my time on the ladder's bottom rung – and experienced all the fire and brimstone of apprenticeship that went with being there – and now I didn't want my chances of climbing to rung two ruined by unexplained ill health.

Raoul came to my rescue, Dr Charles Coombes in the medical world. He was already an up-and-coming breast cancer consultant and researcher. That year the *Sunday Times* had done a feature on his breakthrough research at the Royal Marsden. I don't know why we had become good friends, but we were, and I saw a lot of him and his girlfriend, a potter. He put me in touch with a chest specialist, who did tests at a clinic in Balham and discovered that I had a form of pneumonia. A course of targeted antibiotics soon cured me.

Life in the real world was, at last, on the up. I was 31, I had a proper job, a house that was my own, and the future surely looked brighter and more secure than it ever had before.

Most of Platt's income and profit came from a daily telex providing subscribers across the world with detailed information on the previous day's oil market prices and deals. But Platt's had also gone downstream, as it were, with weekly telex services on the prices for various other chemicals, such as benzene and styrene, which were traded, albeit in smaller quantities. This was my job. It involved making telephone calls to buyers, sellers and traders to collect and trade information with the sole aim of making an assessment on the actual price of each petrochemical product. I would then write this in list form, with a short report for each product. Most players in the market recognised the need for independent assessment of prices, even if those prices were wrong at times, and so participated not only in paying hefty subscription rates for the telexes but also in talking to those like me doing the price assessments.

There was a lot about the job I liked, not least that for the first and last time in my life I had a boss who nurtured me – nothing makes a job better than a good boss. However, my day-to-day work was far removed from writing. Price reporting may be considered a pure form of news reporting, as one is striving for accuracy in a sea of manipulation, but there was no requirement to put words together on the telex in any but the most elemental way. My chief, Jim Trotter, a kindly thoughtful man, kept me happy in various ways. He extended my responsibilities, knowing I wanted to write, by putting me in charge of a weekly printed newsletter providing similar articles to those I'd written for ECN. And he found the resources to hire me an assistant. Most respectful of all, he involved me increasingly in his own internal negotiations with our US masters to the point of taking me to an important McGraw-Hill management conference at Monthawk, Long Island. Indeed, he was grooming me to take over his management job – he said as much.

Our office was a dynamic place, new ventures were being talked of and then started all the time; desktop computers were appearing, and we were sending my weekly newsletter to the printers by modem for the first time. Americans would drift in and out from week to week with ambitious talk of a computer network system to replace telex services, one that would allow traders to trade online. My colleagues all seemed to have a buzz about them, so unlike the ECN office, possibly because there was a smell of money around. We all earned considerably more than trade magazine reporters, and it wasn't unusual for an oil price reporter to leave Platt's to become an oil trader and thus multiply his/her income several fold. There was plenty of travel, business class, and five star hotels, as I was required to go to conferences and hob-nob with our subscribers/sources. In the space of two months in autumn 1983, for example, I flitted from Brussels, to Monte Carlo, to Venice, to Berlin. Moreover, since the job was located in the West End I had any number of galleries, museums, cafes, parks, theatres, shops to explore in my lunch hour or after work.

My diary testifies to a busy social life during this time, but also a constant hankering for more out of life, though this 'more' was then – and always has been – difficult to explain or define to myself let alone anyone else. Until this point, creative writing had been an activity that gave me the illusion of actively seeking the 'more'. In 1980, I had paid for a correspondence course in writing short stories. This involved receiving a small teaching booklet every now and then, and writing stories which I submitted for criticism. I disagreed with many of the clichéd comments I received back, and, eventually, having tried valiantly to get my money's worth, my interest in writing stories to booklet order tailed off.

Between 1980 and 1982, I wrote around 25 short stories, all much longer and/or more thought out than any of the one page shorts I had written in my diary while travelling. From the first stream-of-consciousness efforts, like *The Cruel Garden*, their styles varied hugely, and included a series of Borges-inspired labyrinthine pieces; a series of political satires for a newspaper column I imagined called *Just So*; a series of Anaïs Nin-inspired erotica; as well as the formulaic correspondence course stories. I also tried sourcing plots in the world of my daily work. I wrote one story called *Shame Old Man's Muller's Not Here* about a feud between Norwegian ship owners! Later, as I've mentioned previously, I put together a radio play – *Scarlett's Magic Computer* – with a female oil price reporter who discovers her computer can predict the next day's oil price.

After 1982, from about the time I moved to work for Platt's, there was a marked downturn in my fiction writing. I did have a couple of projects under way, my diary reveals, but these were for novels, and were never completed. I do not remember much about *Angelus* and his purple star: he regularly appears in my diary for many months, but there is no trace of a proper plot for him. By contrast, a novel idea, begun around this time, I called *The Rats* stayed with me for a long time. I kept stalling, unable to make significant progress. Thereafter, I would regularly revisit the part-draft whenever I ran out of other writing projects, and add a few pages or not, before stalling again. The story was set in the early days of the London Underground. It involved a group of rats and a group of blind humans, the former taking just a few generations to evolve higher intelligence than the latter, and to enslave them. Although I loved researching into the early days of the Underground, and, inspired by William Golding's *Pincher Martin*, imagining in realistic detail how a blind beggar could survive underground and develop a relationship with rats, what kept me trying to make the concept work for years was the ambition to write it as a novel about evolution.

But, as I say, by early 1984, I was writing almost no fiction, and it would be nearly a decade, and several years of paternity, before I was regularly thinking up and writing adult stories again. I think, looking back, there were reasons for this. Firstly, positive feedback for my stories was non-existent. Not only did the publishing world show no interest in my writing, but those inspirational forces that had done so much to encourage me towards self-expression, Harold and Mu, were far away in space and time. Secondly, my real world life was fairly busy and fun. I had a job which offered a lot of buzz, not least travelling, and in which I felt valued; and I had my own large house, full of lodgers and activity.

Thirdly, I found another means to search for the 'more': a plan to go and work and live as a freelance journalist in Brazil. I had visited Brazil all too briefly in my travelling days, and I had always told myself that if I could ever get abroad to work, I would go to Brazil. Plus, importantly, I reasoned to myself, by stepping off the McGraw-Hill ladder of management rewards, and transforming myself into a free-lance correspondent, I would be re-routing my career back towards bona fide journalism. In February 1984, I confided to the diary: 'More and more I look to a trip to Brazil to justify my existence. I say in 1985 I will go there to work.' And by July: 'To everybody, I oversell my trip to South America. I'm really boxing myself into this future. But what else do I aim for, what else is there?'

Throughout 1984, I was scheming. I launched into teaching myself Portuguese; and I advertised for a Portuguese speaker wanting to speak better English so we could swap conversation lessons. At work, I nurtured contacts in various ways. I told Trotter that, by the spring, I wanted to be in another job. He tried to hold onto me with his your-my-successor plan, but, at the same time, he helped me fly. McGraw-Hill had news reporting bureaux all over the world at that time, and it began to seem possible that I could be posted to one of these. Thanks to Jim, I had met the company man who managed all the bureaux, so I wrote to him. He suggested a stringer post in Mexico City, and I got very excited – until I found out a bit more about the place, the size/density, the pollution, the corruption. In any case, my heart was set on Brazil, and Rio in particular, and so I turned the idea down.

Brazil was becoming a major producer of oil in the 1980s, and from that oil it was producing large quantities of petrochemicals, some of which were being sold onto the world markets. I not only made telephone contacts in the industry there, but started reporting more on the South American market in the Platt's telex price reports and in the newsletter. That autumn, I persuaded Jim to let me travel to Rio for a major petrochemical conference. Once there, I flew to São Paulo, to meet, and get drunk with, the McGraw-Hill Brazil bureau chief, Jeff Ryser, and one of his São Paulo-based stringers, Charlie Thurston. Charlie returned with me to Rio, and showed me a few ropes, took me to clubs, and introduced me to girls. The trip did nothing to quench my lust for Brazilian adventure. I very much wanted Charlie's life, not in São Paulo but in Rio. As luck would have it, he was, in fact, planning to quit soon. When would that be, and would Jeff and the network chief let me take his place? I had no clue, there was very little I could do back in London to promote my cause.

Then came what I refer to as the steaming turd phone call.

1 January 1985
STEAMING TURD. Before the graphic poignancy of it disappears, I need to talk about steaming (Texas?) turds. Friday morning a message is waiting for me in

my office – ring Ryser. Ryser is at his most sleazy as though his Texan drawl and humour have had a night of it. (I suspect the classic film gambler and womaniser is more sleazy early in the morning then he is during the night, the glitter has not spotlights to shine on, the confidence and arrogance spurred on by drink has waned, and the hair and clothes have become dishevelled.) It can only be 6 or 7am and he is already at his desk with words to write. He tells me Charlie has got a job [in the US] starting 15 January and 'here it is Paul, I want to put this hot steaming turd in your lap'. And not only does he seem keen for me to replace Charlie but he wants me in Rio.

13 January 1985
My mind is full of Brazil – I can hardly contain it. There is no desire to go any-where, see anybody, do anything. [. . .] Where will I live? what will I do in the evenings? how will I get contacts? how will I get a computer there? which computer will I buy and where? and how will I get paid and how will I get the money in Brazil and, [. . .] where and how will I receive telexes. Perhaps all this vulnerability will be my saviour. I have forgotten how to be humble and asking. This is the cycle of life. Up and down, up and down. There is the period of taking and then the period of giving. Unfortunately I have to go through ra-ther drastic upheavals to satisfy my requirements. My mind is full of Brazil – I can hardly contain it.

McGraw-Hill's news network already had a stringer in Rio, by the name of Hank. He didn't work very hard for McGraw-Hill, nor did he produce much copy, but neither would he let go of his strings (i.e. the publications for whom he was supposed to work regularly). Jeff's plan was that I would try and raise the news output from Rio, offering my services to some of the same McGraw-Hill publications that Hank wrote for. This seemed reasonable, especially as, for the bulk of my income, I would be able to rely on the strings Charlie was relinquishing. Oh what a naive young man I was: by February, Ryser had advised that almost all of Charlie's strings had been snatched up by other freelancers, and there would be only two left for me.

Suddenly, there was so much to do, most importantly finding publications that would pay for my stories. I managed to negotiate a small retainer from the McGraw-Hill bureaux network. I also won a slightly better one from my own bit of McGraw-Hill, Platt's, to supply copy for the South American chemical reports that I, personally, had launched months earlier. I made contact with Charlie in the US, for as much advice, specific and general, as he would part with; and I trav-elled to New York to buy a computer. Portable computers – nick-named luggables for they were as big as a small suitcase – were still relatively new and rare. I found tenants to rent my house; and, by early March, I was in Rio – Rio de Janeiro.

It had been nearly five years since my collapse into a sloth of despond, since my psyche had given up pretending and demanded I take action, to get a job, a career, some kind of real place in the real world. But by now work had become the most important – and interesting – aspect of my life.

Chapter twelve

GOLDSMITH IDENTITY
MEMENTO DOLLY, MEMENTO VERA

I like mementoes of a certain kind, generally those that have meaning, are connected to somebody or some place of more than passing interest. A couple of cardboard boxes hold every personal letter I was ever sent/given before computers took over communication lines, and another box has thousands of photo snaps of friends and family. Some photographs – like one of my mother and father on Brighton's Palace Pier – are significant enough to warrant a frame and space on a 'family wall'. A shelf of books holds works written by people I know or have known, or that have specific meaning. I keep, in large glass jars or vases, pebbles collected from all over the place with a date and a location written using indelible ink. Also I have a couple of tins crowded with small trinkets of one sort or another. To pick just three: a napkin ring with the initials P. K. G. which must have been a christening present, since it pre-dates my being called Lyons; a Standard key ring (from that £5 car Colin and I bought together); a crudely carved wooden fish given me by Canadian Jim in South America. I have already mentioned the weavings from South America, among which I consider the multi-coloured poncho as the most precious.

Only one item among my mementoes, though, can be classed as a family heirloom, having come from beyond the span of my own life. This is a rich red mahogany chest, a little over a foot long, and a little under a foot long in height and depth. It contains within an elegant and beautiful-ly made set of games – chess, drafts, backgammon, dominoes, small card boxes, dice, scoring slates, and a tiddlywinks set. It belonged to my grandmother Dolly; and the story of how it came to be mine, involves her oldest son, my uncle Mike, and – I exaggerate not – his being tortured.

Of my other treasures, none is more weighty with memento-ness than a dull, dustcover-less copy of Thelma *by Vera Caspary, my grandfa-ther's second wife. I came to know Vera, a celebrated but by then ageing American author, during several trips to New York in the early 1980s. And it was during these trips that I also became friends with my father Fred, before falling out with him irredeemably. Vera had helped Fred's ambitions as a writer in the 1950s, but, by this time, the two of them had not talked for many years; moreover, on meeting me, they both quickly warned against any efforts at a reconciliation between them.*

There was a strange mix of relations around during my childhood, those from Yorkshire related to my mother who talked funny but whom we saw infrequently, and those connected to my stepfather Sasha whom we saw more often but also talked funny, with German accents and Jewish humour. Time spent with any of them was almost always a chore. But there were also the Goldsmiths, and most often my grandmother, Dolly Goldsmith.

Dolly lived with Igee and their two sons (Fred and Mike) for some years in a large house in Bracknell Gardens, Hampstead. I believe my mother, Fred and I lived there for a short while after I was born, which cannot have been very pleasant for my mother – much later on, before she died, she would talk of that house as a rather forbidding place. By the time I have any memory of Dolly, though, she was ensconced in a cramped flat in Wendover Court, half a mile or so north of Bracknell Gardens. It remains a large imposing, mock Tudor building, near where Hendon Way launches off the Finchley Road.

The flat was crammed full of things, dark furniture far too heavy and large for the space, heavy brooding textiles, giant paintings in baroque frames, ornaments of every foreign kind, and a huge bookcase packed with German books each one dense with Gothic-looking type I couldn't understand. One small room served as a crowded studio, with easel, paints, and many finished canvases. She loved to paint vases full of flowers, and portraits too.

It certainly wasn't the kind of place a child might consider magical in any way, unless they were of an Angela Carter ilk, but nevertheless I have only very fond memories of Dolly and being there. Part of her charm, for me, were the cakes. She did cook the most wonderful Continental kuchen, and the most wonderful of all was Dobos torte. This she always made for my birthday. I never knew its name until, that is, in my 50th year when I decided – in memory of Dolly – to try and make one for my family, and therefore had to seek out a recipe. Named after a Hungarian confectioner, Dobos torte consists of five or so layers of light sponge with chocolate buttercream or jam between them, all topped with a thin caramel layer.

The larger part of Dolly's charm for me though was her love of games, and her willingness to play them. My childhood diary mentions 'Grandma' occasionally, as on 10 January 1963: 'Went to Grandma's and played two Scrabbles, poker, gin and roulette. I dried up for Grandma and found seven differences in Gus.' Gus was a spot-the-difference game in the evening paper, and Grandma would pay me a small amount of hard cash for each one I found. This early introduction to games, and to their money-earning potential might have led me into trouble later in life. I did, indeed, take up poker while at university, but early on in my gambling career I lost a whole £5 which stunned me out of such senseless behaviour. A love of games, though, has never left me.

The other Goldsmiths in my early life were connected to my uncle Mike. Like my father he had married a young English woman, Jacqueline (or Johnnie as she was known), but then separated soon after having one child, Mary in his case. Mike had moved to Paris, so we saw him rarely. Johnnie, however, was my godmother, and got on well with my mother. I know we were all quite close because one holiday I went with Mary to stay at a large hotel at Lac Champex, Switzerland, to be looked after by Dolly who spent every summer there.

Mike Goldsmith, who was a couple of years older than his brother, my father, became a journalist and worked for Associated Press (AP) out of Paris. After divorcing Johnnie, he married a Bulgarian, Claudia, daughter and granddaughter of national heroes. They lived partly in Geneva then, and had two children, Martin and Michael. That marriage did not last either, and Claudia and the two boys returned to live in Sofia. Most often, Mike was to be found in one turbulent part of Africa or another, reporting for AP.

And so to the games box. I have no knowledge of its provenance, but it must have been one of the possessions Dolly and Igee brought with them as they moved from Vienna to Berlin and then to London. Dolly and I must have opened it up and played with the games often, and it seemed common family knowledge that she would give it to me in time, or leave it to me when she died. But this did not happen.

In August 1977, only months after my return from travelling, Dolly suffered a serious fall. According to my diary this happened on hearing the news that her son, Mike, had been imprisoned in the Central African Republic by its self-styled emperor, Jean-Bédel Bokassa. Thereafter, she needed nursing round the clock. By this time, Mike was married for a third time, to Roxanne. She, like Claudia, also came from a notable family, being a niece of Lyndon B. Johnson. Roxanne managed, apparently, to persuade the French authorities to appeal to Bokassa (or she appealed to him directly, I'm not sure) to let her husband free on humanitarian grounds, i.e. because his mother was dying in London. He was released, and arrived a day or so before Dolly died.

I had visited Dolly at least once during her last days, and sat by her bed. Frustratingly, I have only the haziest knowledge of that encounter, other than that she tried desperately to tell me something – something about a key, maybe – but that I left without knowing what it was she wanted to communicate. Mike returned, and I met him briefly. He was black and blue, for he had been tortured, and Bokassa, thinking he was a CIA spy, had personally beaten him. He was in a hurry to get to the States, I seem to remember, so he organised Dolly's funeral quickly, at Golders Green Crematorium. (Needless to say her son, Fred, my long-since absent father, did not bother to come from New York.) Mike also arranged for the emptying of Dolly's home. Having chosen which things therein he wanted for his Paris flat, and having given Mary a chance to do the same, he arranged for a clearance firm to take the rest. He didn't consider that other family members might like anything, let alone a memento or two; I certainly did not interfere or make any claims. Only later did I feel aggrieved about this – the rapid demolition of all that was Dolly's life – but I also came to understand that Mike felt entitled to his unilateral decisions since he alone had supported his mother financially for a long time.

In the years that followed, I would see Mike occasionally in Paris, and I became friendly with Roxanne too. She worked in the nuclear industry in public relations, and I was an energy journalist, so we had a work connection. And Martin, the elder of Mike's two Bulgarian sons, came to work in London, and he lived in my house in Kilburn. We became firm friends for a while, united by something I could call the Goldsmith identity, both of us seemingly more like our fathers than our mothers.

More than 20 years later the veteran German director Werner Herzog would make a film about Mike's experience with Bokassa in the Central African Republic – *Echoes from a Somber Empire*. The documentary simply follows Mike as he revisits the country, and interviews Bokassa's wives, children and lawyers. A planned interview with the imprisoned Bokassa was cancelled at the last minute when the filming crew were expelled from the country. My uncle looks much the same in this film as I always knew him, tall, bespectacled, besuited, serious, but with the possibility of a secret just hidden behind a charming half-formed smile.

Herzog's film was released in 1990, and that same year Mike died, at a hospital in southern France. Processing his estate was a complicated business since he had been domiciled in Morocco for many years, had substantial property in France, but yet still – after a lifetime 'abroad' – had a British passport. For the next few years there would be a legal battle for his money. On one side was Roxanne, Mike's third wife, and their one son Andrew. On the other was Mike's three other children, including Mary and Martin. I mention this because at the outset, before the onset of the years of legal wrangling, they all met in Paris and agreed on one thing: that I should have the games box. Within days, Mary was transporting it back from Paris to give to me – more than two decades after Dolly's death. It was too large to go in the overhead locker or under a seat, so the steward placed it in a spare seat – with its own safety belt.

In a way, therefore, the games box is a memento of both Mike and Dolly. I have no other mementoes of Mike, other than a few letters; but I do have several of Dolly's paintings, both flowers and portraits.

From Mike and Dolly to Fred and Vera. I have no inherited mementoes of my father, Fred, because he very specifically wrote me out of his will, and, after his death – suicide – his third wife, Gail, wished to stick to the letter of his wishes. This is a sad story and takes a little explaining.

By the time I'd reached adulthood, my real and flip-flap father, Fred, had become no more than a distant pen-friend. I sent him very occasional letters while I was travelling, and sometimes he wrote back. This dialogue, involving one or two letters a year, continued during the late 1970s, while I was trying to re-settle in London. A long time after Fred's death, Gail sent me some of his papers, including letters I had sent him over the years. My tone in this dialogue was usually flippant and not a little pretentious. Here's one of my letters.

> January 1979
> Frederic, England shivers under the cold spell of nature and the trade unions, I slowly poke my head out of hibernation. My head is covered with a beret, my neck warmed by a scarf. I am careful not to slip on the ice, or the snow, or the sludge.
>
> I wanted to write to you, tell you what I am doing, keep contact etc., aware that I shall find myself in New York before too long. [. . .]
>
> Harold, a South African, takes refuge in my friendship, he it is who draws me out of the refuge of cushions I made close by the fire. We dance in the street afraid of no one and no thing, we attract the old and the young, the beautiful and the Buddhist, we share lovers and compete for lovers. We fight about practical things and play with words. We love and despise, we cut and caress. For me it is a rare friendship. But now and here, he is important, so I mention him for you.
>
> I gave up my work in market research, the future was too bland and full of compromises. I saved some money and now I work on two projects that I've challenged myself with. One is to write and the other is to set up a Learning Exchange which is a sort of contact and information centre. Both projects have been on my mind some little time, and I shan't remove them without at least giving them a try.
>
> The flat is littered with socks and shoes, cushions and ashtrays. It is a problem to keep warm at the moment. Even the bath water is tepid. [. . .]
>
> Perhaps I bore you. I send my love and regards as ever to you and Gail.

It was clear to me in my twenties that I had no emotional connection to Fred at all. His leaving me at such a young age may or may not have scarred my psyche but if it did, then my very being, my character, had developed, grown up with it, leaving no conscious trace. I had by this time begun to imagine I might go to New York, yet I knew I would never do so just to see Fred, it would impose too much meaning on the meeting, would require too much emotional investment.

(Incidentally, many years later, when a production company was making a half-hour programme, part of a series, about my diaries for BBC Radio Four, the producer urged me to focus my selection of extracts on the relationship with Fred and to provide, in an interview, some emotional context to the story. It was my repeated insistence that I had had no emotion towards Fred which led, I believe, to the pro-gramme being axed, for being too flat and theme-less.)

A perfect excuse for going to the Big Apple came in early 1981. M contacted me saying she was travelling from Central America with her man, and they were going to get married in New York. She wanted me to be there.

> 19 February 1981
> Frederic rang on Sunday night just to say hello and to check if I was really coming to New York. He offered me a place to stay and even 'small amounts of money'. Speaking to one's father for the first time in 23 years deserves a men-tion in the journal doesn't it?

The wedding never took place, but, I believe, my presence was of some comfort to a distraught M. More significantly, I did finally meet Fred. I have several fairly well-embedded impressions of what happened with him. The first is that I felt an immediate empathy in the way our minds worked, and was astounded as to how alike we were, especially in contrast to my relationship with Sasha. He bought me a bicycle – have I mentioned my dependence on, and love of, biking as a form of transport? Since being a schoolboy I had always biked everywhere. Fred and I cycled round Manhattan, usually against the direction of motorised traffic. As we toured the city, he pointed to the very kind of things – reflections, oddities, surreal juxtapositions – that I would notice. One morning before dawn, he took me to the fish market – again, this was the kind of experience I had been accustomed to seeking out on my travels. And another morning, he took me to the Museum of Modern Art where he'd hired out the small cinema to show me the film his father, Igee, had produced (as I've written about in chapter one). This was a man with a mind like mine. We were both, most definitely, Goldsmiths.

Unfortunately, that was the best of him, for me. I was soon aware of disconcerting aspects in his character. At the fish market, a wholesale venture, he ostentatiously pestered the sellers in his search for one small fish of the right type and size. In the streets near his home, he flaunted me as his son to shopkeepers as if those shopkeepers were his best friends, family even. With his wife, Gail, I saw a worrying need to exercise control. This was clearly illustrated one time when he showed me how his small dog would twirl around when a piece of food was held above its head; and then he showed me how Gail would do the same.

I should mention Gail, briefly, who I have been in touch with since Fred's death in January 1989. Much younger than Fred, smaller physically, and rather shy, Gail was Fred's third wife (he'd married a dancer called Judy in New York who I never met or knew anything about). She came from a rich family with inherited money, and owned a sizeable house and studio in Little Italy where she and Fred lived, and where she could work as a sculptress. She has continued to sculpt there, often working towards exhibitions, for many years.

At the time of my first visit, they were scheming, at Fred's insistence I'm sure, to expose how, in the first half of the 20th century, a generation of Gail's family had gone to extreme lengths to hide their Jewish identity. I knew nothing about her background, nor about her relationship with her family, but, nevertheless, it seemed like a seedy project to be so intent on. Fred, I was to find out, was good at feuds, at starting them, and then keeping them going, which was why he had fallen out with everyone in his family, and was soon to do so with me. It is also why an archive of his papers (that Gail eventually forwarded to me) was filled to bursting with detailed correspondence with those – often administrations of one sort or another – Fred felt had wronged him in some way.

It soon became apparent to me that there was a lot about Fred I did not like. Why, thus, it might well be asked, did I continue to see him during my stay in New York, and return two years later. The truth is – and I've never had any reason to doubt myself on this – that I wanted to know more about me. I decided, given our Goldsmith bond, that I might be vulnerable to whatever weaknesses and flaws I found in him. Knowing about them I reasoned, might help me avoid them. Whenever I talked to my mother about this, about Fred and the similarities between him and me, she would unfailingly say I had nothing to worry about, and that I was far nicer and more sensible than Fred had ever been. Still, I wanted to know as much about him as I could find out.

One thing I found out, not from him but from Vera, was that Igee, when he died in 1964 (I was 12), had left me money – I've no idea how much – but that Fred had, what shall I say, absorbed it.

I first met Vera that same trip, and wrote about her in the diary.

5 March 1981
Vera is ageing very fast now, most of the stories she has to tell me are in her book *Secrets of Grown Ups*. She is happy that McGraw-Hill have done such a

lovely job on her autobiography but, she says, they haven't publicised it well. The book is fun and full of lovely stories, most readable. Her life was full and rewarding, she lived exciting times and executed her work in synch with them. She remembers her life with Igee as very happy, she quotes Igee as saying: 'For two worried people we were very happy.'

Now she has Meniere's disease she has difficulty walking and often gets dizzy, like being permanently drunk, she says, without the advantages. She has finished the first draught of another novel but finds the correcting and rewriting difficult, her mind fogs. She realises her body is beginning to fail and swears at herself. She is small and hunched, her straight white hair falls ungainly over her eyes. She almost twaddles around her green apartment in search of photographs, books or spoons. A nurse stays with her, and Vera overpraises her cooking and help.

Laura, Vera's most famous book, is still in print, and in Los Angeles someone is creating a musical from it. If it happens, Vera hopes to go there for rehearsals. Her agent is also trying to get her a ticket to cross the Atlantic by liner in exchange for two 45 minute lectures. Of course I would welcome her to London. I liked her, her honesty, her practicality, her disinterest in all the metaphysical writers, her farts after dinner, her laughter at my few stories, her love of Igee, and the way she talks her age with surprise: 'I've lived so long.'

I did not ask her why she fell out with Frederic (they haven't spoken in over ten years), I felt I had heard enough from Fred to tell me it was complicated. Both she and Fred expressed a wish that I should do nothing towards repairing the breach. Gail has actually never met Vera, even though she only lives a couple of miles away. Imagine a stepmother, so near and so far.

I feel like a flea hopping from Goldsmith to Goldsmith, so much more to the Goldsmiths than to the Todds or the Lyons.

Some 18 months later, in late August 1982, I returned to New York to visit friends, but first went north by train to Block Island, where Gail and Fred had invited me to spend a few days with them at their summer house. I'd only been there a day when I felt things going wrong.

30 August 1982
The atmosphere in the house is stiffening up. I don't think I'm a difficult guest but I feel a difficult one. Whilst Fred was running on the beach and Gail had gone to sketch cows I looked for soap powder but couldn't find any. When Fred came back I asked him for some. He went out and brought me a container. Jokingly, I said, 'Where did you hide it?' He retorted that he hadn't hidden it, it was downstairs. When I said yesterday, I felt it was a warm cosy house, they said, 'and a happy one too'. If I make any observations about the island, I am immediately put in the position of protagonist and the island is defended, even against compliments. The same is true if I say anything about the US. Are Americans super-paranoid, or is it just Fred?

31 August 1982
Writeable of the moment is undoubtedly the complete break down of relations with Fred and consequently with Gail. This morning I sit in the Surf Ho-

tel dining room which serves the best breakfast in town – everybody says so. I get coffee, a choice of fruit juices, a choice of cereals, a choice of eggs, toasts and meats.

After dinner the evening before, Fred told me I had to move out immediately because another guest was coming to stay. No further explanation was forthcoming. It was a downright and obvious lie, but not one I could or wanted to refute. I was told to pack, and then I was driven to the Surf Hotel, where Fred had booked me into a room for two nights. At one point, while transferring me to the hotel, I was introduced to a stranger as 'an acquaintance', and Gail called me 'Mr Lyons'.

1 September 1982
I've thought about it and them more than they deserve. They live under absurd pretensions, to the extent that they think everybody is watching their every move. As though they were famous on the island. Fred is such an old fogey, a fusspot. A complete egoist. Every decision of the day from tiny – choice of vegetables – to larger has to be his. Gail often volunteers or suggests but Fred wiggles around. [. . .] His self-importance and hypocrisy is almost beyond belief. Is this what I am to become. He also believes completely in his own advice and philosophy to the point of advising others. I also. [. . .] Needless to say I left Block Island and the journey back to New York was extraordinarily uneventful.

My sin, I believe, was this, in simplified form. I had wanted to take some photographs of the island at night, and for this I needed a tripod. Fred had not wanted to help me find one, so I tracked down a camera shop, and asked there. I was given the telephone number of the owner, and rang him from Fred's house. I introduced myself as Paul Lyons, an acquaintance of some summer residents. I had used these terms – 'Lyons', 'acquaintance' and 'summer residents' – carefully, sensitively, not wanting to insinuate myself, or be thought of as taking advantage. Fred and/or Gail must have overheard my conversation and, somehow and in some way, taken enormous offence, as though I had tried hard to offend or disown them.

I never doubted for a moment that this behaviour towards me was anything other than Fred's own problem. I felt I had been wise to invest nothing in our meetings and wise now not to bother any more with him: I had no reason then or later to consider trying to repair whatever damage he had caused. That said, I feel sure, I would have responded openly had he ever tried to heal the breach. As it happens, I never saw or spoke to or wrote to Fred again.

The bicycle he had bought me during my visit the year before and which I had retrieved on this second visit was stolen a few days later in Manhattan. Nevertheless, the rest of my stay in New York was thrilling, and Fred never got another mention in my diary during those two weeks. I saw Harvey Fierstein's eye-opening *Torchsong Trilogy*, and was introduced to gay clubs, and to one incredibly pink home. I heard Brownie McGhee and Sonny Terry perform their inimitable blues music. I was taken to The Fifth New York Renaissance Fair where Robin Hood had miraculously been reincarnated as a 20th century American. I had all the pleasure of skyscrapers, the Met, Central Park, and two short love affairs. I cared not a whit that my father had thrown me out of his house and his life for ever.

Of course, I took the opportunity to visit Vera again. We had dinner with her godson Zach. Zach's father, George Sklar, was a leading figure in the theatre of social protest during the Depression, and later had collaborated with Vera on the 1947 Broadway adaptation of *Laura*.

I met Vera one more time, during a business trip to New York in July 1984, this time she was with George.

After Vera's death in 1987, I wrote to the Sklars – one or other of them was Vera's executor – to explain who I was and to ask for a memento, a first edition, perhaps, of one of her books. I did receive a reply, but it was banal, impersonal, and included no more than a book club edition of *Laura*, as though I were some sort of fan to be fobbed off. I felt slighted, and sorry not to have a keepsake.

As with the games box, I had to wait around 20 years before feeling this small but meaningful slight to my Goldsmith identity found a correction. My mother had died, and while clearing out her house I was browsing through her books. There was very little of interest, but I did, by chance, pull out a faded hardback, with no dust cover. It turned out to be one of Vera's books – *Thelma* – and inside it had been in-scribed 'For Barbara and Freddie and Paul – in love – Vera – October 1952', i.e. just a few months after I was born. I could not have imagined a more perfect memento if I had tried.

In early 1989, I learned of Fred's death, but felt nothing, certainly less than several of my own friends who were moved by the news, not least Bel who teared up out of some projected sadness for me.

5 February 1989
So I arrive back near to 8pm and the phone rings almost immediately. It is Mum. She tells me my father Frederic has died, has committed suicide. This gives me a good line of conversation all week – oh, my father committed sui-cide last week.

Well, this is interesting news. Gail rang Mum on Saturday night to tell her the news but was not very forthcoming with details. He died on Thursday, that must have been 26 January 1989, just a week before his birthday on 2 February. Gail thinks he was somewhat depressed. Apparently he took an overdose with drink and may have had a heart attack. [. . .] I feel nothing inside. I have settled my business with Frederic, I have expunged whatever was necessary and remain unmoved by his death. A few minutes later [my cousin] Martin rings [. . he] is more shocked than I. Frederic is his uncle, and he has seen him more recently than I. Although feeling no remorse, I am interested in Frederic. I have always been interested in him. And I find the lack of information about his death rather disquieting.

Given the long-term estrangement between Fred/Gail and myself, I was reluctant to probe for details, but I did find out from others that my father's suicide had taken place in a hotel room, and had followed a separation from Gail. The main thing that disturbed me about the news was that Fred had died without knowing he was a grandfather. I was his only child, and my son, Adam, had been born 18 months earlier. There were half a dozen people who knew me and were still in occasional contact with Fred – Peter and Tony, my uncle Mike, my cousin Martin, and, bizarre as it may seem, my stepfather, Sasha. All of them, it transpired, had either not bothered or not wanted to mention he had a grandson. I would have liked him to have known. Had he known, would he have contacted me? I doubt it.

Two months later, I received from Gail a copy of Fred's will. He had no money of his own, but the will was an extensive document designed to cover the possibility of Gail, who did have wealth, predeceasing him. With that in mind, he left hypothetical legacies to various people (like Peter and Tony) as well as $5,000 to his dog. I am the only person who was absolutely excluded, by name, from making any claim on his estate. A codicil to the will showed that most of the money would have been left to promote Gail's sculpture, with some put aside for a writer to finish the book about the genealogy of Gail's parents! In my diary I called it 'a sad document, the product of a bitter and somewhat twisted mind'.

There is not much more for me to say about the man who was my father. A tentative dialogue with Gail, which had started with the news of his death and the sending of his will, developed slowly into a friendship of sorts. Later, she sent me a large package of his writings which, apart from many complaint letters, contained various projects, a board game, unpublished novels, and heaps of correspondence about them. Attached to the manuscript of Fred's most ambitious fictional work – *The Fairest One Of All* – was a publisher's critique advising against publication but with a concluding remark that the writer 'could do something big.' I wrote to Gail about how I imagined this must have echoed away in Fred's mind for a long time. Also of interest was material that showed how he and his brother Mike had fallen out at a young age because Fred wanted to embrace his Jewish heritage while Mike wanted to escape from it.

We met, Gail and I and Adam, much later in London, but I didn't raise the subject of the Block Island incident, or enquire about Fred's suicide. I suppose I thought it would make Gail uncomfortable, and I had no interest in disturbing the gentle friendship we had established. We still write to each other, once or twice a year, and I keep her informed about the progress of her step-grandsons.

And so, at the close of this chapter, to return to the subject of mementoes. Some years ago now, Gail gave me one of her small clay sculptures. I love it enough to keep it on display; and I like that it keeps her in mind from time to time, regularly prompting me to think of travelling to New York, perhaps with Adam to see her again. I have the hugely meaningful photo of Barbara and Fred on Palace Pier, Brighton, about which I have already written. And then I have a couple of items sent by Fred as parcels to me when I was a teenager, for Christmas or my birthday. I come across them periodically, usually when I'm moving house, and they bring to mind a distant ephemeral sense that pervaded my childhood – the sense of being Paul Kenneth Goldsmith, not Lyons, and that out there somewhere was my real father, perpetually promising to come and visit in the not too distant future. One of these items is a Hungarian stamp collection, complete with specialist album pages. Another is a score of silver Kennedy half dollars. On every occasion they surface, I wonder what on earth to do with them, and then re-pack them in a box, and re-bury them in an attic.

Chapter thirteen

PHOTOGRAPHY
THE PLEASURE OF THE LENS

*On Friday 18 May 1979, a quiet revolution happened to me. I bought –
somewhat spontaneously – an Olympus OM1n camera that cost £200.
From then until now, the taking of photographs and revisiting of the
images taken has added a depth of field, an extra zest, to the business of
being alive, sentient.*

*Early on, with the OM1n, I was much focused on photographs
that captured artful images in the ordinary world around, reflections in
shop or car windows (occasionally of myself) combining with objects
behind the glass, or, perhaps, unexpected shouts of distant colour through
doorways of ruined buildings. I developed a photographic eye that would
be seeking out images wherever I went, even when I didn't have the
camera with me. And photographic projects constantly beckoned, whether it was B&W photos of a nude model in a ruined church, unusual graffiti
in a disued Paris metro station, or displaying the shop fronts of my local
high street along the corridor wall in my house.*

*The OM1n eventually gave way, became faulty, and my arty
phase evaporated in sync. Inexpertly, I chose a dull replacement camera
and, thereafter, never stopped moaning about it, and mourning the
Olympus; though what I was really mourning, I realised later, was having
grown out of my expressionistic, artistically-hopeful youth. In time, I
commented on this photographically with a series of images of trees,
fields etc. in which could be found shadows – not reflections any more – of
my own self.*

*I did continue taking photographs, though all too often the lens
was pointed at my young son, and the film in the camera was for simple
colour prints. Photography became a way of documenting my family and
holidays rather than the interface between the world and some combination of my psyche and imagination. Meanwhile, a number of my 'arty'
photographs got sorted into series, which I then had framed.*

*Whether for family snaps or complex reflections, I have always
felt I had a good eye with respect to composition. By contrast, I have
never had much interest or skill in other aspects of photography. Early on
I did hanker after developing my own B&W prints, and this led to me
creating a tiny dark room in the Kilburn house. I don't think I was very*

good at it, I didn't have the technical craft to produce excellent prints, and I tired of trying too easily. I have never had any interest in hardware, and so conversation with other photographers is usually cut short by my lack of knowledge about camera types, lenses, filters, and so on.

The same is true for much of the magic most cameras can do. I have always had a basic understanding of focal length, aperture, shutter speed, but that was it. These days, even the cheapest of cameras offer a multitude of different ways to fine tune the picture-taking process, and their screens offer a complicated map of colourful icons. I don't really want to bother, all I want to do is compose a picture. In truth, I'm a point-and-shooter. And that's not the limit of my disinterest. I want very little to do with photo manipulation. Tinkering with photographic film, in the dark room, was once the preserve of professionals or skilled amateurs. Nowadays, everyone can adjust every image in any way they wish, so much so that original images are but Cinderallas in the digital age.

The revolution wrought by the coming of digital photography is surely the most dramatic and widespread since the very first images were fixed on paper in the 1830s. It certainly felt like a tremendous upheaval in my own life when I switched to digital – I recall spending most of one holiday talking to anyone who would listen about how deeply it was affecting the very way I looked for, thought about, and took photographs. The transition was painful; but once converted I never looked back: I'd no more use a film camera now than I would choose a typewriter to write with or a gramophone player for listening to music.

Occasionally, I have crossed over from clicking purely for my own pleasure, to doing so for some other purpose. Working as a volunteer, as mentioned earlier, I took a large number of images of listed buildings for English Heritage to put online for a vast database. For The History Press, I took photographs of Brighton to match views found in old prints to be published in a then-and-now book.

I have a faint memory of owning a Brownie camera, but have no evidence of this – apart, possibly, from a handful of old, fuzzy photographs of friends which I could have taken or which could have been given me. I have remarkably few photographs of myself or my siblings in childhood – taking photographs then was not an every day occurrence as it is today. There are a couple of me being christened, and some ten years later of me in the Black Forest. I cannot bring to mind a single photograph of me as a teenager. In my 20s, I know, I affected a dislike of being photographed, so it's possible I took on this attitude much earlier in my teens.

The first time I recall having any awareness of, or interest in, the world of photography was at university. Before then, I doubt I had ever discussed the character of a photograph, been to a photographic exhibition, talked cameras or been aware that any and every photograph had a history, a provenance, had been taken by someone, somewhere, with some kind of camera, with some kind of purpose. Thus I can trace back my awakening to Cardiff and my friend Philip, as I've already written about. He took photographs for the student magazine, developed them, and was involved in selecting images for publication. Occasionally, I borrowed his camera, and helped in the dark room, and with laying out the magazine.

I took a definite decision not to take a camera when I left London to go travelling. This was partly practical/financial, because taking a camera meant bother: a valuable to protect (from thieves and from damage in the rucksack); film to buy and process; prints to carry or mail home. Partly, also, I was clear about wanting to give priority to a diary, to write about experiences, rather than collect images for them. Decades later, my only regret is not that I don't have pictures of the places I went – a simple internet search will find myriad photos of almost every place I ever went – but that I don't have images of the many people I met and became friends with.

A photograph of a person can bring with it layers and layers of otherwise buried memories. Without pictures, I cannot bring to mind a face or anything else about most of the names in my travelling diaries. I do have a few photographs of people, given to me by others, from my time in New Zealand and Chile, and these feel disproportionately precious. Today, of course, I could snuck into the rucksack a tiny camera and a few memory cards with very little practical cost or bother, and return from three years of travelling with tens of thousands of photographs. It is difficult to say whether my diary would have suffered if I'd taken a camera, whether I'd have been tempted to write 'see photograph' every other day.

It must have been Marielle who sparked awake my photographic self, after all she not only awoke much else creative in me but she is the only person from this period I remember with a camera. We met, as I've described earlier, in Amsterdam, and when she came to stay with me in Kilburn, it was with camera in hand. She lived, I believe, for people, and made friendship an art form. Characteristically, her lens was never focused on things, always on the people around her, trying to find a beauty in their form and/or spirit. The only photographs I have of myself from this time (apart from the reflections) are ones she took, and which today I still find flattering. I also have photographs of her friends, the ones in the commune, and they are equally pleasing, sensuous, generous to the angels she loved.

In May 1979, I travelled to Barcelona to carry out freelance market research for MORI. On the first day there, I wrote in my diary about the previous day being 'one of the busiest days of my life'. I was clearly somewhat manic, and despite having to pack, do a ton of stuff, and see many different friends, I found time to buy a camera. In a long list of other things done my diary records: 'Spent £200 on an Olympus 1 with f1/2 lens'. This was in fact a 55mm f1.2 lens. In the same diary entry – so soon, so quick – I am aware of a consequence for my diary habit: 'My imagination disappears into the photos that I take. In South America, if I saw a stuffed horse doll lying in the gutter, I would have made a story, but now in an instant it is gone, finished in a photo.'

A week later, I made the same point to a friend, Luis, who had promised to show me some of Barcelona's magic, notably two 'esquinas' (corners) with stone carved heads, 15-20 feet above street level, once used to mark entrances to the Jewish quarter. I'm impressed by the first, but Luis cannot find the second – he swears it was there 15 days ago. Having already explained to him the new conflict I was feeling between photograph-taking and diary-writing, I now please him by saying I have a story to write in the diary because I can't take a photograph of an unfindable esquina.

Any potential conflicts I'd been worrying about between my diary-writing and photographing selves failed to materialise, or else they vanished quickly. I soon found these two modes of self-expression happily reconciled and anxious to play along with each other. Indeed, now looking back, I can see from my diary how this photographic side of myself had been yearning to be let loose. Two years before I bought the Olympus, for example, is this entry.

4 June 1977
Photos from Portobello Road: The crowds of people staring into the sky with super quick clicking cameras as an air-ship (Goodyear) passes overhead; an escape artist escaping from sacks and chains to appear as an old tired man, working so hard for his bag of gold; the Indian sitting on a small car playing his steel pan sweetly and saying thank you to donors with his cross-eyes through his cross-glasses; the 'Free Shop' being the most boarded and barbed-wired and locked up of all the shops.

In pursuing the new side of my efforts at self-expression, this seeking for photographs to take, I became more conscious of the visual world around me. Thus I had found a new dimension to my sporadic travels, and more to write about – i.e. photographs, those taken and those not taken – in my diary than I had before owning a camera.

13 April 1980
Out for a trip, hitch-hiking around the marshes of Essex – Wallasea, Burnham, Wickford. The bright sun, the brilliant green fields hiding hard-baked earth, people's smiles, kite-flyers, dog-walkers, the strollers along dykes, and the gardeners. [. . .] One of the high spots of the day was taking photographs of a derelict boatyard using it to frame the bright colours of the sails as they passed by in the waters beyond.

5 October 1982
I have just looked again at the slides I took in New York. Sheer poetry. Why am I not a photographer? I never say I do things do well. Therefore, I am impressed by my own impressed-ness at the photographs. Poetry.

By the time of this 1982 trip to New York – the one during which my father Fred chucked me out of his house – I had begun to focus my camera on various photographic styles or themes. Inspired perhaps by that early trip to the Essex coast, one of these themes was distant concentrations of colour in an otherwise bland or uniform landscape. I loved colour and shapes, though that says little since every photograph is made up of colour and shapes, but I liked to find and capture symmetries, coincidences, conjunctions of colour or shape, or conversely amusing contrasts. For some reason, I found undertaker shop fronts very photogenic, especially when the undertaker's name had a punning resonance. It seemed to me there was an unnaturally large number of undertakers with strangely apt and/or comic names, such as Newman or Truelove or Wakely. I found much to photograph among non-chain shop fronts, too, their 'landscape' shape window displays seeming so often to demand attention by my camera.

Of all the themes, though, the one that I felt most passionate about, the one that – according to the evidence above from my diary – seemed able to bring out in me a touch of self-addressed immodesty, was that of reflections. I loved taking photographs of reflections in glass so that the subject of the reflection combined or contrasted somehow with what could be seen behind the glass. I had taken many such photographs before that trip to the Big Apple, but the images I gathered there seemed better – more startling, surprising, interesting – than any others. That year several of my photographs were included in the Greater London Council annual photography competition and exhibition. Occasionally, I captured myself in these reflection photographs, and, later, I used three for a set of framed self-portraits – enthusiastically trying to expose myself as an enigmatic being with depth and hidden colour.

One constant debate I had during the early years of my photographic life concerned the relative merits of using B&W and colour slide film, and which film to buy and use next since I had no wish to be wasteful by switching film before a roll was finished. My photographic brain would thus be clicked in to one form or another seeking out whatever type of photograph might be suitable for the film currently in use. There was no point in looking out for reflections or other colour-focused images if I had B&W film in the camera, but, on the other hand, there were several advantages of B&W film. At the time, colour had become so ubiquitous for holiday snaps, that B&W was often considered the film of choice for art or arty photography. Also, because I liked the idea of developing my own photographs, I installed a tiny but serviceable dark room-cupboard for B&W photos in my Kilburn house, and was determined to use it.

I did persevere with B&W, off and on for years. I still have a few memorable photographs that I took and developed, mostly shot in Kilburn. As I sit and type now, there is one in a clip frame on the wall opposite. Looking slightly down, a black youth is framed against a grid pattern of paving stones. He wears a sweater, half white, half black, with black stripes down the white side. His 'white' arm is outstretched to the photo's edge, and his black arm is folded at the elbow with a flat-palm hand underneath his chin, as if comically miming a cut-throat action. He is grinning his head off, with the most beautiful white teeth matching his white trainers.

A memorable set of B&W photographs from Kilburn – very much not on my wall, but tucked away in a folder and box somewhere – feature Mitzi, a girlfriend of the time, and a ruined church with heaps of rubble and broken brickwork inside but stained glass windows in tact. I'd had the idea of photographing Mitzi topless inside the church, but when I asked her if she was game for taking all her clothes off, she replied 'anything for art'.

Of all my B&W photographs there is only one group that I framed as a set. During a trip to Paris, Colin took me into a deserted metro station where we found the most intriguing graffiti on the walls – a variety of naked human forms created by and with hand (as opposed to finger) prints. I developed them myself as A4 prints, put six into clip frames, and the set decorated my bathroom walls for a decade.

Generally speaking, though, I struggled with B&W. The results I achieved in my mini dark room were always technically poor: I didn't have the patience for perfection or for repetitive experimentation; nor was I willing to invest in a decent (and more expensive) enlarger which might have helped. I had liked the idea of having my own dark room, and developing photographs, but the reality proved less appealing.

In 1983, I bought a zoom lens for the OM1n. It cost £150, and I used up more space in my diary writing about its high cost than why I bought it. A week later we were in Ireland for a week's touring.

15 September 1983
We stayed for too long in the city, chiefly because I was racing around trying to find the perfect photo to encapsulate Limerick's Irishness. Of course, I didn't find it. The sun came out crackling against the wet surfaces and travelling low along the east-west roads. One block was almost entirely taken up by a factory painted white with yellow sills and drainpipes – the sun highlighted the building happily if not dramatically. In one barred window, a bright yellow mac lay on a table in an otherwise empty room. But for the bars it was a lovely picture. I write it because I didn't take it. [...] A pink cottage by the roadside is not unusual but one we passed sported a bright red Volkswagen immediately in front. Now that's the sort of photo I like to take. I didn't because the car's owner came out and began waving at me as though he knew I was going to reverse back to the house and snap the picture.

Though most inspiration to take photographs surfaced when away from home, visiting new places, I did continue with photographic action in my own backyard.

24 November 1983
I have an idea to photograph all the shops on Willesden Lane and transform a corridor wall in my house into a Willesden Lane junior.

16 April 1984
I slipped out just before dusk last night in my quest for photos of Kilburn. The light in spring, especially at dusk, combined with the orange and red glows of sodium lights, make for interesting photos. As it happened, streams of people were making for the Catholic Church on Quex Road; the same swarming of people I had seen about 11:30pm the previous night bustling at the entrance to the National Dance Hall. There is a solemnity about the way Protestants approach their temples, but these Catholics were more dressed for a good time and less formal and less conscious about their time-keeping. The service was well under way but the people kept coming. In the distance, towards the back of the church, I could see, through the doorway, the crimson red priest. It reminded me of the coloured yacht sails I photographed through the derelict framework of a house – the central show of colour piercing the average column of brown and earthly greens.

And then I was off to live in Brazil, a whole new land and culture to experience, write about, and, of course, to photograph. For an Old-Worlder like me, Brazil was a country so full of zest that everywhere I went, everywhere I looked seemed to demand I point the camera – to click and collect as much of the colour and culture as I could. My days of trying to take arty, clever photographs were over, but the obvious world in front of me now demanded as much of the lens as the un-obvious one had once upon a time.

> 2 July 1985
> On Sunday, the Junina festival really came alive. I was heading out of Urca when a stream of people entering the peninsula convinced me I was going in the wrong direction. So I followed the crowd. The cause of all the bustle transpired to be the cute Modigliani-style statue that sits strangely in the middle of the water [Botofogo Bay] like the hand of the lady in the lake. It is in fact São Pedro, the saint of fishermen. And it is to him that the people (not the people in Urca for they are but spectators) in boats, hundreds of boats come to give thanks. When I rushed back to get my camera, I thought that three gaily crowded boats was sufficient to warrant pictures but very soon the entire bay was bustling with boats bedecked with bunting. [. . .] There was a wealth of photographs for me. The spectacle of the bay crowded, the display of dancing groups on each brightly coloured boat, but better, the multitude of people lined the low wall along Avenida Portugal leaving the rocks below devoid of all but a few persons, which left me free to jockey back and forth along the whole length taking photos of the audience as well as the show.

Of many such experiences I had in Brazil that were enriched because I was looking for and taking photographs, none are more memorable than my interactions with the Rio carnival parades. I went twice – in 1985 and 1986 – with press credentials allowing me to mingle among the samba school processions along the famous Sambadromo parade ground.

> 4 March 1986
> I arrived in time to see the second school and stayed right through to the seventh, and then saw most of the eighth (Mangueira) before it entered the parade ground. Tomas arrived about 1am and we moved slowly together through one enormous spectacle of feathers, coloured plastic, naked bodies, incredible fancy dress, huge floats of colour and vibration, thousands of people dancing singing together in chorus, streamers and confetti flying through the air, the sound of drums fill the air never ending, going on and on in repetitive cycles of the eternal samba.
> I walked along the backstage areas, after the second group had finished, to see if I could find any photos but there really wasn't enough light. Estacio de Sa were preparing themselves, almost ready to leave. [. . .] Mangueira, the last group, came on parade about 90 minutes later than scheduled because of the inevitable delays. I could barely keep my eyes open. The sun was already shining forcefully adding discomfort to the tiredness. I went backstage to have a look at the floats and fancy dress, what a mass of green and pink – the traditional Mangueira colours – very lush. I took a few pictures, including one of Chico Buarque who had joined the Commissao de Frente and was rehearsing movements in line. The best photos were taken just after dawn with gorgeous metallic blue skies as a background to the fancy dresses.
> The following night I did not take the camera, but regretted it right at the end, again when it was light and the Mocidade school was waiting to come

on, then there were some fantastic pictures to take – the school being so colourful and imaginative.

Of the slides I had printed for framing, two sets remain – a quarter of a century later – on display in my home. One consists of four views of Botofogo Bay: the Junina festival, showing several overcrowded boats decorated with coloured bunting; New Year's Eve on the beach with a low sun highlighting a myriad of offerings to Iemanjá, goddess of the sea; the sails of beached windsurfers in the foreground, echoing the shape of the Sugarloaf behind; and a sunset view so golden it looks hyper-real. The other set consists of four portraits of carnival participants, two groups taken on procession through the Sambodromo and two taken back stage.

Finally with regard to Brazil, there were two developments in my photography-related life worth mentioning. Early on, I discovered a book of photographs by Marc Ferrez (1843-1923) who had documented Brazil maturing into a nation as well as Rio de Janeiro expanding into a city. Because the book included a description of where each photograph had been taken, I was inspired to try and reproduce some of the views. I encountered any number of difficulties, some of which I was to re-experience many years later working on a book of then-and-now photographs of Brighton. The most striking of Ferrez's photographs were of wild, empty beaches, unrecognisable today as Copacabana and Ipanema. This was the first time I showed any interest in early photography and photographers. Thereafter, whenever on holiday or abroad for work I would seek out books of old photographs of whatever city I was in. I also found myself buying new and second hand books on the history of photography. Much later, 19th century photographs would be a significant motif in *Kip Fenn*, one of my novels.

The second development occurred in late December 1985, for this was the first time I placed a photograph (or any extraneous item) into my diary. Although the photograph was not even mine, and had no attributes as a photograph, this marked a physical uniting of the two modes of self-expression, and opened the way for very occasional insertions thereafter. My mother had telephoned from London to tell me Aunt Johnnie (Mike Goldsmith's first wife, and my godmother) had died. We weren't close but we wrote now and then. A few days later, a Christmas card arrived from my now-dead aunt. I glued into the diary a snap, taken by my brother, of her and her only daughter, my cousin Mary. I noted at the time Johnnie's face was out of focus, as if already fading away.

My first son, Adam, was born to Bel in London on 4 August 1987. Throughout his childhood, my camera lens never lost its impulse, its yearning to capture his beauty, his smile, his poise, his comic poses, his being. Concomitantly, other subjects got demoted, as it were, in relative importance. That said, a trip abroad always felt like an opportunity for photo-catching.

31 March 1988
Coming to the end of a tiring day. It is far more tiring being a tourist than being a journalist. At 10pm I'm ready to doss, yet I didn't get up until 8:30.

What is the purpose of wandering around endlessly just looking. I make purpose by searching for photographs. With slide film in the camera I impose a fairly rigorous quality control over which pictures I take, thus if I do take some there is an achievement. I also make purpose by trying to capture part of life, of the day, part of my experience, my thoughts, part of what I see in words on this paper. But truth will out and so much of tourism can be defined as dross. Already I have found it more interesting to write about the seediness of the hotel than the beauty of Stockholm. I have taken one or two pictures around the city but they were hard won, i.e. I walked a lot to get them.

In any case, my words, my pictures are what? No more (and no less) than my self-imposed purpose. Without those twin expressions I could barely bare to walk another city again.

1 May 1988
I took a few photographs of tombstones in snow, trying to capture some of the essence of Finland – rather an arrogant thing to do since I'd only been in the country two hours.

Also, a new place in England – Aldeburgh – came in for much lens action when I bought a small cottage there for Adam, Bel and I to spend weekends together (as we lived in separate houses in London). Again, as with those taken in Brazil, I organised the best photographs to be framed and to hang together as a set of six. By the time we sold the Aldeburgh cottage and bought a house in Brighton, so Bel could study for a degree there, my photographic self was very definitely on the wane. I'd been a regular visitor to Brighton for years, and the place, though photogenic, was not as fresh a subject as it might have been. Moreover, I had much else to do in my working life. Here I am in Brighton, trying to face up to the waning.

24 November 1989
Usually, I find it quite hard to discover photographs, even more so when I have black and white film in the camera – it is more difficult to get inspiration from just shapes and contrasts than from unusual colour schemes or the extra reality of an image that needs colour for effect. But this morning, with the sun low in the sky and streaming down alleyways, and through chimney stacks, I found myself more photographically inspired than for some time. However, as

I shot and stuffed my images away into the camera's film, I was also aware of how someone might critique my art. 'Rather desolate photography,' they would say, 'people only stray into the picture as extras, for some light relief from the stark house facades or intricate urban landscapes. Yes, he has a sense of shape and uses depth to contrast patterns in an interesting and surprising way (a sense of the surreal is never far away) but the spirit in his art is a mathematical, logical one, born of calculation and intellect rather than one connected directly to his emotions or feelings. As such, he shoots from the head not from the heart.'

And, as if it knew that my (and its) arty photographic days were numbered, the OM1n began malfunctioning. I didn't know exactly why, or how, for it had become quite inscrutable, but it was letting me down more and more often. Finally, in 1994, I let the old and beloved camera go; I took it to Jessops. There I let myself be persuaded to part-exchange it for a brash, sparkly new Minolta, but I'll let my diary take up the narrative.

27 November 1994
[…] In the end I got £175 for the OM1n and the two lenses plus an extra £25 for buying a camera with a trade in deal. So I ended up paying just over £100 for a £300 Minolta including a three year warranty; and, I was assured, the £300 itself was a special deal devised between Jessops and Minolta. The salesman also assured me it would take as good pictures as my OM1n [. . .] So, the upshot is that I now have a fully automatic Minolta – automatic aperture, automatic speed, automatic film roll on, automatic wind back (when the film is finished) and the lens has automatic focus, and a power zoom. Indeed, it even takes the picture on its own – I close my eyes and it decides where to point itself. […] Oh, but I am sad to have said goodbye to my OM1n, it has been so many places with me and I have taken so many pictures with it over the last 15 years.

The Minolta served me for about 10 years (until the digital revolution finally won me over) but I was never happy with it, we never got on well. Bel, Adam and I had moved to live in Elstead, a large village in Surrey, and our lives had become altogether more rural, more countryfied. I found a modicum of renewed interest in taking photographs, by focusing the lens on shapes and colours to be found on and around the peaty wild heathland filled with heathers, gorse, silver birch, Scot's pines, oaks, and, in autumn, mushrooms. Our new house was larger than the old, with many walls that needed decoration, so I embarked on a project to frame a select few of my photographs – most notably a set of nine that fit together in a three-by-three shape (though this can be tricky to hang).

27 April 2002
The most creative thing I've done for ages is to have hung my triple triptych of Elstead photos [. . .]: three pictures of purple heather (*Hither*, *Thither* and

155

Wither), three pictures of grasses (*In red, In blue, In green*), and three pictures of oaks with shadows of me taking the photograph (*Thin and Twisted, Old and Gnarled, Small and Fallen*).

The latter three – the self portraits and their names – were a conscious response to the bright and colourful self-portraits I had taken some twenty years earlier, and were meant to reflect how I felt about the state of growing old, jaded, faded and grumpy.

A couple of years later the Minolta and I were sparked into life by seeing an English Heritage advertisement for volunteer photographers. I signed up, attended a training session, and was given photographic film and a long list of targets within a 20 mile radius. The aim of the *Images of England* project was to collect a single 'defining image' of every listed building in the country, and make them all available as an online public record. An army of volunteers like myself were recruited, and we were only allowed to take one photograph of every listed building target. The film when finished was posted back to English Heritage with the relevant paperwork and notes, and many months later the images appeared on the *Images of England* website. This is still available as I write today and describes itself thus: 'Images of England is a "point in time" photographic library of England's listed buildings, recorded at the turn of the 21st century. You can view over 300,000 images of England's built heritage from lamp posts to lavatories, phone boxes to toll booths, mile stones to gravestones, as well as thousands of bridges, historic houses and churches.' One hundred and seventy five of these photographs are mine.

On paper this seemed an easy enough task, in practice it proved anything but. Often, locating the building or structure from the information given was problematic. Many times, too, it was impossible to take a reasonable photograph from public land, and so permission would be required from the owner. Sometimes he/she could be found, and then refused permission, and sometimes he/she couldn't be found. Sometimes, too, the light was all wrong on a first visit. Yet, the challenge of all this suited me and, indeed, my way of taking photographs – no fancy equipment, no multiple shots. When English Heritage told me there were no more targets in my vicinity I asked if there were any in northwest London, for I was spending one or two nights a week in Willesden at the time. It did. Coincidentally and serendipitously I was given a new set of targets that not only included one of my first schools, but also several in The Hill garden on Hampstead Heath – my secret garden – about which I've already written.

Around this time, or soon after, I began reading about digital cameras.

3 January 2004
Digital cameras seem to be sweeping the photography world, but I feel the technology is getting away from me. I've never been happy with my Minolta automatic, and I've been wondering whether I should buy a new camera – a more expensive one. But part of the reason I haven't got on with the Minolta is that I'm not one for fancy adjustments, my interest is in the creative way of choosing the photograph not in making it: I'm interested in making what I see more visible (showing something that is there but which might not have been seen); I am not interested in making, in recreating what is there in a different way.'

By 2007, I had succumbed, bought a mid-priced digital camera and taken it on a holiday tour of Cambodia. However, for the first few days I found myself preoccupied by the new technology.

5 March 2007
I did not take as many pics as I would have liked. In fact, the relationship with my new digital camera is in crisis! I've tried to explain this to a couple of people but not succeeded very well. The first and major problem (which is understood well) concerns the viewing screen. In strong sunlight it's not visible, so composing a shot becomes not just difficult but impossible. I am left to snap randomly, and this is the other problem. With my SLR I seek out photos, I try and compose them – the art and the interest is in the finding and choosing. But now with digital you can take as many photos as you like regardless of quality, and delete all or none or some. The picking and choosing comes afterwards, not before. Perhaps some people took film photos like that but I didn't. And this change affects when and why I get the camera out, or don't. [. . .] Not getting on well with my digital friend.

In fact, it did not take me long to adjust, and to fully appreciate the striking advantages of digital photography over film. I've got very used to a photographic life without any ongoing costs of buying and developing film. I love having a camera that can take high quality pictures and still fit comfortably in my pocket. And, truth be told, I like having the freedom to take a zillion pics. And I do take a zillion pics, but these are all of my young family, and our holidays and outings together. The taking and the viewing of such pics gives me and us enormous pleasure and satisfaction. Sometimes we use modern digital services to put them in albums or make calendars; and often we simply browse through them on a computer, which is far easier, and gives a better quality show than the old cumbersome business with a projector and screen. Occasionally, we post a pic or two online, on Facebook perhaps, wanting to share the beauty of our kids with friends, or bizarrely embarrass ourselves dressed up in wigs or doing silly dances.

I like to think I haven't lost a modest ability to compose a decent photograph, but the days of trying to make art with my camera, and being impressed enough with the results to frame them, are long gone. A couple more projects have come my way, though not as satisfying as the *Images of England* gig, but enjoyable nonetheless. I wrote a book on diary extracts about Brighton, and the publishers, The History Press, wanted an illustration for each chapter. For several of the chapters I couldn't find any usable portraits so I supplied photos of Brighton. On the back of this, The History Press asked if I wanted to author one of their *Then & Now* series for Brighton. The skill of this was choosing 45 mostly Victorian photographs (from a limited range of scenes) and taking a modern photograph of the same view that showed change, whether for good or bad. Taking the modern photos was a challenge, thanks to constantly inclement weather, awkward road alignment *vis-à-vis* the light on sunny days, scaffolding, road works, parked lorries, traffic and traffic signage. Although I was obviously not confined to taking a single shot as I had been with the English Heritage project, it was still exacting, and sometimes impossible, to find an interesting way of capturing the modern scene to emulate the old.

Finally, I should mention *Graffiti Brighton*, a project I embarked on because of the possibilities opened up by both the internet and digital photography. Once a year, or so, when I have the time, I zip out on my bicycle every day for a month or more and take photographs of graffiti found around Brighton. I upload them to the *Graffiti Brighton* website, with street names and made-up oddball titles for each one. At the time of writing, I have nearly a thousand such photographs on the site.

I do, it seems, given half a chance, still like to be a photographer, even if all my arty pretentions have dematerialised with time. I may use but a tiny digital camera, and point it mostly at my family, yet the pleasure of the lens remains, whether in the snapping itself or in the enjoyment of the photos, recent and past.

Chapter fourteen

BRAZIL
A NEW WORLD OF ADVENTURES

Looking back, my two year period working in Brazil seems very much like a colourful escapade in what had become, to my mind then, a relatively black and white life; a half-time interval of fireworks, perhaps, in a dullish game; an intermission of adventures in the otherwise regular flow of life. At the time, however, I believed I was heading to live and work in the New World to renew myself, to find again the man who had taken risks, who had travelled so widely, who had met and engaged with so many different people, the man for whom, once upon a time, every day had been different and brought new adventures.

Ever since returning from my three year travels, I had talked of going back to Brazil, but this time to live there. It was not until I went to work for McGraw-Hill, with its worldwide operations, that I had any inkling this dream might be possible. Over the course of a year or so I built on the inkling, schemed at work, and when a slight opportunity actually arose, I hesitated not.

With rigorous intent, I planned and executed my move to Rio carefully, I would say, and professionally. On arriving in Rio, I was full of focus, all business. My priorities in order were, first, to find a place to live (shining luck and persistence led me to the most wonderful apartment); second, to establish communication links to clients (which proved unbelievably complicated); third, to get in touch with those local contacts I already had (most of which proved how difficult my work would be); and, fourth, to accelerate my learning of Portuguese so as to read the business newspapers, and make new contacts. It was two weeks before I allowed myself the luxury of a swim in the sea; yet only another week before I was regularly filing stories, including for The Economist.

Without doubt, I had come to Brazil to work, and this remained my priority for the duration – all the renewing and re-finding of myself was to be done this time, as opposed to during my hippie 20s, through or alongside a working life. I had no intention of reverting to peripatetic ways. Life as a freelance correspondent was a brilliant compromise; I loved the freedom, the variety, the need for self-discipline, and being self-reliant. There were a few downsides: lack of a reliable regular income, a tendency to fret if ever the leads dried up for a day, and a lack of respect from many, but not all, editors in their New York or London offices. I focused on specialised articles about Brazil's exciting and upcoming industries such as energy, chemicals, transport and metals. In time, I built a good (and lucrative) network of publications that wanted regular material from me.

I did enough travelling in and around Brazil to be satisfied that I was making full use of my time, and that I was getting to know the country a little better than I had first time round with Nene and Christian. Most of my more distant excursions were work led – petrochemical plants in the south, a uranium processing unit in the interior, huge iron mines in the northeast, an experimental agricultural station in the Cerrado – but I travelled locally too, up or down the coast with friends, to Buzios or Paraty, for example. And, of course, I had Rio itself to explore, its extraordinarily beautiful setting, beaches and views; the mind-boggling contrasts between rich and poor, privileged and ragged; and its many magic places off the tourist trail. Mostly, I moved around the city on a Yamaha trail bike that I bought, loving warm wind in my face, and the freedom to ride wearing only shorts, a t-shirt and flip-flops, no helmet.

Socially, to begin with, I felt disconcerted. My diaries reveal a chronic carping at myself for not managing to meet or befriend more people, or more interesting people, or for not having a wilder time of it. Yet I can find this kind of chronic self-criticism in the diaries at most points of my life, and on closer inspection I'm usually not quite sure what it is I am wanting – unless, of course, it was the unsustainable high of those special times in Fordwych Road, with Harold, Marielle and clown make-up on my face.

I made early contact with other journalists, and with ex-pats through the British Council, but what I most wanted was to become involved with Brazilians, and Brazilian society. Within a month I was seeing Elaine, a flautist and music teacher from the northeast, who – perfectly – spoke almost no English. We remained friendly, and more often than not very friendly, throughout my two years in Rio. I have much to thank her for, not only in terms of learning Portuguese, but in learning about Brazilian people and their ways.

Brazil was first discovered by Western colonialists when a Portuguese fleet landed in Porto Seguro in 1500. Portugal's early interest in the land lay in monopolising trade in pau-brasil red wood, used for making dye – and it is from the tree that the country is named. The indigenous peoples proved unwilling labourers, and so slaves were brought in from Africa. Around mid-century, a capital was established at Salvador, and remained there until 1763, when Rio de Janeiro was chosen as the new capital. By this time, the Portuguese had staved off various at-tempted invasions, and Brazil had become roughly the size and shape it is today. Moreover, precious minerals, emeralds, diamonds and espe-cially gold had been discovered in the interior which led to the rapid and rich growth of many towns.

When Napoleon chased the Portuguese royal family out of Lisbon they settled in Rio, modernising the city and opening the port to trade. Then Dom João VI returned to Portugal, leaving his son Pedro I to govern. In 1822, Pedro declared independence and established the Brazilian empire; but it was not until the second half of the century, under Pedro II, that a stable regime allowed the economy to expand, and a parliamentary system to evolve. His daughter, Princess Isabel ended slavery in 1888; soon after unhappy landowners sided with the military to dispatch the monarchy, and to form, in 1889, Brazil's first republic. For the next 100 years or so, the republic was run mostly by military dictators, and occasionally by democratically elected presidents.

Getúlio Vargas, the longest serving leader (after Pedro II), and remembered as 'father of the poor', served first as dictator, before winning a second democratically-elected term. Juscelino Kubitschek, another elected president, nearly bankrupted the country through building Brasilia, inaugurated in 1960. The military again took over in 1964, with its tanks and technocratic approach to development, and was still in place when I first visited the country in the mid-1970s. Compared to the junta that had ruled in neighbouring Argentina since 1976, though, Brazil's regime was benign: whereas official statistics blame the Brazilian government for around 300 political deaths in the 1964-1981 period; it is thought 30,000 people disappeared in Argenti-na between 1976 and 1983.

I arrived in Brazil in late March 1985, just days after the formal and peaceful transition to a democratic government presided over by vice-president José Sarney. Yet the country's joy at finally shedding military rule was overshadowed by the sudden illness – on the eve of his inauguration – and then death of the man they loved and who had been elected president, Tancredo Neves. It was an extraordinary turn of events. I wrote home.

We are all in mourning. As far as the Brazilian people are concerned the death of Tancredo is the greatest tragedy there has ever been. On Monday, two mil-lion people were in the streets of Sao Paulo following his funeral cortege, yes-terday one and a half million thronged through the streets of Belo Horizonte and forced open the gates of the Palacio de Libertade in order to be able to see him one last time. The people to a man loved Tancredo. He united this huge country of poverty and riches, Africans and Germans, military and com-munists. He gave hope and direction, and more or less singlehandedly guided the powerbrokers from authoritarianism to democracy. The hope of 120 million people for a better future rested on this one man's shoulders and then, then on the very day [before he was] to assume power he falls fatally ill.

A few months later I attended a press conference with Sarney, he who had so unexpectedly found power, and he who would remain the country's president throughout my stay. 'So many journalists and so much buzz, constant clicking of cameras, the television crews rumbling at the back,' I wrote in my diary. '[A colleague] said he presented himself better than expected. It all sounded pretty wishy washy to me, and the three people on the platform with him looked pretty washed out too!' His presidency proved pretty wishy-washy by the end, and he was replaced in 1990 by Fernando Collor de Mello. Having been one of Brazil's foremost oligarchs, wielding enormous power in the state of Maranhão, Sarney finally retired in 2015, after serving in elected office almost continuously for 60 years.

My first task on landing at Rio airport was to navigate through customs without my luggable Kaypro computer – the size and shape of a suitcase – being confiscated indefinitely. Many were the tales I'd heard of this happening, but my strategy was to scribble pen marks and stick labels all over the metal casing making it look old, used, and of very little value. It felt like I'd won the jackpot when I emerged outside the airport buildings, my passport and work visa all duly authorised, and all my belongings in tact. I installed myself in a cheapish hotel in downtown Rio, and for the days I was there worried constantly about my room being robbed, or my own self being mugged on the way to or from the building, whether by foot or taxi – there being no safe way to store or look after valuables.

I focused exclusively and intensely on the search for a place to live, and in less than a week I had found the perfect, the most perfect place – a beautiful, spacious, light, relatively cheap, two-bedroom apartment in an art deco building, overlooking Botafogo Bay, just metres away from the water. I wrote about how this happened in my diary under the title 'Anatomy of luck' because there seemed so many random and coincidental events that had led me to this good fortune. The event chain started with a Brazilian girl ringing me in London, only days before I was about to leave, to exchange language conversation – we did once. She gave me the name of a friend in Rio, who I also met only once, but who taught me how to ask building porters about rentable apartments (rather than scour newspaper ads or use agencies). Having done this in restless Copacabana and Ipanema without success, I tried quiet Urca – which hugs the rocky shore line at the base of the Sugar Loaf – after a first visit to the British Council there. I walked along the sea front road, randomly asking any porter I could find for news of vacant flats. I was about to abandon the quest when I spied one more porter. He nodded me towards another man cleaning his car, who further suggested I seek out someone called Senhor Mucio, further along the road. He wasn't in. It was such a long shot, I might easily not have bothered to trek back to Urca later that day, but I did. Mucio immediately walked me along to another building a few blocks from his own, where he owned an apartment that had just been vacated. He spoke good English, which helped a lot, and he liked that I was British. When, a few days later, I found it would cost hundreds of pounds (I didn't have) to 'buy' a telephone line (demand being so high), he agreed to help me out by financing the line out of my deposit.

The apartment had a large windowed balcony front, overlooking the bay. This is where I worked for the next two years, regularly popping down to the rocks for a swim, and occasionally stringing a hammock above my desk to read or nap. Behind the lounge area, with its old-fashioned furniture and polished wood floor, there was a small kitchen and a shower room. I soon found Maria, referred by another tenant in the block, who came three days a week to clean, to do my washing and to cook. She was something of an angel, always good-humoured, efficient and hard working. She made such simple tasty foods (and cakes) to be eaten on the day or later, that I barely had to do any housework myself. If, to begin with, I was uncomfortable with the idea of having a maid, someone doing things for me all the time, I soon got used to it thanks to Maria's easy way of being. But she did more than simple house duties. She helped me with speaking and understanding the language (for she spoke no English), and through her I was able to find out much about normal, every day life in Brazil. And as my Portuguese improved, so she was able to help me interpret more subtle aspects of the society around me, my relationships with neighbours, tradesmen, and even my girlfriends. Moreover, on days when I might otherwise have felt too alone, or even lonely, I felt reassured by her presence in the flat.

Maria rarely brought any of her own private life to my apartment or to our conversation, but I did find out that her father had pressed her to marry at 14. She had had one child with her (violent) husband but left them in the northeast and come to Rio. She married again and had two more children, but had separated from their father also; and she was still only in her mid-20s. Of course, I paid her significantly above the going rate, but it was still a pittance by Western standards.

With the apartment sorted, the next challenge was establishing lines of communication. Mucio's help with the telephone was the first and most important step. The next was to head downtown to the Reuters office, from where – thanks to an agreement with McGraw-Hill – I was able to use the telex machines, to file stories. This was a laborious process. Having typed an article out once already in the writing, I had to type it out again on the clunky telex keypad. Sometimes, also, I had to wait until the machine was free, which could be a pain. On the upside, this gave me a chance to chat to Silvio. While I found the English journalists at Reuters rather stuck-up and self-important, I had a lot of time for Silvio, a locally-employed salesman, who spoke perfect English, and did so with much humour.

Undoubtedly, having a computer to write on was a boon. Throughout my first job, at *European Chemical News*, we had all used typewriters; then, at McGraw-Hill, we had begun to use computers, and we had pioneered sending text to printers by modem. The Kaypro computer I had bought in New York – one of the very first that could actually be transported easily – had a green screen no larger than a postcard, but, nevertheless, I loved it. I loved the ease of writing, being able to change and rewrite without the text looking a mess, and I loved how efficient it made the writing process. It was hooked up to a printer, but also I was hoping I could link it, by modem and telephone, to a computer in New York, and file stories direct from my apartment. Doing so proved far more difficult than I had hoped, and it was only after six months, once I'd discovered a Brazilian firm that was starting to manufacture modems that functioned with the Brazilian telephone system, that I was able to make progress.

8 October 1985
When talking to anyone outside of the business I call them magic boxes. The method in which they transmit the material stored in my computer to any reception computer in the world is surely magic. Who will send letters one day when all you need to do is write on your mini-television and press a button. Hey presto it's on your friend's TV screen half way round the world. Well, the idea is but a hair's breadth from reality.

A modem salesman came to my apartment, and set up a trial with my computer – it worked. I was joyous, but when my own modem arrived, could I get it to work? Of course not. It took weeks of trial and error, of fiddling with buttons, trying every one of a large number of possible settings and then making expensive international phone calls to test them. When, at last, the computer-modem connection functioned, I wrote in my diary: 'I finally got the fucking modem working.' Any exasperation was short-lived, for the modem did indeed prove to be a magic box, saving me so much time and effort, and, perhaps, doubling my productivity. It also attracted attention: soon other journalists were wanting to see it in action. At that time, I was still only able to file stories in this way to McGraw-Hill's New York based publications; McGraw-Hill in London and other publishers I worked for did not have the capability to receive text sent by modem.

Work itself proved challenging and rewarding. I felt I had done the right thing professionally, by escaping from the narrow confines of oil and chemical price reporting, to become more of a real journalist, writing real articles for real magazines. But gearing up the work, at least at the beginning, proved tougher than I expected. On arriving in Brazil, I had, or thought I had, three types of work: regular reports on the petrochemical industry for my ex-boss in the London McGraw-Hill office; freelance strings (i.e. informal but committed arrangements to provide copy) for a range of McGraw-Hill publications based in the US; and strings for various other (non-McGraw-Hill) London-based publications. For the first of these, I already had contacts, and knew exactly what was wanted and when.

But the US strings proved a different matter altogether. Although Jeff Ryser, McGraw-Hill bureau chief in Sao Paolo, had implied I would be able to take over Charlie Thurston's strings, by the time I got to Rio, other freelancers had already pinched them. I was left with McGraw-Hill's oil and nuclear publications, both of which already had a Rio stringer – Hank. However, the editors were dissatisfied with the amount of copy, i.e. news, they were getting on a regular basis. McGraw-Hill, or Jeff in particular, had tempted me to Brazil with the hope of boosting supply for the publications – but without actually being clear about the Hank situation. The role was a poisoned chalice, since Hank had no intention of letting his strings be filched by an incomer. Not only did he re-invigorate his efforts at getting oil and nuclear stories, but he tried to use his press contacts of old to make life difficult for me. I liked Hank, he was a real old timer; and it soon became apparent that he had so many clients that he couldn't match the time and effort I was able to put in for the oil and nuclear publications.

The string for McGraw-Hill's daily oil bulletin proved most lucrative. Brazil's oil exploration and production industry was already booming, with huge finds in the Atlantic, and a fast-growing refining and petrochemical sector taking good economic advantage of the oil, so there was much to write about. The state-owned oil company, Petrobras, based in Rio, was one of Brazil's most powerful. It had no history of communicating regularly with foreign correspondents, though it had a well-established group of Brazilian journalists with easy access to a press room and arrangements for high-level interviews. I struggled, initially, for acceptance among the press staff, and then had to pretend, in briefings, I understood more than I did. Nevertheless, my interest and perseverance paid off as I landed more and more articles in McGraw-Hill's oil bulletin.

The nuclear string was a different story entirely. McGraw-Hill's highly respected *Nucleonics Week* paid an impressive $3 for every line it published, but it did not confine itself to industrial matters and loved scoops and rumours on secret programmes to develop a nuclear bomb. The 1970s had seen both Argentina and Brazil embark on rival programmes, acquiring enrichment technology, ostensibly for nuclear power production, but which also could be used to make fuel for nuclear bombs. I arrived in Brazil at a time when a first, but troubled, nuclear power station was starting up, and when the authorities were denying any secret programme to develop bomb capabilities. I made good contact with the state-owned organisations involved in the nuclear industry; but this was to no good purpose since they all had a strict policy of saying nothing of any import to the press. Indeed, *Nucleonics Week* published more ($3-a-line) news about Brazil's nuclear enrichment and power developments, or lack of, written by a rival correspondent in Buenos Aires than it did from me. It was not only that Rik Kessler, my opposite number in the Argentine capital, had good contacts, it was that Argentina had a different, more complicated, policy on dealing with the press on nuclear matters, and was not beyond deliberately trying to embarrass Brazil for its own political ends. When *Nucleonics Week* failed to publish a long piece from me, based on a one-to-one exclusive interview I had had with a vice-president of the Brazilian nuclear company in favour of a sexier piece about Brazil from Argentine sources, I gave up in a fit of despair (and angry letters). Instead, I filed stories to a highly-respected, UK-based nuclear monthly. Its editor loved my articles, and published every word I sent (but paid a quarter as much).

This was an interesting lesson to learn about myself. I worked harder and better for editors who took the time to remember who I was, to be pleasant, and to be respectful of the work I was doing for them. Asked nicely to do something, I was anyone's stringer; treated in a dismissive or disrespectful manner, I was nobody's fool, even for $3 a line.

Apart from McGraw-Hill publications, I wrote for several UK magazines, the most well known of which were *The Economist* and *Flight International*. I never quite got *The Economist* house style right, and my stories for the business and science sections received more editing than anything I wrote for any other publication. At times, I considered the editing excessive, even to the point of introducing errors. Other times, an article would be held back from one week to the next, by which time it had evolved, leaving my text dated. The effect of this was amplified because every *Economist* article on Brazil was translated and published, a week or two later, in a similar Brazilian publication *O Senhor*. No one ever complained to me about mistakes or outdatedness, and *The Economist* continued to take my stories. Each one took a lot of work, and £90 a piece never felt like adequate financial recompense; but I liked the editors – Matt Ridley was science editor at the time – and I liked the kudos of being an *Economist* freelancer.

I also had a lot of time for David Learmount at *Flight International*. He was the most nurturing of editors, and very much encouraged my writing on aviation, which, again, was an industry experiencing exciting growth in Brazil, both in terms of aircraft construction and transport demand. A couple of the features I wrote for Learmount are among the most memorable of my assignments. One was about the so-called Air Bridge between Rio and Sao Paolo, which claimed to be the world's first air shuttle service. For another, I went to Belo Horizonte to interview José Afonso Assumpção, the founder of Lider, the largest air taxi service in Latin America at the time. I learned that he and the founder/president of the famous TV channel, Globo, had swapped advertising time for aircraft hire – 'Air time for airtime' was the catchy headline. Another interesting, but frustrating, trip took me to Brasilia to find out more about the Brazilian air force, and future aircraft orders. Defence ministry interviews were cancelled or delayed and in my spare time I became frustrated by the city's futuristically impractical layout, and I found the architecture dispiriting from a human point of view.

Occasionally, lucrative assignments came my way. One of these saw me flown into the Cerrado, a vast tropical savannah hinterland, where Shell Brasil – the largest private company at the time – had a major government-backed reforestation project. My task was to write a feature – for Shell's flagship international publication *Shell World* – about Fazenda Jacoba, covering 70,000 hectares, of which 30,000 had already been planted. On returning to Rio, I delivered my copy in good time, and expected to hear nothing further until a cheque arrived. Unfortunately for the young press officer who had recruited me, something was wrong. I didn't know what, but an interview was arranged for me to meet with a key executive. Having no inkling as to the reason for the interview, I had no questions prepared, and started by asking the executive why he wanted to see me. The interview was terminated without further ado, and in consequence, I suspect, my friend in the press office was sacked. I realised too late that diplomacy had been required of me, the bigwig simply needed to be consulted, and, perhaps, to be quoted in the feature.

Another fascinating trip was to the north, to visit what became the world's biggest iron ore mine at Carajás, controversial because its owner, the state-owned mining concern, CVRD, had to unsettle native tribes. The open cast mines were then, and later, huge scars in the Amazon rainforest. Ugly.

I delayed my trip back south to take part in a weekend tour of a beautiful and unspoilt island situated at the mouth of the Amazon, Marajó. During the press visit, I'd got on well with one of the CVRD staff, a lawyer named Edna, and it was she who suggested I join her for a bit of tourism. We journeyed for several hours through the night on a ferry, before reaching our hotel, and then spent two days travelling quietly on river boats and canoes along narrow tributaries watching out for strange fish and noisy monkeys. Beautiful and mesmerising.

It is hard to be precise about how much I managed to earn as a freelancer in Brazil, partly because the dollar-pound exchange rate fluctuated such a lot, and partly because inflation has significantly reduced the value of both currencies. At a peak, I was earning $4,000 a month, and for the second year, I think, I averaged above $3,000 – probably £4,000-5,000 in today's money.

I loved living in Urca. Apart from the views across the bay, and being able to swim from the rocks in front of my apartment, it had other benefits. It was one of the safest places in Rio, being a tiny closed-off suburb with a single road entrance, all traffic having to pass a police point. There was a small beach just a few minutes walk from my building, with a great little cafe, Garota da Urca, and a little further along, at the end of the peninsula, some kind of quasi military establishment. This was one of Rio's secret places, for it opened up on Sundays allowing locals to ramble round the old fort ruins, and to take advantage of a fabulous beach, nestling quietly and peacefully at the foot of the Sugar Loaf.

Through a friend, I met a geologist, Robbert, who also lived in Urca. He was obsessed with the Sugar Loaf, and would climb it every day, sometimes more than once. There were several routes, some easier than others and even walkable – another Rio secret. Once at the top, I was certainly impressed with the view.

7 April 1985
The view from Pao de Azucar is extraordinary. Probably the most extraordinary vista in the urban world – 360 degrees of spectacle. There is the fat crowded beach of Copacabana, the empty beaches on the other side of the channel, the pocket beaches directly below Urca showing the difference in populations between the public beach near me and the two beaches in the military compound at the far end of Urca, the many deserted islands, the rocky outcrops, the boats, the airport, the forts, the drilling rig, the bridge to

Niteroi, the panorama of Niteroi itself, Corcovado of course, and so on. Quite extraordinary.

I bought a bicycle soon after settling in Urca – having never lived without one – but I soon found it tiresome to use. The heat was one problem, distances were another, and traffic speed/density was a third: on leaving Urca, to go downtown or to Copacabana, I was obliged to cycle on dual carriageways that were more like banger race tracks crowded with duelling buses and taxis than urban routes. Before long, I'd bought a motorbike – a Yamaha 180 DT trail machine. I knew nothing about motorbikes, and only bought this model because a neighbour was selling it. With a lifetime of bicycle road-sense in my subconscious, learning to control the thing didn't take long, and in days I was merrily racing through traffic, high on the speed and freedom of it, and getting anywhere I wanted in minutes. There seemed to be little policing of road traffic rules in the city (cars regularly ran red lights, for example), and I was able to ride the bike, when it suited, in nothing more than a pair of shorts and flip-flops, though it was easier with stouter shoes. I did have a helmet, but hated wearing it. Once, and only once, the police at the control box entering Urca pulled me up for a helmet infringement. I pulled out a small amount of money bills, and was immediately reprimanded for being so blatant – they had expected me to palm the backhander not flash it.

For a year, I lived a charmed life, but eventually I was stopped – some 20 miles from Rio on an inter-city road – where the traffic police, I found out to my cost, were less 'flexible' than those at the Urca police point. I was pulled over for not wearing a helmet, and then the bike was impounded because I didn't have a licence. This created a highly awkward problem for me since I was due to fly to London in 10 days or so, and I feared if I left my bike with the rural police for that long, I'd never get it back. I spent most of the next week trying to get a licence legitimately, which meant jumping through all kinds of hoops, written exams, lessons, then a final afternoon with over 100 prospective bikers and various examiners dressed like road diggers, all milling around a large testing area. The actual riding test was short and easy, but the bike assigned to me broke down while I was navigating a figure of eight. Earlier in the week, I had asked the driving lesson company whether I should bribe the examiner, as friends had suggested this was normal, but had been told it would not be necessary if I thought I had passed. I thought I had, but was given a fail. I lost my temper, mostly with the company that had organised me through the process, for it was their motorbike and, I also realised, they had mis-taught me on some points. Writing in my diary later, I felt I had handled the situation dreadfully.

27 June 1986
I left the site fuming, although, had I controlled myself and discussed the situation humbly with the examiner, it may have been possible to find a jeitinho. In my vague memory, he seemed interested in what I had to say, whereas I was tensed-up with all these people around – too tense to stand around calmly discussing my situation when there were so many others waiting to take the test. I may pretend a Brazilian manner but in a crisis out pops that tense little English arrogance.

The word 'jeitinho', by the way, comes from the expression 'dar um jeito', i.e. 'find a way', and is a particularly Brazilian way of managing situations by circumventing rules or social conventions.

Without a licence, there was no way the highway police would give me back my moto. So, instead, I inveigled a Brazilian friend, Neco, to help, and a friendly taxi driver I knew, Chico, to drive us up to Petropolis in the hills far from Rio, where the bike was impounded. Though we did have permission from one office, a vindictive policeman refused to release the bike, and I had to rely on Neco and Chico negotiating a jeitinho before Neco was allowed to drive it away. He stored it in his own garage while I was in the UK, and on my return I opted not to go through the whole examination procedure again but to buy a black market licence.

With the motorbike I was able to explore Rio with ease. Apart from the famous beaches of Copacabana, Ipanema and Leblon, there was much else to enjoy: Ilha das Cobras in the centre; a large and picturesque cemetery in Botafogo; the botanical garden and Jockey Club near Lagoa; rich enclaves in Gavea; windy narrow streets and colonial houses in Santa Teresa; the journey to Corcovado through Tijuca Forest. Occasionally, I took the moto out of Rio, to Petropolis for example, or Buzios along the coast, where I shared a weekend cottage with friends, but the trail bike wasn't comfortable on long rides.

Festivals. Brazil is famous, of course, for its February carnival. As a journalist, I was able to wangle a press pass (even though oil and metal publications didn't really need a samba correspondent). This allowed me free access throughout the Sambodromo, a purpose-built arena with concrete seating rising up on either side of a long wide parade route through which the samba school processions dance, drum and sing in their thousands. It is an awe-inspiring spectacle, about which I've written in chapter thirteen. But carnival is more than the official competitions between samba schools and the formally organised processions, for the streets everywhere are also full of music and dance and costumes.

I've also mentioned the Festa Junina, and the hundreds of crowded bunting-strewn vessels that filled Botafogo Bay. Each boat moved in a circular direction, passing in a channel between a cute statue of São Pedro, the saint of fishermen, and a small church on the Urca roadside. A master of ceremonies with microphone attached to immense loudspeakers welcomed each boat, big and small, as it gently nudged past, and the crew of each craft cheered as they heard their boat's name. In the evening, many giant hot air balloons made of paper (some as big as houses) were launched into the sky, this despite being illegal because of the considerable fire risks. One balloon I witnessed being launched was about four metres across. The air inside was heated with a burner until fully expanded, after which scores of little brightly coloured cups holding candles were hung around the lower half of the paper sphere. A very long tail of string and wire, with more candle-cups, was also attached. Finally, a kind of cradle of burning material was wired into the mouth of the balloon. This heated the air inside, and soon the whole thing slowly and grandly lifted into the air. The balloon paper was blandly coloured, but the candle cups around it were all bright yellow, while those along the tail were bright red. It was spectacular for a few minutes, but, unfortunately, the balloon burst into flames before even the tail had fully lifted from the ground. As midnight approached, though, the Rio sky became alive with hundreds of custom-made balloons and tails dazzling, sparkling up, up and away through the night.

Candles feature prominently on New Year's Eve, too, when Cariocas flock to the beaches to pay homage to Iemanjá, the goddess of the sea. Starting long before sunset, they build small and large personal offerings in the sand, with candles, white flowers, mirrors, shells, food. However, Copacabana has long since turned New Year's Eve into a much bigger party, and even the non-religious come, dressed in white, carrying flowers, willing to press their way to the water's edge just to wet their feet. Thousands of sea craft jostle for position as close to the beach as they can get. Music blares out from the hotels, and immense and impressive firework displays fill the sky as midnight approaches.

Oh, but how I loved tripping through Brazil. I went a couple of times with my neighbour Cecilia to Paraty Mirim, close by the pretty colonial town of Paraty. Access to her house, built on stilts by the water's edge, was by rowing boat. A minute's walk, round a bend hidden from view, was a deserted beach of golden sand, and turquoise waters.

When Julian, my brother, visited for a holiday we travelled by coach to Salvador in Bahia, which was full of churches, mostly looking dilapidated on the outside and full of baroque ornamentation on the inside. It was on this trip that I read Jorge Amado's brilliant and ultra-Brazilian novel, *Gabriela*; and for my diary I turned several chance encounters into my own Gabrielas. One was 'a husky, dusky mulatta with strong beautiful features and thick long black hair falling across eyes that would otherwise open and shine on you'. Another was the girl we met on the beach, 'who stretched out her lanky body of unblemished skin, so scantily clad, close to mine'. Many years, later, I wove a story line about one of these Gabrielas into *Kip Fenn*.

When Bel came out to Rio, for two weeks, we explored more distant parts of Rio de Janeiro state, like Itatiaia National Park, where we stayed in a log cabin, and went in search of dream-like forest waterfalls. In my diary, I wrote about one drive through a valley so remote, so quiet and unpeopled, it made me think of Erewhon, the eponymous forgotten land of Samuel Butler's world. And there were a couple of trips also to the gold-rush towns in Minais Gerais, like Ouro Preto, and to Ilha Grande, a small undeveloped island west of Rio, once notorious for pirates, lepers, and more recently for an isolated prison.

I discovered much about Brazil, New World life, from my journalistic work and from my travels. Here was a culture, a society, surprisingly unbeholden to the West, so large in itself, so brimming with confidence (industrial and artistic) that it seemed to pay little attention to Europe or North America. And yet, everywhere one cared to look the new, the modern, the fast enriching was rubbing shoulders with poverty. Favelas were everywhere in Rio, especially on the hill tops, and often in the news, but I probably learned more about favela life many years later in the film *City of God*, than I did when I was there.

Finally, for it seems I have dallied too long in this intermission, in this Brazilian dreamtime, I must also write a little about the people I spent time with. By and large, they were split into two groups, the journalists and ex-pats in one, and a few Brazilians in the other. I could not have done without my ex-pat friends, contacts and acquaintances, but I never stopped complaining to my diary that I seemed unable to find and integrate myself into a Carioca network of people I liked.

In the ex-pat group were several other freelancers, like myself, a couple of whom had children with Brazilian girlfriends, only to find themselves adrift after a while, and returning to Europe alone. A loose group of ex-pats played volleyball regularly, and though the gameplay was mostly ragged I felt needy of the social contact. We also gathered sometimes at the weekend for a feijoada, the Brazilian national dish, a stew of beans and pork, a party of a meal which would take all afternoon and half the evening too. And on Sunday nights, there was a gafiera at Circo Voador – gafiera being a samba-type dance, or, more loosely, a dance hall or occasion – where Brazilians of all classes and all dancing abilities came together to dance till they dropped. Though I was usually very reluctant to actually dance, the music was so alive it was impossible to stay still. I have always been overly self-conscious about dancing, my head steps in to monitor if I'm keeping rhythm rightly, and even if I am then I lose it. Apart from the music and the electric atmosphere one could spend all night just watching the better dancers, many of them showing off with flamboyant steps and twirls.

Through the British Council, I met British Consulate diplomats, and their wider circle, and received invites to parties, cultural events, and even a cricket match. By far and away the most fruitful connection was with Stan, a retired Shell man, who owned a large and very beautiful, wood-built sailing boat called *Tuna*. Stan was a member of the exclusive Rio Yacht Club, and Tuna was moored out in the bay where I could see it from my apartment. Although I had no sailing experience, Stan soon co-opted me to join his crew for occasional races, and taught me what I needed to know. These races were a lot of fun. Stan would direct operations in between serving up cocktails and preparing a meal. Once fed and well-watered, as it were, he would sit on deck, flabby top exposed, smiling broadly, and admire his crew's progress through the blue waters, and fabulous scenery. Sometimes, the weather was a little stormy, and we all got rocked around a bit, wet, fed up; yet I always looked forward to a call from Stan.

I should also mention the Royal Ballet, who on tour came to perform at Rio's Teatro Municipal in March 1986. I met, and fell in love with, several of the troupe at a British Council welcome party, and thereafter acted informally as their social secretary. The tour manager, Clair, found me a ticket for the gala night, so I was able to witness Rio's finest put on their best glitter, dazzle and costume for a visiting Princess Anne and the Sarneys. In exchange, I took Clair and some of the dancers to the gafiera at Circo Voador for a most wonderful night. Well, I was in heaven, surrounded by several beautiful women, all of whom had taken to me so warmly, except for the fact that they all kept trying to persuade me to dance with them. As I've said, I've always been insecure enough about my dancing that it was a bit of a nightmare suddenly being pressed to dance with professionals, such gorgeous professionals at that. Damn, it had never occurred to me I might have to dance with them. After, in the middle of the night, they wanted to know if it was safe to walk back to the hotel. As long as they stayed close together, I said. So they bunched up very close and stepped in time picking their way carefully along the pavement, while I shepherded them on my motorbike. Very funny.

While work, travel, and ex-pat/British Council connections all brought me into contact with Brazil's highlights, if I can put it that way, I came closest, I suppose, to being fully in, and part of, Brazil through girlfriends. Charlie Thurston had said I would need a revolving door, implying that Brazilian women were not difficult to meet, at least for young Americans or Brits. I'd met Charlie, a McGraw-Hill freelancer working in Sao Paolo, during my 1984 conference trip to Brazil, and it was being with him that had turned my dreaming about moving to Brazil into more of a concrete plan. Charlie made the idea seem not only possible, but more exciting than I had envisaged. But I was no Charlie, and I suspect Charlie needed a revolving door wherever he lived, not just in Brazil.

That said, I did slip into affairs more easily than I had done for years in London. I felt that, like everything else in this country, there was a New World character to social interaction; relationships seemed far less weighed down with worries about the future, or indeed the past, than they did at home. Elaine – dark-skinned and small, with wild black hair and bright red, smiling lips – was already a part of my Rio life before a month had passed, and she remained a regular visitor to my apartment, sometimes more sometimes less, throughout the two years. She had been brought up in the northeast, played the flute, and worked as a teacher. I don't think Maria ever approved of her, and Elaine was always rather disrespectful of Maria (and even more so of her own maid), though she didn't mind quizzing her about my other liaisons. But Elaine was fun, undemanding, sensual, available, and spoke so little English that we always communicated in Portuguese, much to my benefit.

Then, confusingly, there was Eliane, who picked me up at a party, and for a few months we went about as a couple. I had a much better time of it socially with Eliane, as she took me along to meet friends, to parties, on outings, and through her I became friendly with a few other Cariocas. Despite my half-hearted entreaties for her to do so, Elaine never stopped visiting. Once, this double-timing led to Charlie's revolving door metaphor whacking me in the face. Early on in the relationship with Eliane, she arrived at my apartment an hour earlier than planned, while Elaine was still hanging around, draped in but a sheet. The building porter had let Eliane in, unwittingly or wittingly, and the door to the apartment was unlocked. Somewhat phased, I quickly ushered Eliane back down to her car, enquiring, my diary says, 'pitifully' why she had arrived so early. I don't think either women was as unsettled by the experience as I was. After a while, though, it was Elaine's easy loving that outlasted Eliane's social whirligigs.

I had one other significant relationship in Brazil, with Rosa, and through her absorbed much ordinary stuff about Brazilian life and culture. I met her at dance classes. Having decided to face up to my fears, I took a weekly, and terrifying, samba class. Everyone else at the class had rhythm in their soul, could move to music without any complications, so learning the steps was a relatively easy process. Not so for me, I was too tense to remember the bloody steps, try as I might. (Interestingly, though, I took Bel along one time during her short visit, and danced much more easily and unselfconsciously with her than I had done with anyone else.)

Rosa did not seem to mind my awkwardness, and her head must have been turned, I suppose, by my Englishness; or perhaps it was my age, she being more comfortable with someone considerably older. Rosa accepted a lift home on the motorbike one evening, and the feel of her breasts pressing into my back stayed with me for many days. We became lovers soon, spending as much time as we could together. She knew from the outset that I was heading back to London – this is what I mean about the easy way with relationships – and why I was going. She, and I too, simply wanted to have a good time in the couple of months left to us. And we did. When I got back home to England, there was a small part of me that missed her like crazy. We wrote often at first, and continued exchanging letters for many years, till she herself married and had a child.

I loved most everything about Brazil, its geography, its people, the colour, the dancing, the music, the food. I loved, in particular, the New Worldness, the fact that everything was possible, that culture and society was infused with an optimism lacking in Europe where every aspect of life is weighed down by history and where the ancient and old so often set the standards. By then, the mid-1980s, Brazil was growing fast and confidently in every field – politics, science, architecture, industry, music, sport – and the country felt like a world unto itself. But I never lost sight of how privileged my ex-pat life was, earning wages on a different scale from locals, and being able to take advantage of distorted money markets. I had never planned to stay away for more than two years, and, as luck would have it, I had good reason to return to the UK when this time was up – back to the Old World, but a new life.

Chapter fifteen

BEL
WHY ONE RELATIONSHIP PROVED FRUITFUL

Whereupon one arrives at the point of significant compromise – in one's life, and now in writing about it. While my spirit was gallivanting in every direction looking for love, my sensible head eventually brought me through the emotional gales to find a calm landscape, one in which my youthful wildness could be kept tethered and become tame in order to reap benefits I might never have found otherwise. To tell of this, I must write at some length of Bel. Yet because she is so very much a private person – hence the pseudonym Bel – how can I do so, honestly from my point of view, without being disloyal, without betraying confidences or confidential and intimate matters? I fear, as I set out on this most difficult of self-analyses, that to avoid disturbing her feelings, I will pull too many punches.

And it is not only Bel's feelings that I wish to care for, but those of our son, Adam. Indeed, Adam is likely to have more strident opinions about my writing of his mother, and of him too – in the chapters of a second patchwork to come – than she will. That said, I fear more that the punches I'll be pulling will be to protect myself, the image of myself that I'm projecting by writing this memoir.

Bel lived near Salisbury when we first met, and then near Oxford. We only saw each other occasionally, but were head-over-heels in love when we did, acting like newly-weds. I was able to indulge in this relationship alongside several others because, presumably, I was fickle, promiscuous – nothing much mattered to me. I hadn't grown up to the point of taking anything seriously, least of all relationships, and when I did analyse them, I found myself scared of becoming like my flaky father Fred. Bel coped, I believe, by keeping the relationship a special, precious thing, highly compartmentalised in her mind. She said she was able to ignore any uncomfortable realities – professing, for example, not to care about my other affairs, of which I made no secret.

In mid-1982, Bel came to live in London, and soon after I bought the house in Kilburn. This was when we began to spend more time together, as a couple. It felt good to have Bel's companionship as I was decorating and furnishing the new house. It felt good also to be loved so well, so innocently, so generously. By this time, I had no other relationships so Bel and I progressed to going away for weekends, and then for a week to

Ireland in autumn 1983. Yet, I never thought of myself as coupled, and continued to yearn for other emotional excitements. I never believed we could have a future together; and Bel, accepting this unilateral judgement, appeared to accept whatever density of togetherness was available.

Inevitably, our honeymoon times started to give way all too often to friction, argument, sadness on Bel's part, ennui on mine. I had fallen into Bel's arms and I didn't know how to fall out of them. We tried several times to split up, and Bel made an effort to date, but within a few weeks one or other of us always found a reason to get together.

Have I pulled any punches yet in this rather extended intro? I'm not sure. Certainly, on a superficial analysis, there was one immature cad in this relationship and one beautiful, lovely and largely innocent lady. In my defence, all along I felt more experienced, worldly, ambitious than Bel, and that the loving between us was unreal, unsustainable. I could see forward. I'd experienced enough of the world, of relationships in real life, and absorbed plenty of intelligence through literature, films, drama, to know we were completely mis-matched, and that the differences between us would inevitably create chasms of separateness. Social and cultural norms would have had us marry, live in the same house, but in trying to be a couple, all the joy and love between us would have been poisoned. I imagined I would be a victim in such a scenario, but also – and this is the main point of my defence – I was crystal clear in my belief that Bel would come to suffer as much or more than me. If we followed the rules, and the expectations/guidance of our families and friends – I was sure – there'd soon be little love left for, or in, either of us.

As the relationship went up and down in 1984, Bel occasionally talked of marriage, and we did discuss children too. In mid-1984, Bel thought she might be pregnant. I surprised myself by noting in my diary that I felt elements of excitement, and questioned, 'Am I really a man? Could I be a father?'.

And then Brazil beckoned, and my move abroad seemed a perfect excuse to bring our relationship to a permanent end. There were many tears – Bel's and mine – before I finally left. At this time, also, I first raised the idea of us having a child, not only out of wedlock, as they used to say, but out of couplelock – i.e. us not living together. Bel couldn't or wouldn't accept such an idea. On my second trip home to London, I found Bel depressed, and we talked a lot about her career and future, and that what she most wanted to do was go to university and study for a degree. A few weeks later, though, she telephoned me in Brazil to say she had changed her mind, a degree would take too long, she wanted a child first!

Within a couple of weeks she had organised a flight to Rio, taking much care over the dates. We travelled, loved and laughed for that two weeks, and a short while after her return she phoned to say she was pregnant. How amazing, how astonishing, not only that Bel had flown to Rio, for she had barely travelled anywhere in her life, not only that she had believed in me and was courageous enough to take this momentous step, but that she got pregnant at the very first time of asking. I started to wind down my affairs, and I arrived home after just two years in Brazil. I felt like Bel's love had saved me in some way; and our beautiful son Adam was born in August 1987.

Meeting Bel in the summer of 1979 proved to be the most important encounter of my life up to then – though I wouldn't understand this for several years. It was six months or so before I waltzed off to Corsica to try and be a writer, and a year before my 'breakdown'. It is thanks to Jean-Christophe that we first met. Jean-Christophe, a gentle Swiss man, and his French girlfriend Cecile were renting a spare room in my Fordwych Road flat, where Harold and Roser were living too. I'd met him in Battersea Park a couple of years or so earlier, one Sunday morning when I'd gone out for a walk leaving M to sleep in our small Chelsea bedsit. I was playing the recorder (just as I had been when M first noticed me on the boat from Argentina) when Jean-Christophe found me. I liked him immediately, and we stayed friends. He became a masseur, and was always trying to interest me in alternative stuff, growth therapy sessions, EST, vegetarianism. Memorably, he and Cecile were worried about me being alone and lonely one night, so together they invited me into their bed.

Incidentally, I met someone else in Battersea Park on my Sunday morning walks – Victoria. This has nothing to do with Bel, who I wouldn't meet for nearly two years, but where else should I include this name-dropping anecdote? I was very taken with this Victoria, she was beautiful and exciting and secretive.

20 November 1977
I dressed up warm, took my [recorder] and played a little by the river to the cold. It beat my fingers so I put on my gloves and wailed on. This lady speeded past (maybe she is thinking about me now). She looked twice and apologised for staring. I told her I was me, and that I was sorry that I was me. She sped on past. I watched her hoping she would stop. Nearly at the end of the park she did. She waited for me. Victoria, 33, heroin addict for seven years and now starting a new life, today, without tobacco – afresh – very exciting attractive lady – addicted to travelling – we sped through the park, she was excited with life, with the trees, with the cold, with dogs, with feeling the air, she had been a slave to a drug for so long and now she was feeling really strong to beat it all. We laughed and gave each other little bits of information. She was glad she had waited for me. She had never been alive like this – and soon it will be very bad for her, she will have very bad times.

1 December 1977
I met Victoria again, for an hour in a pub. As she talks of her lover that isolates himself from the world and how she cannot leave him because she has spent so much of her life with him – it would seem like she was throwing it all away. I met Victoria again. I sent her a note and she came and maybe she will ring me one day.

It was not until years later, in 1983, when I read a feature in *The Sunday Times* magazine on the Getty family, that I learned Victoria was none other than Paul Getty II's lover, and later his wife – they lived close by in classy Cheyne Walk. No wonder she had been so unwilling to tell me much about herself.

Jean-Christophe supplemented his income as a masseur with decorating jobs, and in the summer of 1979 he invited me to join him at a country house in Downton, Wiltshire, to help with a painting contract for a titled Lady. I am not exactly sure how they knew each other, but the link was through EST, an intense group therapy training devised by Werner Erhard, and The Hunger Project, also founded by Erhard. The plan was that we would occupy the house while the Lady was away, and complete the painting work in a week or two. Out of working hours, I planned to write, to walk, to read.

On arriving at the property we found two reclusive young women, employed as gardeners, living in a tiny outhouse. This was still my pre-breakdown phase when every day was bristling with self-made adventures, seductions, excitements, and here was another for the making and the living. I did not have much time for one of the gardeners, but I fell for the other – Bel. I fell for her short cut gingery hair, her freckles, her brightness, her youthful beauty, her innocence; and I set about courting her – maybe, seducing is a more accurate word.

Bel was born in Devon, an only child, and brought up as a strict vegetarian. Her parents had moved to south London at some point, and she had left school at 16 and become an assistant librarian. Dissatisfied with this, she fantasised about becoming an enlightened Zen master, which led her to study various eastern disciplines, Chinese language, karate, tai chi – this was in the early 1970s. But, after a while, she said, she had opted for gardening as a way of getting close to nature.

Despite Harold, despite my clowning antics, despite the travels and the three Ms, I was still, at heart, a shy man, timid, innocent in a way, scared of rejection. And Bel saw this, and it was part of why she fell in love. On the last night of my stay, Bel and I talked and walked in the moonlight; anxious for intimacy, I persuaded her we should sleep together. She wouldn't use any of the bedrooms, and instead we made up a makeshift bed on the floor in the large lounge.

I must have sent a letter to Bel soon after returning to Kilburn, for I still have a letter from her (ornamented with tiny pressed flowers and their Latin names) in which she says: 'You mentioned in your letter (thank you) coming down sometime. Well – I would welcome you with open arms, so to speak, anytime!' But, for the rest of that year, there is no record in my diary of me visiting her or she coming to London, though I'm sure she did. Not till I am in Corsica does my diary reveal any emotion towards Bel.

29 November 1979
I think of [Bel] and tears come to my eyes. I think to write her a letter, but the things I would want to say to her would sound so silly. How can I say I love her, but could never love her, how can I say I cried for her, how can I say that it is one of the most wonderful things for a person to find such purity. I am tempted to write her to come. But she might, and how would she handle that if E came or M. Funny how she makes me cry so. I shall write her about the maquis and the fruits and about my own stupidity.

Through 1980 and all the inner turmoil I was experiencing, Bel remained a treasured, beautiful part of my life. We started to spend a little more time together, whole weekends, sometimes in London, other times away, in Aldeburgh (where we could borrow a friend's holiday house). But I was carefully compartmentalising the relationship, keeping it in a bubble, never willing or able to mix it in with friends. Bluntly speaking, I suppose, I felt the affair was wonderful, but it wasn't what I wanted for the rest of my life – as several (reduced) diary entries indicate.

17 April 1980
We lay in the Hampstead Cemetery, sheltered from the wind by tombstones, just loving and smiling at each other [. . .] it was a happy chance to find at least some quiet on such a day. The odd days we meet are always boundless in laughter and love. She is a jewel for me. The rest of Good Friday we re-potted plants, cleaned windows and hoovered.

6 August 1980
Softness and sweetness of three days together with [Bel . . .]. By the end I realised that, on balance, I was not good for her – I was disturbing their [Bel and friend] routines, their peace of mind. Tears came and guilt came and bye byes were full of 'do you think we should see each other again' and 'please, please don't write to me'. [Bel, Bel] I would give you more if I could, if I only could.

14 July 1981
To [Bel]: Still in beauty you simplify my complications, never let me complify your simplications. Tis little love I can give but tis love.

In the early 1980s, as I've written about elsewhere, I sought out my real father in New York, and then I fell out with him. But I had spent enough time in his company to know, to the core of my being, that I did not ever want to let myself become like him, especially how he was in the relationship with his wife. He and his wife may have been happy then, I don't know, but what I saw was a relationship that had deteriorated into unnecessary, petty and possibly cruel dominance by my father, and a chronic nervous submissiveness by his wife. It seemed all too possible that this is what would become of Bel and I were we to follow the usual path into coupledom and marriage.

My mother – who, after all, had known Fred far better than I ever did – always claimed that I was nothing like Fred. She was making practical comparisons, between our attitudes to money, to being on time, keeping promises, being thoughtful, that kind of thing. But, I knew better, I'd had that unsettling moment of revelation when first cycling around Manhattan with my father; and I'd also come to understand how very different I was from my mother, step-father, and many of the people I had grown up with. I might have had a more normal childhood (whatever that is) than Fred, but, I felt, I was still a Goldsmith – a restless individual, ambitious for change, for the new, unwilling to settle in any sense. It did not really matter whether this was a good or bad thing, what mattered was that I accepted it, made allowances for it. Fortunately, my mother's influence – nature and nurture, both genetic and behaviourally – did temper, did attenuate this restless gene, if that is what it is; and I consider myself lucky that it has never led me into the kind of darkness experienced by both my father, Fred, and grandfather, Igee.

Here I am grappling with this in my diary.

17 February 1982
As my loneliness becomes more acute, I am tempted – no – I want to see [Bel] more, [. . .] But I am afraid, for I see too many parallels with Frederic [. . .] Besides she would not have me. She is by far the stronger. Last night I was thinking how much stronger she is than me, because she can take the position of giving like that – as I could not with Ann, I could not relinquish control. And it's probably just as well, although by relinquishing control one can often win it, I suppose. Matters that still lie well outside of my understanding.

23 May 1982
[Bel] confessed some weeks ago that I was the most important person in her life. She cried and I loved her. She then decided not to sleep with me any more. But, in spite of my own fears that she loves me too much, I seduced her to forget such silly ideas. I need her so terribly, for without her, I have nothing. And yet I cannot live with her, can I?

181

11 June 1982
Oh [Bel], I can cry to think of you. On Monday, she was moping, head bent down, eyes curling towards tears. I could not bring her out of herself. Until we came back here and then we fought, fists and nails, and then we lay quietly, recovering, letting 'Rite of Spring' curse us. She says she fights so desperately against needing me.

4 September 1982
New York. I do think of [Bel]. I might have telephoned her this morning if she'd had a private phone. What a jewel she is, even in thought among these egoists. Altruism at its worst, its most obvious. But what does worry me is Vera [Caspary] saying Fred's second wife was insipid. [. . .] I tell Vera I'm afeared to be like Fred, and she says there are no similarities. But my affair with [Bel] frightens me. Why is it I am drawn to this woman, and continue with her, involving deeper and deeper? Is it because she is weak and giving and gives in to my egoism, as Gail does to Fred? Do I need someone weak, or else I sink into the mood of insecurity. I do not have the machismo, drive, ruthlessness, ambition to find, let alone, bed, or marry a difficult woman. Did Ann love me? Were all those jibes about commitment questions? I cannot survey my past affairs without horror at my own lack of involvement, trust.

16 October 1982
Aldeburgh. A weak mind. As nothing compared to the incessant purging of the pebble beach by the waves of the North Sea. The scuttle of surf on stone much like the grating of philosophy on practical realities.
   I am acutely aware of the limitations of my relationship with [Bel]. How much more I want and need from a partner. I cannot resolve this dilemma in me. I am so horrible to her. I do not want take every decision myself. I am trapped into egocentricity. Rilke says, in his 8th elegy, never think that fate is other than the condensation of childhood. [Bel's] humility is frightening. I have to frighten her into decision-making. I am always correcting her. I remember me of old. Unchanged. So now I find myself here in Aldeburgh, not in my usual peaceful mode, but feeling weak, weak in the knees, weak in the head. But yet she is so lovely in her gentleness and innocent approach to life. So much so that I punish her. I love it when I provoke the fire in her. But maybe I burn her up.
   [Bel] comes to me – she is going out for a walk – I ask for a kiss before she leaves. I feel lighter now that I have some time alone. Later she asks me if I am happy. I have to say no. She wants to know what she can do to make me happy. There are times, many times, in my life when I yearn for someone who would love me so and give me so much and with whom I could find the sort of intimacy I now have with [Bel]. But now I have it, here captured, mine, alone with it, it is not enough.

The year 1983 arrived, and with it a more sober, 30 year-old me. I bought my first house. I moved from my first job as a journalist which I hated and stayed with under sufferance to a much better job and working environment. Work became the most important aspect of my life for the first time. Bel had moved to London in mid-1982. She found a room in Kilburn, and before long I had organised for her to take over the garden flat in Sumatra Road, the one where my friend Harvey had gotten into such trouble over a bribery allegation. Around the same time, she found a job in London, as a librarian again.

Our relationship continued to see-saw, usually to my inconstant and selfish demands, but there was a lot more see and less saw in 1983, after I'd taken ownership of the house in Aldershot Road. It seemed natural that we would spend more time together, scouring junk shops, visiting garden centres (the house had a small yard and flower beds) and going to auctions, especially in Tring on Saturday mornings, to buy paraphernalia for the house: second hand furniture, ornaments, books, pictures. I loved Bel's company on these expeditions, and our romance continued and progressed towards taking a holiday together in Ireland. Indeed, I remained constantly and faithfully attached to Bel for the whole of 1983. But I did struggle against the domesticity of it all.

> 12 September 1983
> Ireland. Several times I want to cry without any real reason. But I know it has to do with the future, my future. I cannot sustain this ordinariness that we live together. There is such a banality of our existences. No spark in the moment, no change. [. . .] There is so much of a problem here, that it denies formalisation in words but rather wells up in tears. [. . .]
> Here I am sure is the dilemma of many a person. The to and froing of mind for and against the situation. Now, here on Garnish Island with birdsong and gardener's clippersong soothing me, I feel indeed that this, she and I, should not be. We have reached the limit of usefulness to each other. But so much fear stalks within me. To say go, do not love me any more, I have no more patience, is like trespassing on secret burial grounds and thus releasing a multitude of evil spirits.

> 13 February 1984
> Will I look back on these days with [Bel] as the happiest of my life. They are so inconsequential, so ordinary, and yet I am nothing else. Nothing burns within me, to flame other than this simple life.

The novelty of being a house/garden owner wore off in time, and in 1984 restlessness was nagging me for change, new experiences. At work, I was beginning to think seriously about moving abroad. Meanwhile, Bel and I tried periodically to separate and not see each other. Inevitably, and before long, one or other of us managed to find a reason – being unwell, a house problem, an issue at work – to break off the break up. And thus, despite my intellectual efforts to avoid our relationship deepening and becoming more serious, it did. One consequence of this was that I found myself less able to be hurtfully crass and honest with Bel, as I had been for so long, and having to resort to a kind of deceitfulness to be more gentle with her feelings. I only recall a couple of times I was properly duplicitous, but I'm sure there were more. I had never promised any commitment to Bel, but I had, in fact, been faithful for 18 months when a one-night stand with a work colleague came, effortlessly, my way. I did not feel guilty, more relieved that there was still a bit of spice in my life.

A few weeks later, I wrote a prose poem for Bel in my diary, but I don't think I ever gave it to her.

> 8 July 1984
> [Bel], Know that wherein we are but human minds and bodies and wherein we are thus victims to a multitude of forces more powerful than we
> and that wherein the concepts of love and truth and peace deserve attention lest they be forgot altogether
> and that therein we are subject to constant and dismal failure being but more full of ego now than ever before
> and in consequence of all this bearing the knowledge that I then am succour to unceasing impatience within this seething panic of life, I say to you that
> I do and will love you for such beauty and generosity of spirit I shall ne'er meet again.

And a few weeks after that comes this diary entry.

> 30 July 1984
> I tried to call you twice last night. I felt justified in order to check on the state of your period or lack of same. It excites me to think you might be pregnant. Am I really a man? Could I be a father? Of course it would upset me deeply too but I have to confess to those inner feelings.

The rest of the year passed, off and on, together and not together. On a work trip to Geneva I met a young nurse in a park, and was invited to eat with her and her boyfriend. Half way through the evening, she told me her name – Mireille – and, my diary says, 'I exploded with joy'. Very recently (and thanks to my uncle Mike in Paris) I had fallen in love with Gounod's opera of the same name, and had been listening to it on this very trip. At the end of the evening, I asked them both to come to London, in the hope that Mireille would come alone. And she did, a few months later; but this was not the worst of what could be called my cheating.

I do not think – from this distance in time – that my decision to leave Britain, and go to Brazil to work as a freelance journalist had anything to do with Bel. I believe I would have done so regardless of the state of any relationship. I had, after all, done a similar thing, albeit in a minor way, when I had gone to live alone in Corsica, thereby effectively interrupting several sparkling liaisons. Nevertheless, the move came as a legitimate excuse, for both of us, to bring the intimacy, finally, to a clear end. Ha ha.

Well, we still had a month or two in which the pressure to resolve our relationship was entirely removed, leaving us free to indulge our passion as of old. And it is in this period that I was tempted into deceit, for which I was fully and properly punished. Mireille and I had fallen a little in love, fantasy love on my part, played out in warm sexy letters, so when she wrote suggesting we go to a chalet of a friend for a week to ski, I said yes, yes. The time should have been Bel's, but I stole it: I had learned to love skiing in New Zealand, and the thought of it combined with a week of nights with Mireille was impossible to resist.

I booked time off work, and bought the tickets, and eventually had to tell Bel of my plans. We were at the theatre, and the information took a while to sink in, and the show had started, when she lent over and whispered, 'If you go to Switzerland then you can say goodbye to me now!' I hesitated before whispering back' with the information that her boyfriend would be going too. It was a lie, the biggest I had ever told her – and, of course, my diary had to know about it.

10 February 1985
So this was the biggest lie I've ever told, and I knew it as I told it. But what would have been the point of allowing her to be miserable. I have been as honest as any man, in the sense that I have exposed my feelings in their crudity and self-ishness to her, I have not given her false hope or dreams, I have not pumped her full of future only to prick it with inevitable unfaithfulness of a future imperfect. The sexual aspect is so painful, we are such primitives in this aspect of our rela-tionship – I have said it before and will say it again. I believe in a monogamous relationship bound by the limits of our own ability to cope with sexual jealousy – but where that monogamous relationship is not extant then a few lies and half truths can save a lot of pain and discomfort. There is self-justification in these words, but I am my own harshest critic, and this lie I forgive myself.

I do love this story – many would comment with the single exclamation, karma! I arrived at Mireille's flat full of expectations, only to find her very girlish, coy. When I asked for an explanation she told me she was in love with her boyfriend (new one), who, it transpired, I DID have to spend an evening with. I did not see a problem since we would be escaping the next day to drive to the ski field, and once alone together I was sure Mireille's coyness would dissolve. But the gods were against me: Geneva suffered a huge snowstorm that night, and its access/exit roads became blocked. Meanwhile, Mireille's boyfriend had become acutely jealous, apparently, of me (though Mireille had done nothing untoward), and he made a very crude attempt at suicide. Yikes. We then had to stay longer in Geneva so Mireille could look after him. As angry and frustrated as I've ever been (these being valuable days before my departure for Brazil), I would have returned to London if my ticket had been transferable, but instead I stomped through the snow in search of open museums, and paced around my room in Mireille's flat like a caged tiger. Eventually, we did get away. We drove to the friend's chalet, but the few days left then passed in a sour fog of the resentment and frustration I couldn't let go of. Mireille and I lost all connection, and never wrote again. Served me right.

Back in London, Bel and I became slowly sadder and sadder at the impending separation. I wrote her a letter, first in my diary, and then I sent it. (The second half of this letter – which I've decided to exclude – is egoistical and uncomfortable reading for me, but I have the curious thought that it reminds me more of how I suspect my father was as a young man than of how I really was.)

> 23 February 1985
> My Dear [Bel], I have thought much about you today (in fact it seems I always do when I go away). This morning I wept in anticipation of no longer knowing you were round the corner, to lose such a great friend and lover is not easy, and I do not think I think it might be easy for me. I wept very much in remembrance of such beautiful times we have had together. And then this evening, I was thinking about children again. How serious were we when we talked about children, I don't know.

I do not remember exactly, nor do I have written evidence of, Bel's thoughts on these matters. She probably felt it was simply a whim of mine, as I was flying high towards new pastures, and that, in any case, she had no wish to be a single mother, or have a child with a wandering father, wandering in body and in mind.

Separation – at least at first – did little to diminish our ardour, and in September, when I returned to England for my sister's wedding, we took up where we had left off, with a joyful tour to the West country – Cornwall, Devon – including many walks, visits to gardens and beaches, and a memorable picnic in the rain. Again, there was a vague possibility that Bel might be pregnant, which prompted mixed emotions in both of us. Thereafter, communications between us did diminish, as though our physical distance was finally whittling away at our emotional closeness.

> 25 May 1985
> From this distance, our love seems to be rich, so caring, but it is a mirage caused by the desert of emotions around me. I think to write to her but see I wrote only seven days ago, and a long letter once a week has to be too much.

> 7 October 1985
> [Bel] rings. She is far away from me. Says so. Cannot write. Depressed. Like me. What can one say. The Phone Rings Again. [Bel] to give me a big hug. This is eas-

ier now, lighter. I am almost tongue-tied in response. But the real message of the first call. NOT PREGNANT. Of course, I never stashed away hope there – but . . . she says. She says, the coming of her period was a confluence of emotions: relief. Relief and disappointment. But which is the greater, she says, I do not know.

21 November 1985
I called [Bel] last night. We rubbed the margins of our depressions together to no good effect. I love her so it destroys me to think of her unhappy. I am less guarded than her, but even so I know it makes her unhappy even more to know I am too. What a fight this life.

I returned to London for a second time, this journey arranged to coincide with my mother's 60th birthday in July 1986. A small family lunch was organised at her house, and with everyone assembled I rang the doorbell. My mother, having no idea I'd flown back from Brazil, demonstrated the most rewarding and comical hysteria as well as joy. Nevertheless, I believe most of the pleasure was mine, for I'd had weeks in which to enjoy the anticipation of the surprise. Bel was there, too, looking lovelier than ever, for she had been firm friends with my mother for years by then.

Reticent about spending too much time with me at first, Bel softened and we went on a couple of day trips, and then on a long weekend to the Peak District. It transpired that a depression she had been feeling for months had deepened, yet she had little clue as to the cause. Much discussion brought us round to the possibility that she felt stuck in her job, and longed for a university degree to progress, possibly to become a chartered librarian. This triggered us together into research for colleges, courses; and, before I had left again for Brazil, she had filled out several application and grant forms.

Then came a phone call. Some 18 months earlier, Jeff Ryser's New Year call had triggered my move to Brazil, and this one now was to trigger my return. It was Bel. The more I think about going to university to do a three year course, she said, the more I know I want to have a child first, and to study later. I tried to remain calm, and suggested we spend a few days writing down our thoughts and thinking through potential problems. With letters exchanged, I called her, and then wrote this in my diary.

23 August 1986
Not only has [Bel] now been offered a place at North London Poly this year, but her grant application has succeeded already and so quickly. She is full of beans. She has thought about it carefully and decided not to go to college this year. Her reasons are not convincing until she comes to the last, she is determined to try for a child. If that is the case then, I say, she must come out here as soon as possible. This will mean carefully monitoring her periods and stealing holiday time from next year – it will take planning and a package of good luck.

> At least one thing has been achieved – [Bel] is active and alive again, her depression having lifted.

Bel wanted to come for a month, but I suggested two weeks and as soon as possible. I sent her the money. It was a crazy gamble, looking back, and we had no right to expect success at the very first try.

> 24 November
> The two weeks have passed and [Bel] has left. Once again we have lived out a romance as if we were in the first throws of an infatuation. Hardly a minute went by during the whole two weeks when we did not adore one another, whether in passion, or walking through the forests of Itatiaia to a waterfall, collecting stones on Buzios beach, eating a tasteless meal in a 'natural restaurant' or riding the motorbike through the Rio streets towards some market or panoramic spot, or reading Jane Austen or Jorge Amado together on the sofa.

Not a whisper of doubt fell between us – it seemed so right and perfect that we should be doing this thing. In the first day or two we discussed briefly matters we had already raised – her parents, money, flats, etc. – but the conversation soon dried up to be replaced by passion (full of significant moments, any one of which would be the perfect romantic beginning for a child), joy and much hilarity.

> 9 December 1986
> [BEL] RINGS. IT IS 5:30AM. THE HOME TESTER BOUGHT FROM THE CHEMISTS THAT PROMISES 99% VALIDITY HAS GONE DARK BLUE. SHE IS SURE SHE IS PREGNANT.

> 15 December 1986
> I call [Bel] to ask how she is feeling. She sounds so excited identifying dozens of symptoms of pregnancy, telling me that within a few days already the foetus will have been formed, if only one inch long. I try to calm her excitement – so much can yet happen. I tell her I have written to Mum but asked her not to mention it to anyone for the time being.

Within a week, I had booked my passage back to Britain the following March, four days before my work visa would expire – the timing was impeccable. But then, almost immediately, I felt terribly impatient, to be organising the end of my work arrangements, to be packing, to be heading back to London, for to start a new kind of life.

To begin with, Bel was full of the joys of pregnancy, and speaking to her always left me happy too; but then tiredness and being alone bore down on her spirit, and speaking to her left me anxious, full of conflicting thoughts competing for attention.

In February, I wrote to her parents as follows.

'Dear Mr & Mrs _____, Strange times. Strange times that a man and a woman can decide to have a child outside of marriage. And it must be stranger indeed that [Bel] is now pregnant by a man you have not even met. I regret this.

But you know that [Bel] and I have been close friends for seven or eight years. In that time I have never ceased to love her, and my feelings towards her have become deeper and richer to the point where I care for her as much, if not more, than members of my own family. This is the way it should be in a partnership that brings new life into the world.

Of course children SHOULD be brought up inside a marriage. That is the ideal, but these days marriages are no longer what they used to be, people have become more demanding, more selfish and so very often couples live out relationships that are fights, battles. My childhood left such scars on me. And I see little in the world to change my ideas.

I do not believe that marriage is impossible just difficult and especially when the couple are so very different as [Bel] and I. I have thought long and hard many times, but do not believe that a marriage between us would work. Perhaps we are both destined to be single people. Yet I have never considered having a child with any one else, nor has [Bel] as far as I know.

This situation then between your daughter and myself is a kind of compromise: we don't believe a marriage between us would work, yet there is no one else we want to marry, and we want a child.

In deciding to have a child, I think [Bel] made a brave, mature decision. Although we will not live together, I expect to be close by, with emotional, practical and financial help. Neither of us expect it to be very easy – there will be all sorts of difficulties and perhaps because of this we will need a little more understanding and support than an ordinary family might.

Just as I have felt a need to write a few words to my own parents, being so far away until now, so I write to you. Yours affectionately.'

No sooner had I arrived back in London than Bel and I went away for a weekend, to Aldeburgh, to discuss as many practical details about our impending parenthood as we could muster. On money, I said I would open an account to provide a regular income for her and the child; on food (I was worried about her vegetarian diet), Bel said she would be happy, when the time came, to feed our child fish (later, she came to widen her own diet to fish also); on the baby spending time with me, Bel's position was unequivocal: she wanted me as involved as possible. We were very happy.

That same weekend, I found a two-up two-down terraced property in Aldeburgh, and after some reflection, bought it – to be a home of sorts for the three of us at weekends. Indeed, as it happened, in early August, we would be there, in Aldeburgh, when Bel went into labour late at night. We set off back for London, and having no clock or watch with us, we timed the contractions by keeping to a steady 60mph, and counting the miles per contraction.

... To be continued ...

www.pikle.co.uk

Printed in Great Britain
by Amazon